The Campus History Series

THE THACHER SCHOOL

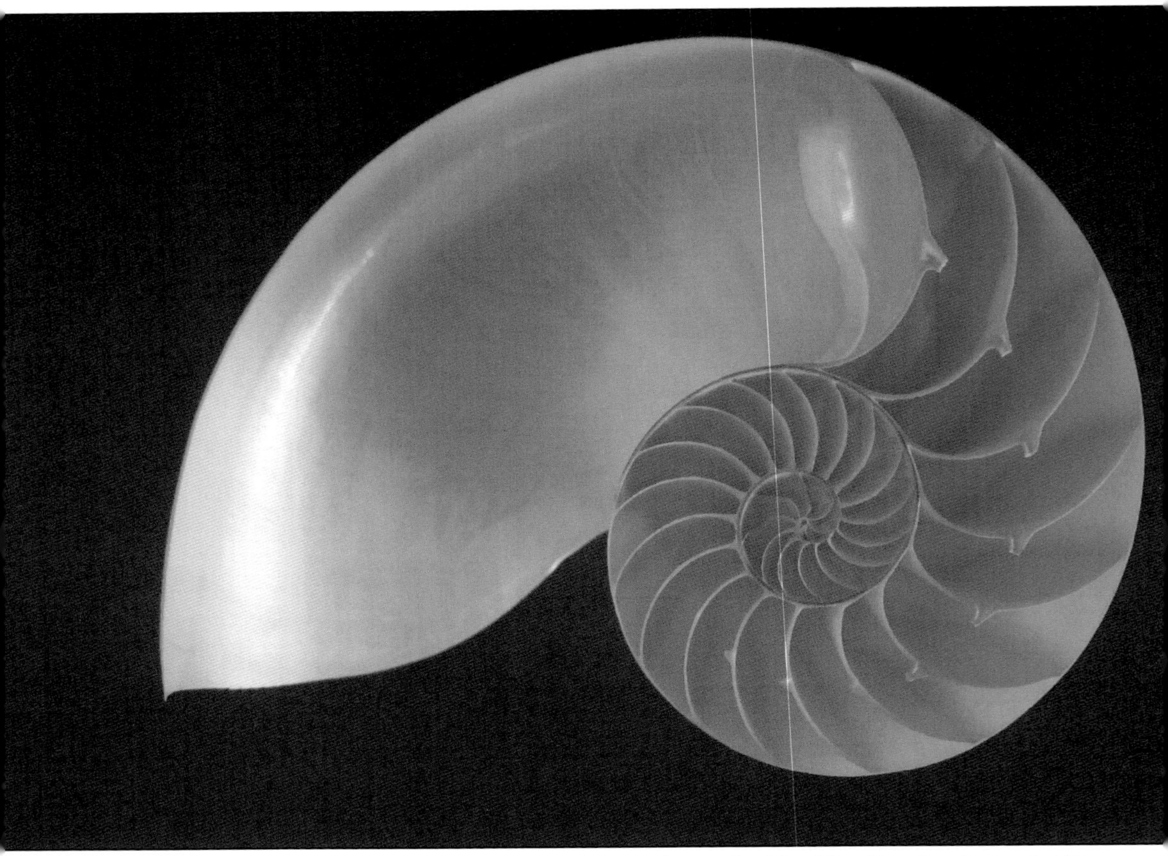

The chambered nautilus has become something of a symbol for The Thacher School. Oliver Wendell Holmes's poem by the same name is read at the first assembly of each new year. The closing stanza is particularly apropos of The Thacher School's mission of preparing students to do the greatest good: "Build thee more stately mansions, O my soul, / As the swift seasons roll! / Leave thy low-vaulted past! / Let each new temple, nobler than the last, / shut thee from heaven with a dome more vast, / Till thou at length art free, / Leaving thine outgrown shell by life's unresting sea!" (Courtesy of The Thacher School Archives.)

On the Cover: Thacher horseman Bill McNabb CdeP 1954, riding Sage, retrieves an orange during one of The Thacher School's signature gymkhana events. (The CdeP designation for the graduating class is a vestige of the original name for The Thacher School—Casa de Piedra.) (Courtesy of The Thacher School Archives.)

The Campus History Series

THE THACHER SCHOOL

JOHN TAYLOR

ARCADIA
PUBLISHING

ISBN 978-1-4671-3069-1

Published by Arcadia Publishing
Charleston, South Carolina

Printed in the United States of America

Library of Congress Catalog Card Number: 2013937626

For all general information, please contact Arcadia Publishing:
Telephone 843-853-2070
Fax 843-853-0044
E-mail sales@arcadiapublishing.com
For customer service and orders:
Toll-Free 1-888-313-2665

Visit us on the Internet at www.arcadiapublishing.com

This book is dedicated to my classmates from the storied Thacher class of 1965, and to my wife, Lynn, whom I met at my first Thacher dance in the fall of 1961 and whom I married in Thacher's Outdoor Chapel in 1987.

Contents

FOREWORD

Like many heads of schools, I could spend my entire day answering e-mails or dictating text messages. As the technology revolution has unfolded before our eyes, who has not benefitted from its wonders and suffered from its ceaseless demands? It is, therefore, all the more rewarding to read the descriptions of Thacher alumnus John Taylor on the rich history of the West's oldest college-preparatory school and browse the fabulous pictures of this unique institution. This volume takes us back to simpler times when a headmaster read to his students under the light of lanterns, played recess baseball with his charges, and handwrote missives to parents at the end of the semesters as he bid his students goodbye and they rode their horses to the stage and rails in Ojai.

Yes, much has changed both at The Thacher School and in the rest of the world. But what has not changed is that students learn best when they are supported by devoted, caring, and passionate teachers and are held to the highest standards by these teachers. In these important ways, Thacher has not changed. It also has not changed in one other important way: the horse remains central to a Thacher education. Founding headmaster Sherman Day Thacher discovered early on that horses were excellent teachers. Thacher students quickly learn that they can only succeed with a horse by transcending their needs and understanding a horse's unique ways. In so doing, they learn to care for and love these incredible sentient beings. It is educational magic at work. As Sherman Thacher famously said, "Something about the outside of a horse is good for the inside of a boy [or girl]."

John Taylor captures in images and prose both the old and the new. He brings to life the old school and expertly depicts its progress and evolution into the 21st century. In these pages, you will return to more innocent and simpler times, and you may also give thanks to educators and teachers everywhere for their work in helping young men and women learn, as Thacher exhorted, "to live for their own greatest good and the greatest good of their fellow citizens." We at Thacher thank John Taylor for his excellent work.

Like the aroma of the Los Padres sage and the Ojai orange blossoms, it will leave you both more at peace and better acquainted with what generations of students and teachers have experienced at The Thacher School.

—Michael K. Mulligan
Head of School
The Thacher School, Ojai, California
June 2013

ACKNOWLEDGMENTS

I am hugely indebted to Bonnie La Forge for her assistance with accessing Thacher's extensive archives and to Chris Land, Thacher's director of communications. This work would also have been much more challenging without the extensive research by Leroy McKim Makepeace and Jack Huyler in their seminal works, *Sherman Thacher and His School* and *The Stamp of the School*, on the history of The Thacher School. Reviews by Sam Eaton, Ruth Huyler Glass, Nicholas Thacher, and members of The Thacher School's administrative team were also detailed and much appreciated. All photographs appear courtesy of The Thacher School unless otherwise noted.

INTRODUCTION

The young man reined in his horse, stood up in the stirrups, and stretched. The sweet smell of sage tinged with a hint of orange blossoms drifted by on the afternoon breeze. He looked back down the trail as the last of his friends rode up onto the ridge road. Below them to the west stretched the valley. He could see the town of Ojai in the distance, awash in a sea of orange trees. Below Twin Peaks he saw the distinctive features of The Thacher School—Jameson Field, the Upper School, the Outdoor Chapel, the Pergola, the stables. They were small but comfortably familiar. Dismounting, he checked his horse's feet and stuck his fingers under the girth. Smiling to himself, he noticed that the gelding was sweating but that his breathing had almost returned to normal; despite the steep switchbacks between Horn Canyon and the Pines and the final climb up to the ridge. The weeks of trail riding had paid off; there would not be any conditioning issues on this Mutau Loop.

Turning to the pack mule that he had been leading, he checked the diamond hitch. He and his classmates had thrown hundreds of them at Camp Supply or during the packing races over the years, but he knew that a loose pack could be disastrous on the talus slopes on the other side of the ridge. He took out his canteen, poured some water into his cupped hand, and offered it to the horse and the mule. The gelding nickered quietly. This would quench his thirst for the time being, but they would need to get on down to Middle Lyon, where they could really get a drink.

"Let's go, guys," Beise said. "Hey, Taylor, have you read ***Moby Dick*** yet? That sucker is long!"

"It's shorter if you leave out the parts about the whale," Taylor chuckled as the group crested the ridge and headed down the trail into the Sespe. "By the way, did Sam tell you that he persuaded at least three smuts to bring swimming trunks for the pool at Pine Mountain Lodge—one even packed his tennis racket!"

This experience has been shared by thousands of Thacher students since Sherman Day Thacher first established the Casa de Piedra Ranch School in 1889. The institution, with its impressive academic record and unique horse program, has transformed nearly 5,000 boys and girls into local, community, state, and national leaders since its founding. This book commemorates the rich history and traditions of The Thacher School from inception to the present day.

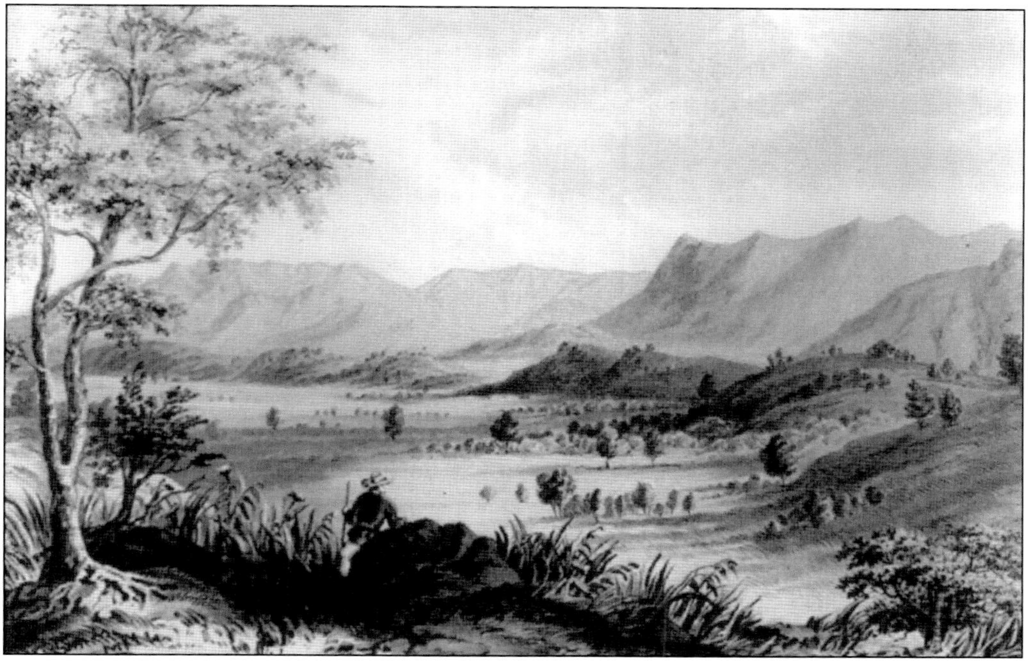

The Thacher School is located at the east end of Southern California's Ojai Valley. The name *Ojai* is a transliteration of the Chumash Indian name *A'hwai*, meaning "moon" (not "nest," as is often reported). The valley was first settled in the 1830s by Mexican farmers and ranchers. The lithograph shown above looks west from a point near the eventual location of The Thacher School. Drawn by A.H. Campbell during an 1854 survey for a railroad from Mississippi to California, it is the earliest known image of the Ojai Valley. The image below shows downtown Ojai in 1900. Note that the village was named Nordhoff until 1919. (Courtesy of the Ojai Valley Museum.)

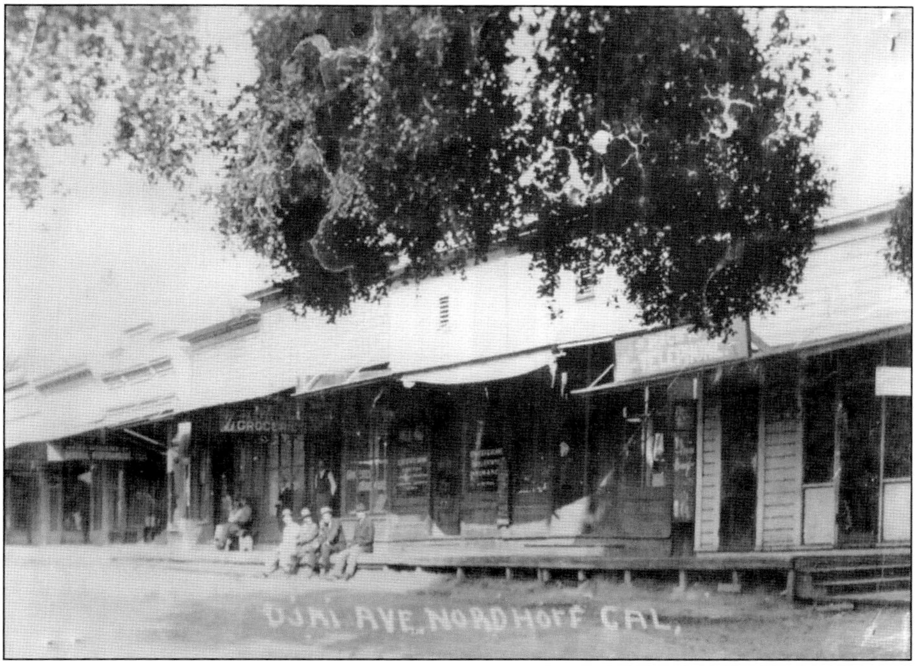

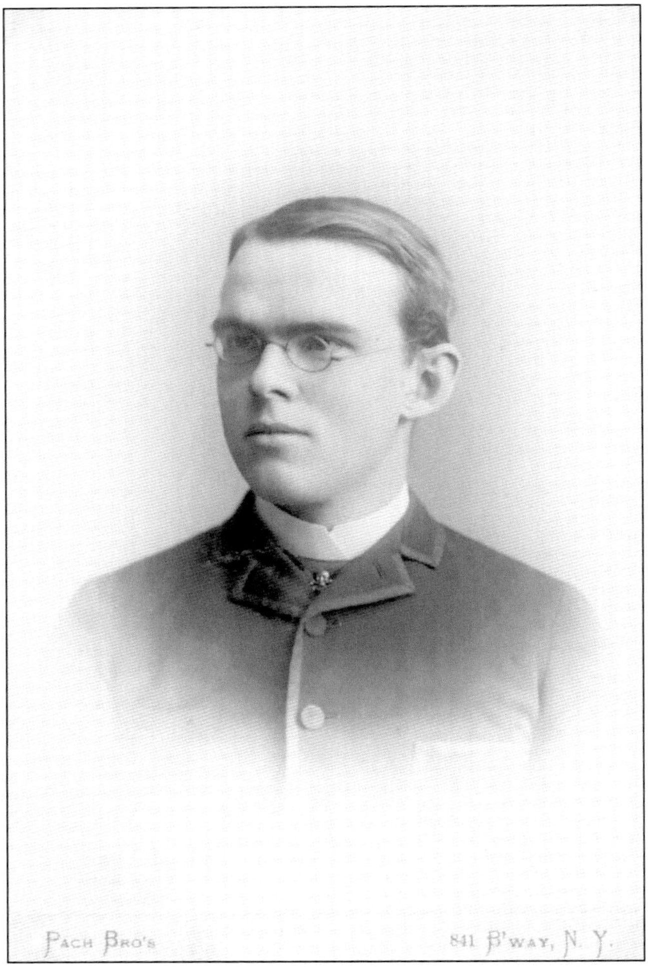

Sherman Day Thacher was born in 1861 in New Haven, Connecticut, where his father was a professor of Latin at Yale. Sherman graduated from Yale and from Yale Law School (law school portrait shown at left) and came to the Ojai Valley in October 1887 with his brother George, who suffered from a serious heart condition. Their brother Edward managed an orchard at the east end of the valley, and Sherman decided to stay to help care for his brother and try his hand at orange cultivation. He bought 160 acres adjacent to Edward's ranch and built a small, one-story, three-room stone house (below), which he moved into in January 1888. (The famous stone house burned in 1944 and was not rebuilt.) With the help of Chinese workers, Sherman cleared the land and planted five acres of orange trees, fully intending to have a career as an orange rancher.

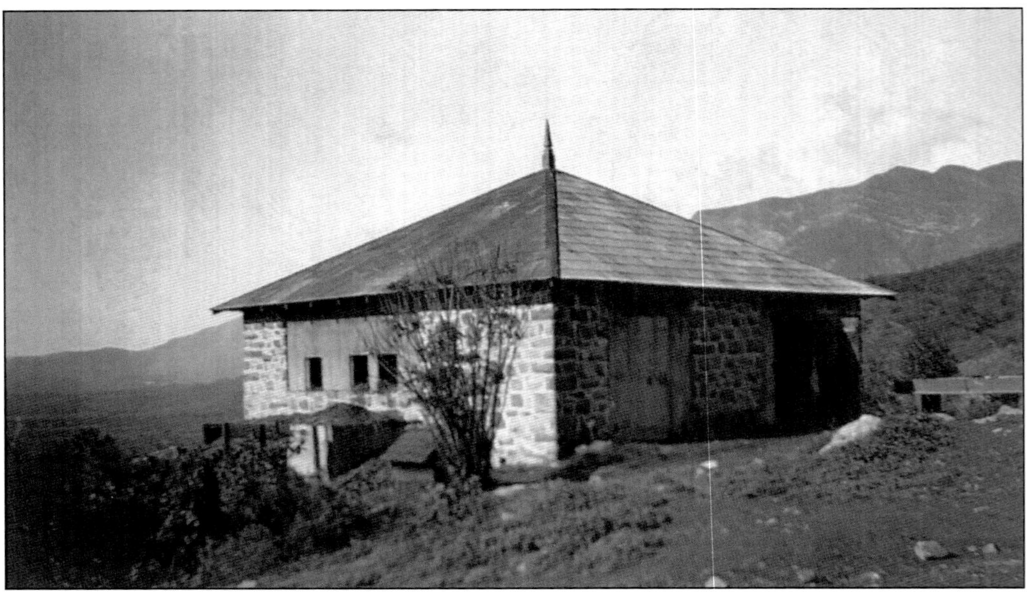

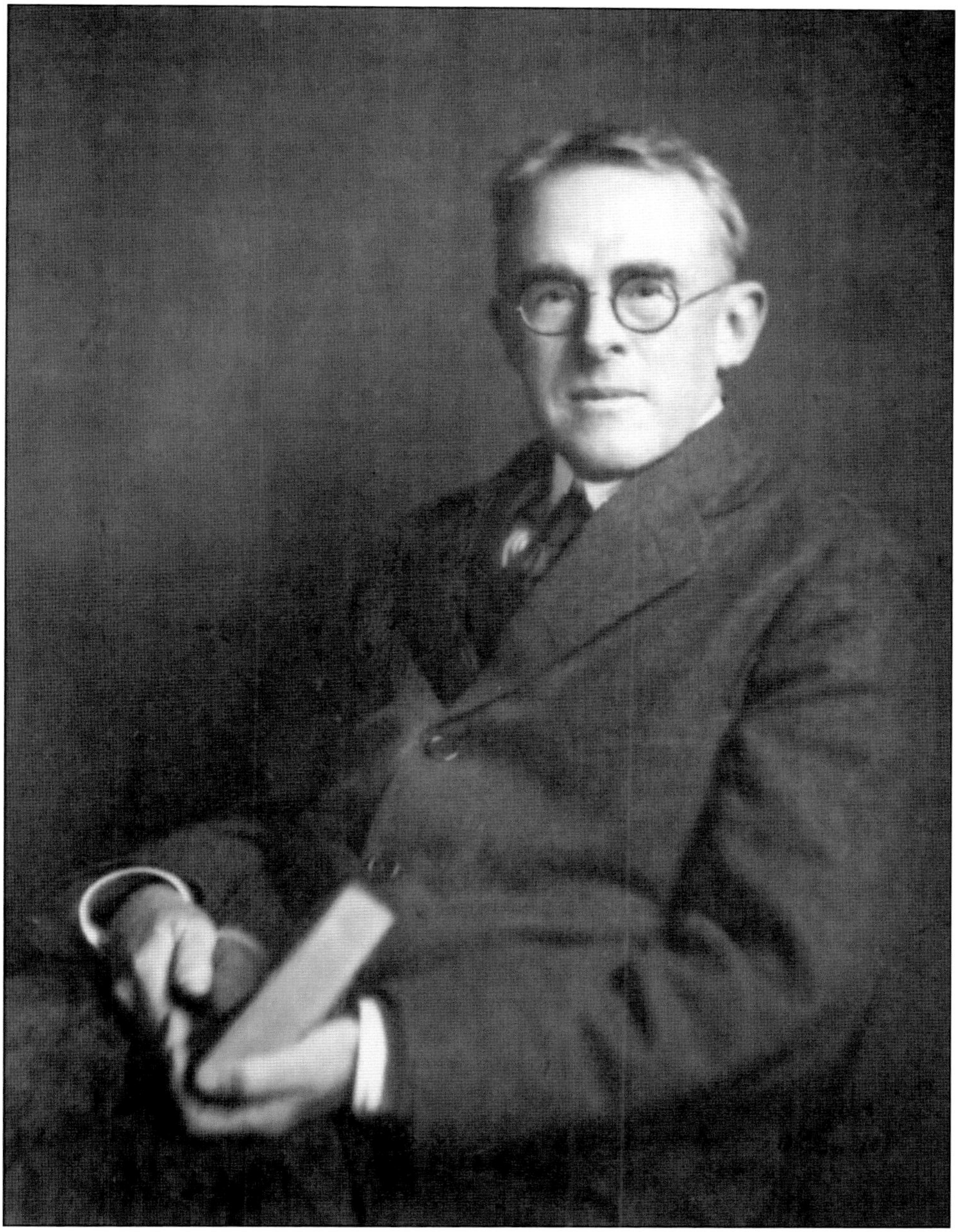

Sherman Thacher's life forever changed in 1889 when he was asked to tutor the nephew of one of his friends from Yale. This tutoring arrangement would eventually lead to the founding of The Thacher School, one of the most famous and successful college-preparatory institutions in the country. Sherman Thacher, shown above in his classic portrait, would lead The Thacher School for the next 42 years. Under his direct leadership as headmaster, The Thacher School grew from a single student in 1889 to nearly 60 by the time he stepped down in 1931. In addition, the physical plant expanded from a few small buildings to an organized set of classrooms, dining and dormitory facilities, laboratories, faculty residences, playing fields, barns and stables, and administrative offices. The faculty grew from Sherman alone to 19 instructors, and the management changed from a family business to an incorporated, nonprofit educational institution.

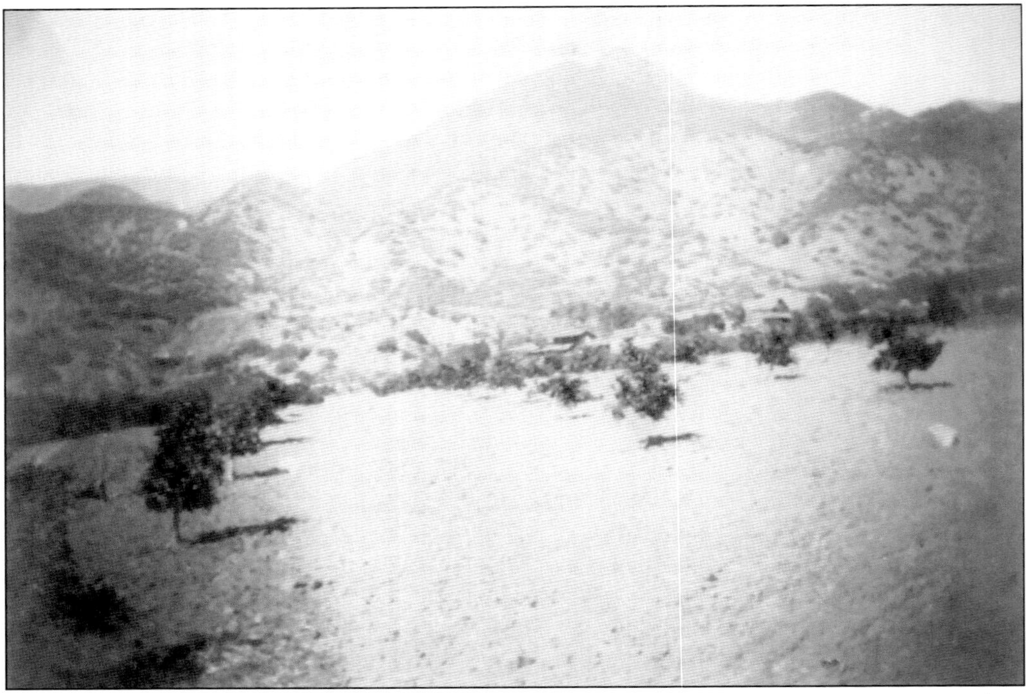

These 1892 images are among the earliest taken of The Thacher School. The above, taken looking to the north, shows Sherman Thacher's orange groves with Thacher School buildings in the background beneath the familiar outline of Twin Peaks. Below is a close-up view of The Thacher School buildings themselves, looking to the east. Note Casa de Piedra ("the stone house") to the right center and the dining hall/dormitory/classroom building in the center. Another characteristic worthy of note is the rocky nature of the landscape. Clearing land for orchards or buildings was always a challenge in the face of the boulders that litter the area.

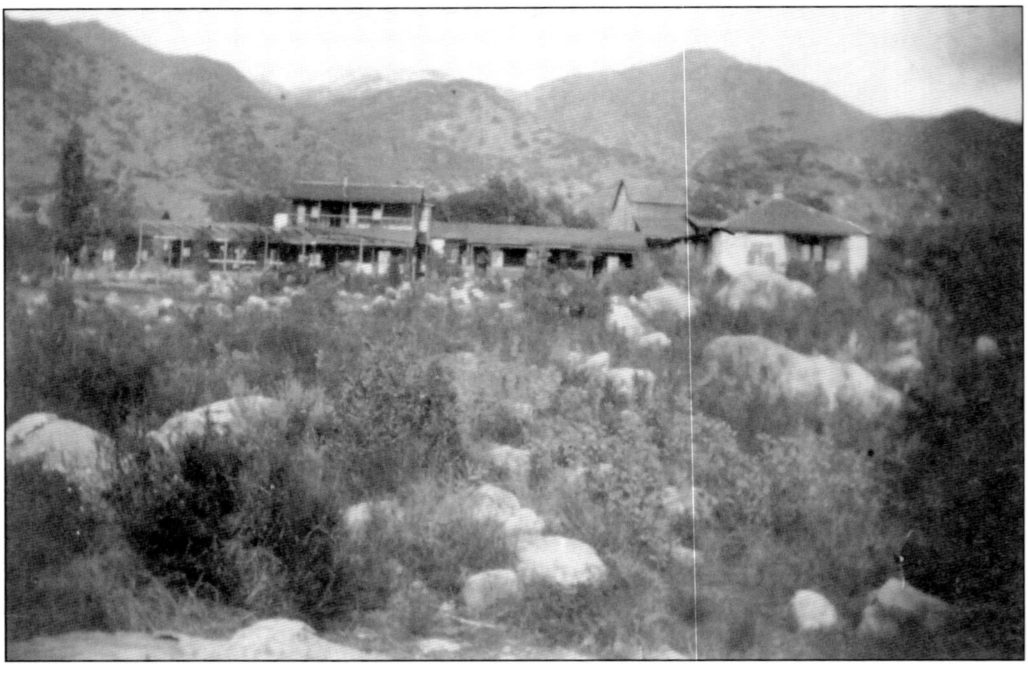

One

Beginnings and Growth

Although the request by Sherman Thacher's Yale friend to tutor his nephew came as something of a surprise to the young orange rancher, it was not a burden, nor did it upset the day-to-day routine in the newly planted orchard. Sherman and his brothers had tutored for pocket money while they were at Yale, and this seemed to be a good way to balance the books while his orange trees matured.

However, news of the arrival of this well-educated Yale Law School graduate soon spread across the county, and Thacher had several requests to take on more students. Initially, he politely refused, but the requests were plaintive and overwhelming. By 1890, he had five students and soon decided that cultivating young minds was a better pursuit than raising oranges. In June 1891, he published a simple advertisement for Casa de Piedra Ranch titled, "Out of Door Life and Study for Boys—Casa de Piedra Ranch." (Note that by 1899, the name had changed to The Thacher School.) In the one-page pamphlet, he said that "the aims of the place are in three directions: toward health and enjoyment, toward unselfish, manly character, and toward accurate, thorough, and self-reliant habits of thought and study." Tuition was $650 per year plus the cost of keeping a horse.

The Thacher School continued to grow, and with expanded enrollment came new facilities—dormitories, classrooms, the dining hall, faculty residences, stables, playing fields, and more. By the time The Thacher School celebrated its semicentennial in 1939, it was recognized as one of the premier boys' schools in the West, if not in the country. By 1950, it had weathered several fires, the Great Depression, and two world wars and was entering its seventh decade with a solid enrollment, extensive facilities, and a good financial position.

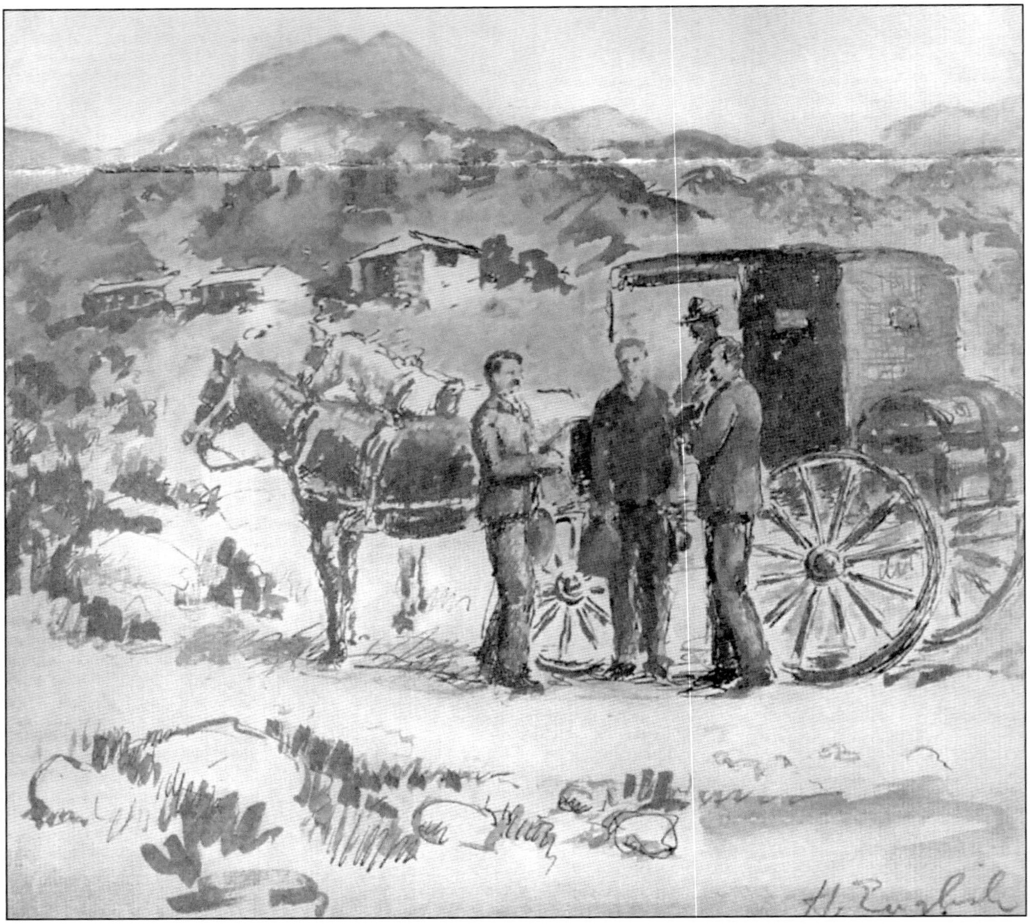

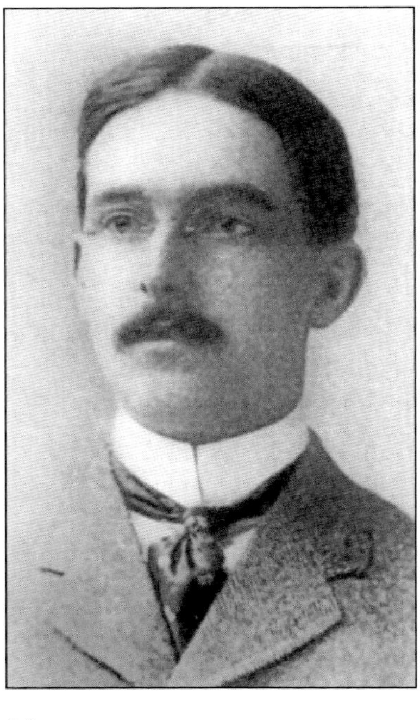

In 1889, one of Sherman's Yale friends, professor of political economy Henry W. Farnam, asked if Sherman would take his nephew Henry Farnam "for a year of outdoor life combined with study in preparation for college." Sherman agreed and began construction of a larger building made from the rocks and boulders that were strewn across the ranch. Henry Farnam and his nephew arrived on August 7, 1889, and the younger Henry took up residence as the first student at the Casa de Piedra Ranch School. Henry spent the 1889–1890 school year there and then went on to graduate from Yale in 1895. The image above shows Sherman welcoming Henry and his uncle, and the image at left is of Henry as a student at Yale. (Above, courtesy of The Thacher School Archives; left, courtesy of Yale University.)

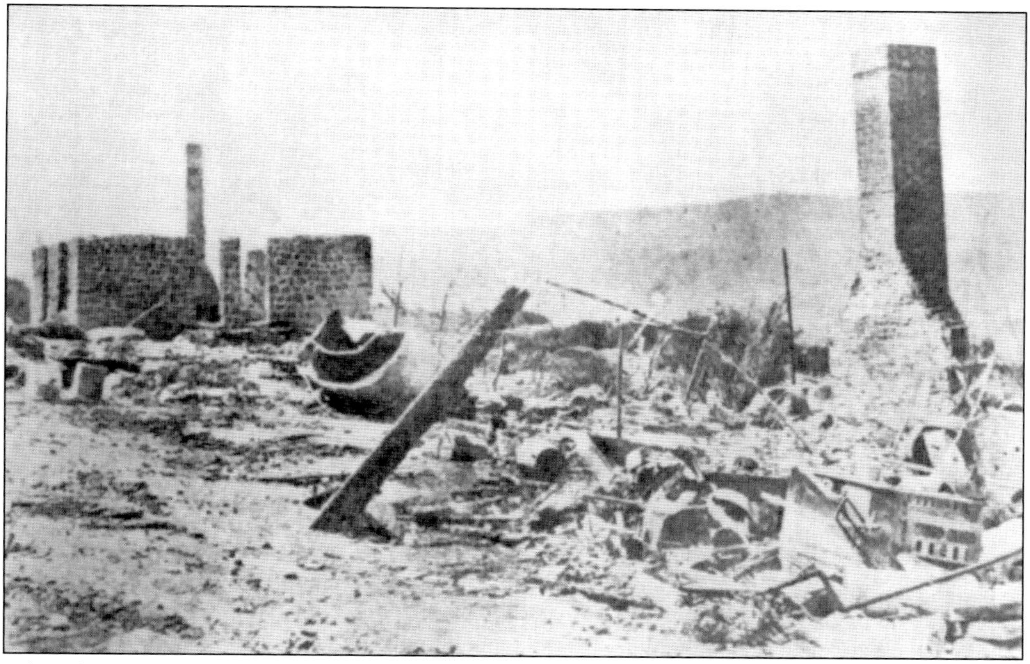

A fire that began in the kitchen swept through The Thacher School on June 18, 1895. With the exception of some minor burns, no one was hurt. However, the wooden buildings burned to the ground and the stone house was badly scorched. Despite this setback, Thacher rebuilt his school with the help of his growing student body, as shown in the 1899 photograph below. To accommodate the enrollment of 25, the infrastructure now included not only dormitories, classrooms, and a dining room, but also tennis courts and stable facilities. A reservoir, which doubled as a swimming pool in the hot days of spring and summer, was also available.

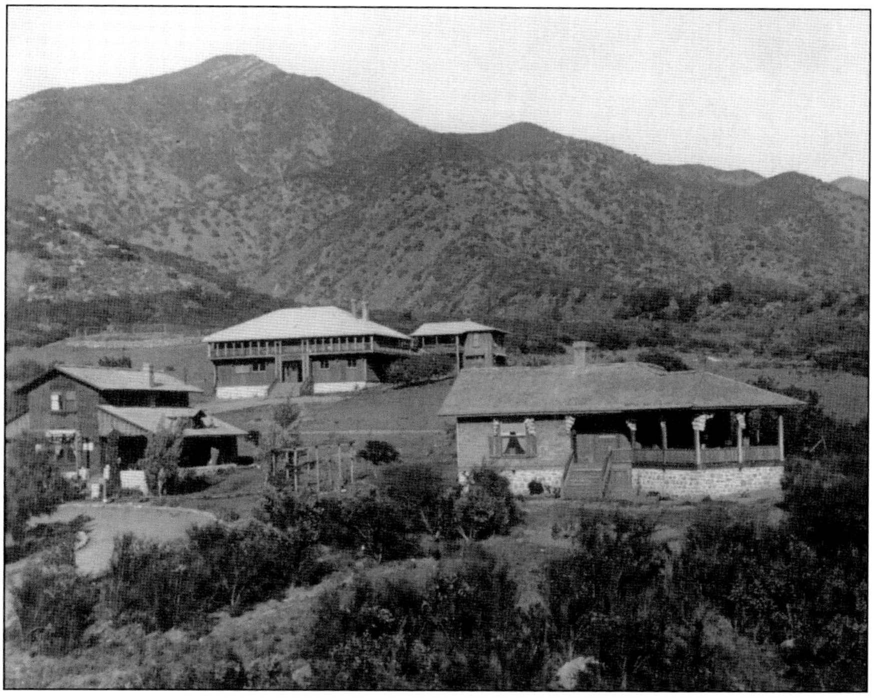

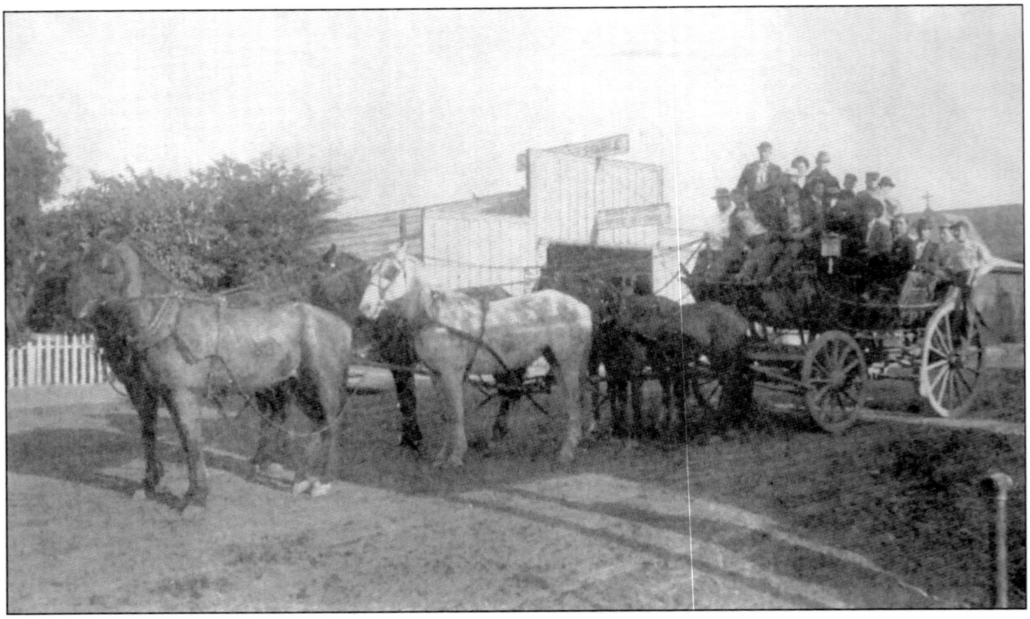

The first train came to the Ojai Valley in 1898. Despite this breakthrough in access to the valley, Casa de Piedra was still isolated at the far east end, and Thacher's students, parents, faculty, and visitors had to travel the five miles to the depot in downtown Nordhoff by horse and carriage before they could access the train to the outside world. Below is a 1905 image of The Thacher School and the valley looking west across the campus. Note the reservoir/swimming pool in the lower left.

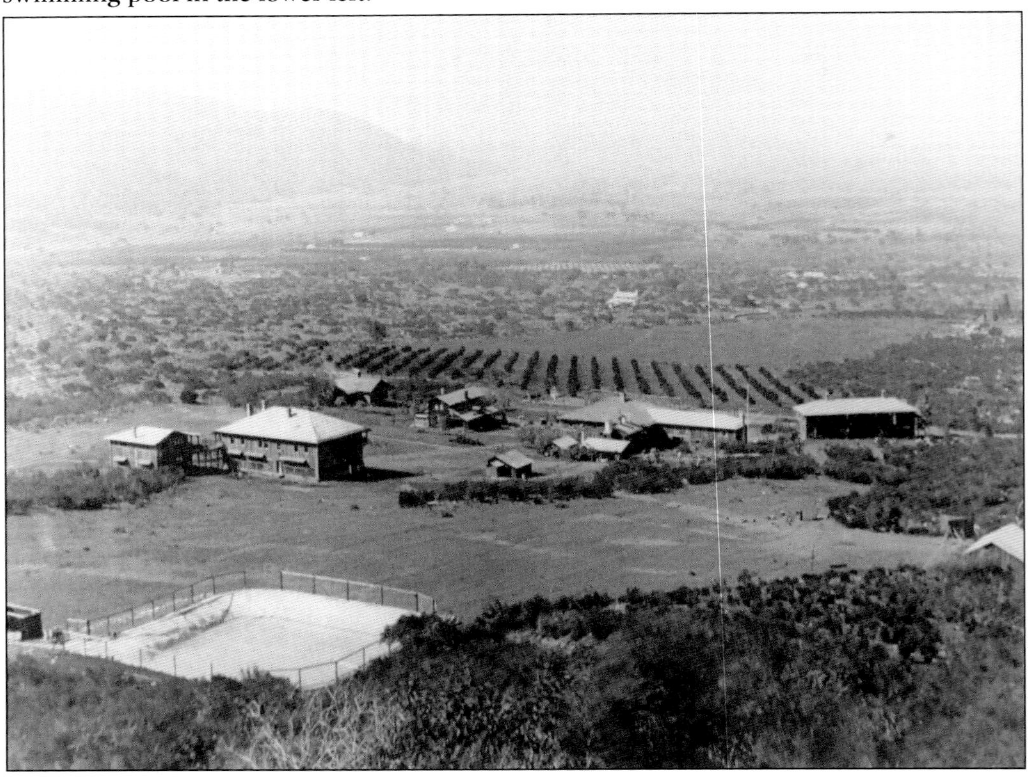

Sherman Thacher, Thacher's founder and headmaster from 1889 until 1931, emphasized a complete and well-rounded education, as illustrated in the 1899 advertisement. The references cited included the presidents of Yale, Harvard, and Stanford as well as the world-renowned author, historian, social activist, and theologian Edward Everett Hale. In another early flyer, Thacher described a typical day: "The mornings are devoted to recitations, with a liberal recess for ball playing, in which all must join, and the afternoon to study until 4 o'clock. Light gymnastics and breathing exercises precede each recitation. It is the custom to read aloud in the evenings some good authors and to keep track of current events."

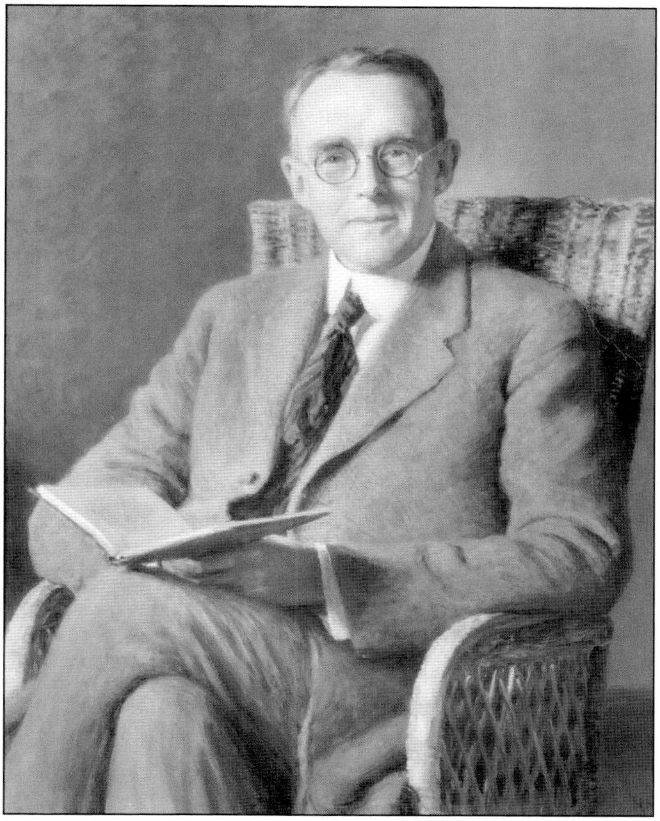

Out of Door Life and Study for Boys

▲ ▲ ▲ Casa de Piedra Ranch School, Ojai Valley, Southern California.

The next school year begins Sept. 25th. Boys over twelve years of age will be admitted if properly recommended, and may receive preparation for any American college. Special attention is paid also to sciences, modern languages, manual training and music, and to physical development.

References: President Dwight, New Haven; President Walker, Boston; President Kellogg, Berkeley; President Jordan, Stanford; Rev. Edward Everett Hale, Boston; Charles Nordhoff, Esq., Coronado, California.

Address— SHERMAN D. THACHER, Nordhoff, California.

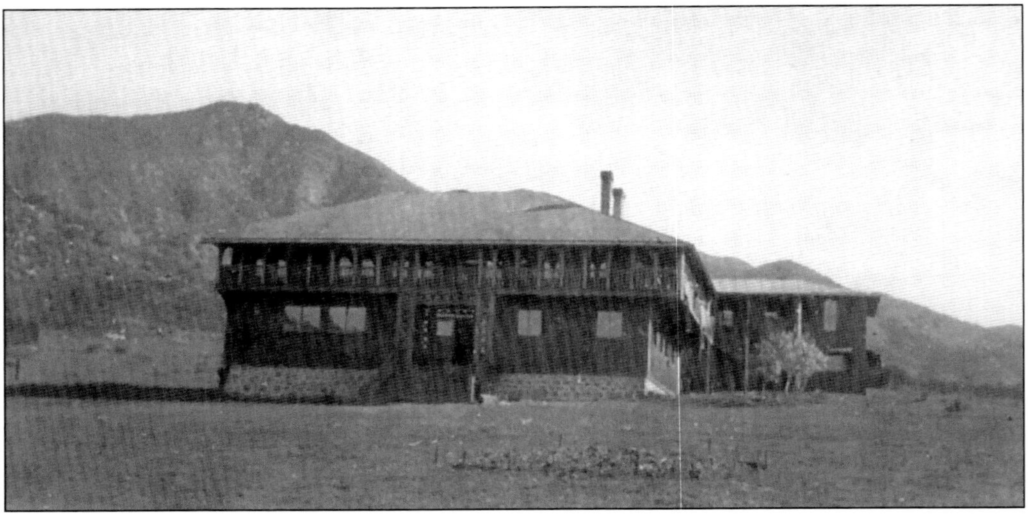

Fire was a constant threat in the dry Southern California environment. This was especially true for wooden buildings such as the Upper School and the Upper School Annex (shown above), both of which utilized fireplaces and wood stoves for heating. That scourge struck again on November 22, 1910, with a fire that began in a stove on the first floor of the Upper School Annex and burned the Upper School, the Upper School Annex, the Appendix, the Main School Building, and the Rough-House. Once again, the faculty and student body pulled together to keep Thacher going, holding classes and study hall in the library until the structures could be rebuilt.

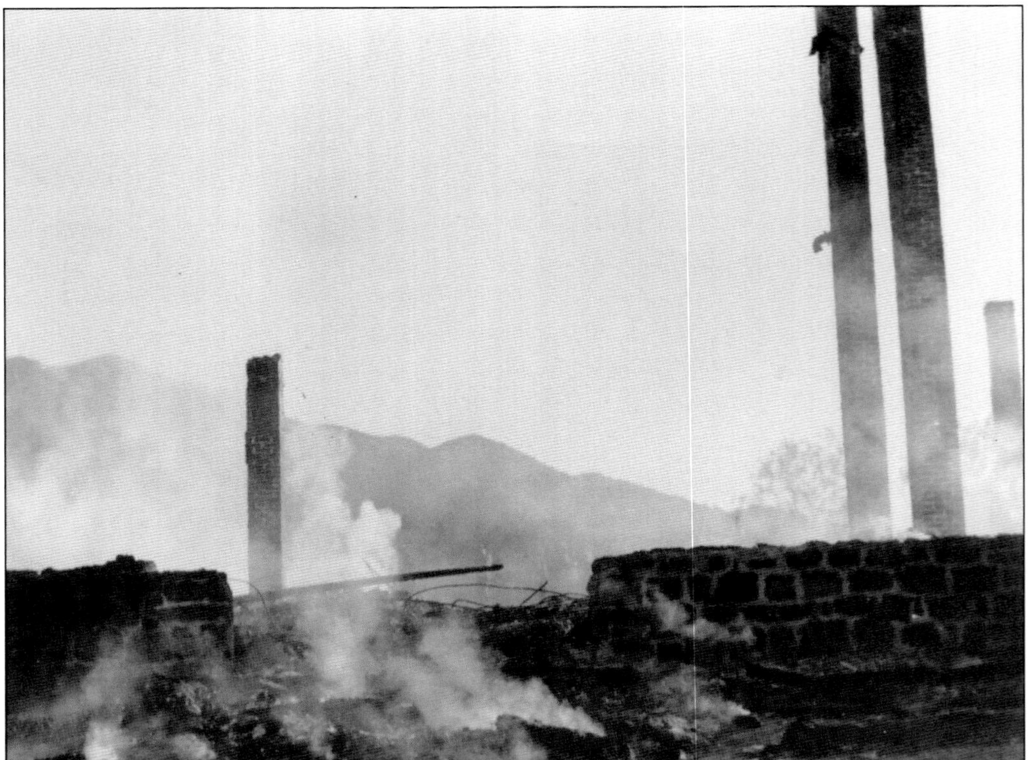

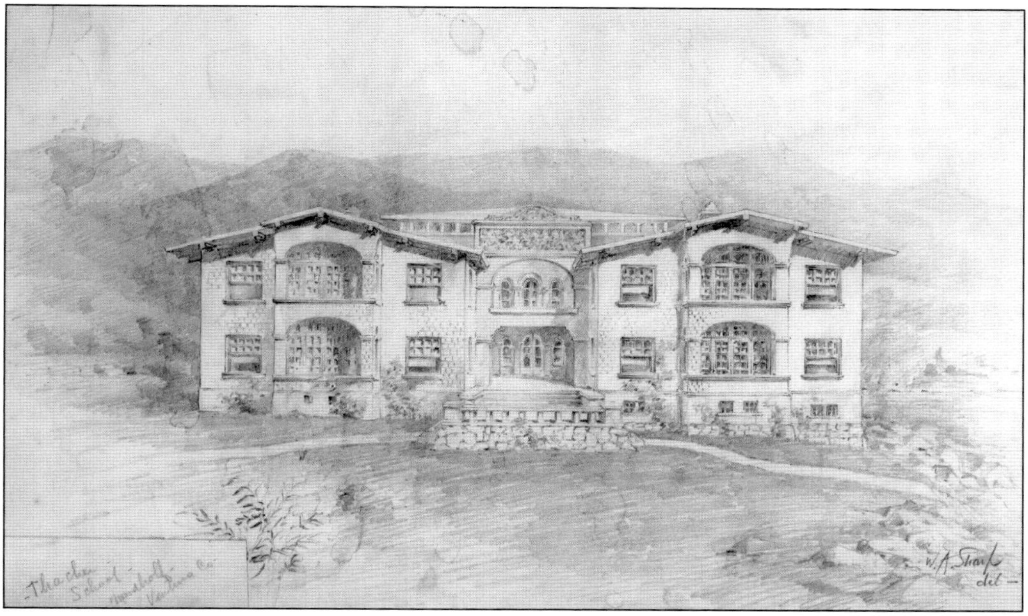

After the dormitories were rebuilt, seniors lived on the top floor of the Upper School (shown above, probably around 1911) and were, therefore, referred to as "upper uppers." Juniors inhabited the first floor and were, logically, "lower uppers." Freshmen were the youngest students and were referred to as "lower schoolers," or, affectionately, as "smuts" because of their tendency to get covered with fireplace ash. Adjacent to the dining room was the sophomore dorm, and sophomores, being between freshmen and juniors, were "middle schoolers." The photograph below was taken in 1912 on the Pergola in front of the dining room (now known as the dining hall). Sherman Thacher is seated to the right with his wife, mother, and children. Students are arranged by class, with lower schoolers under the pepper tree and upper uppers, faculty, and staff on the Pergola.

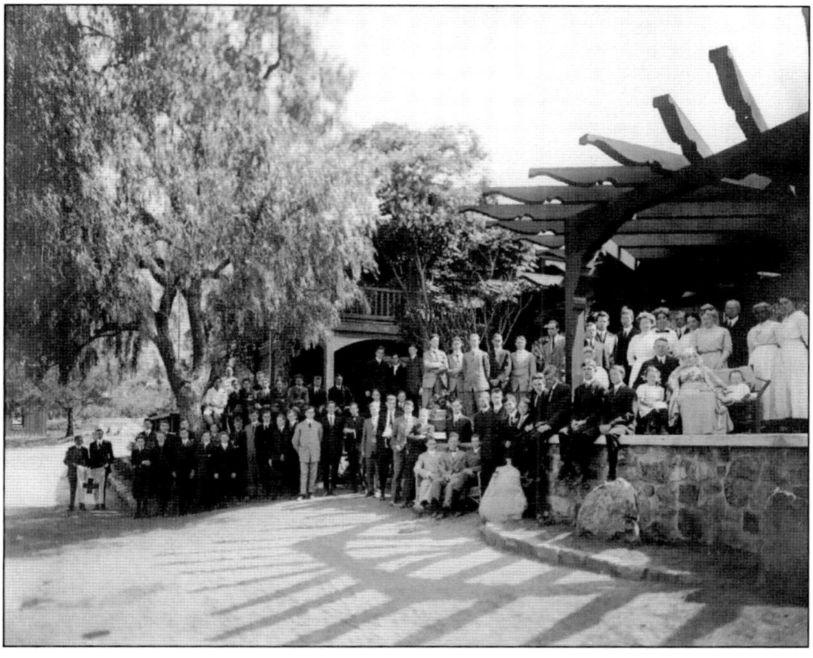

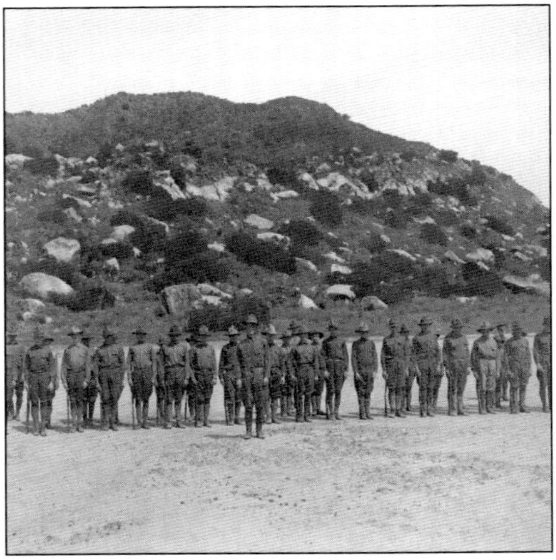

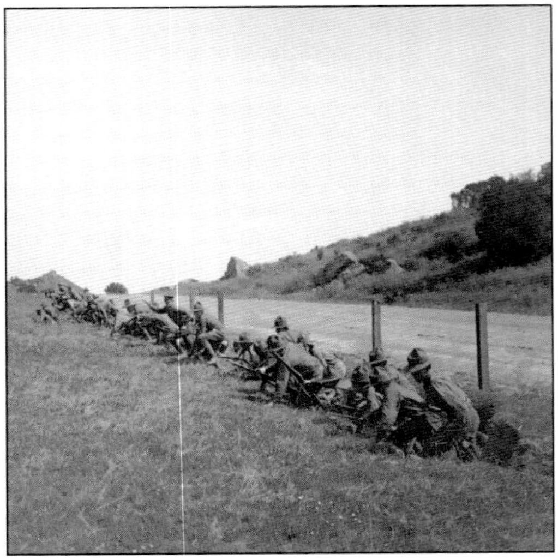

The world went to war in the second and fourth decades of the 20th century, and Thacher did its part. The images above show Thacher boys in uniform drilling on Jameson Field in 1918. During World War I, 11 Thacher alumni gave their lives. World War II was equally costly, with the ranks of the Thacher family reduced by 12 (one of whom died as a result of the atomic bombing of Hiroshima). Two additional Thacher alumni died as a result of the Vietnam War. The Memorial Pergola, shown below, was built after World War I to commemorate these brave men.

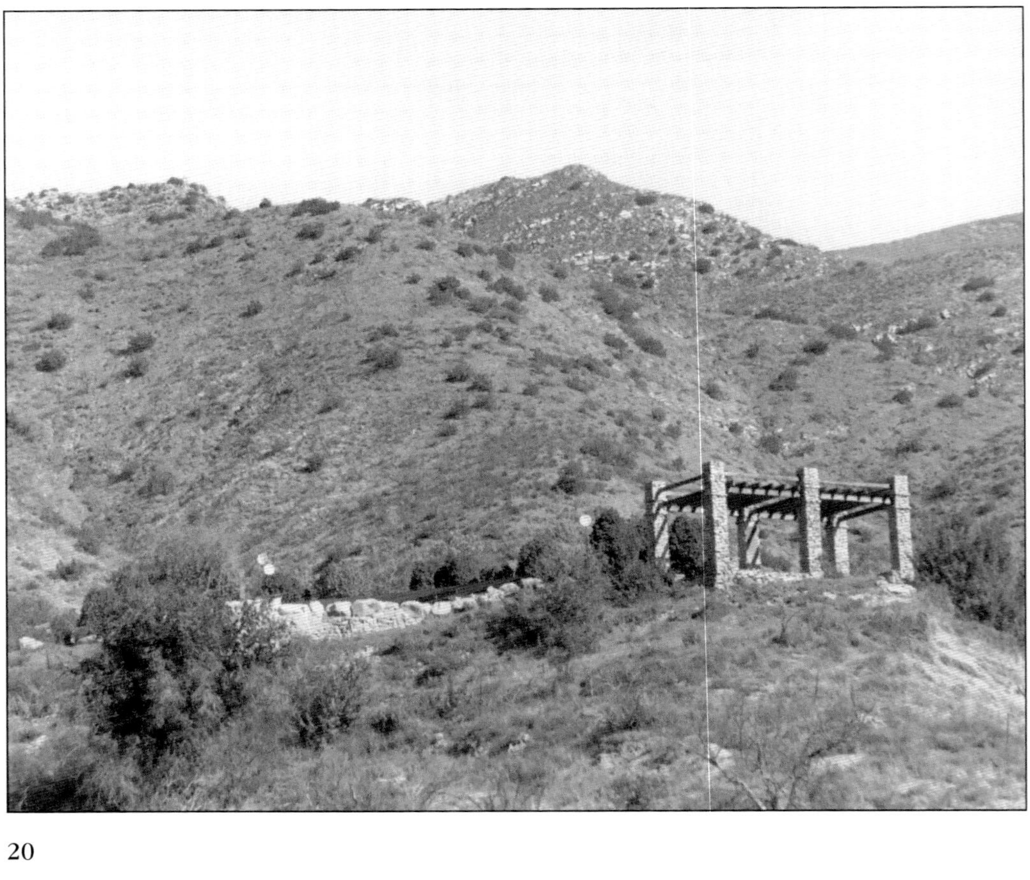

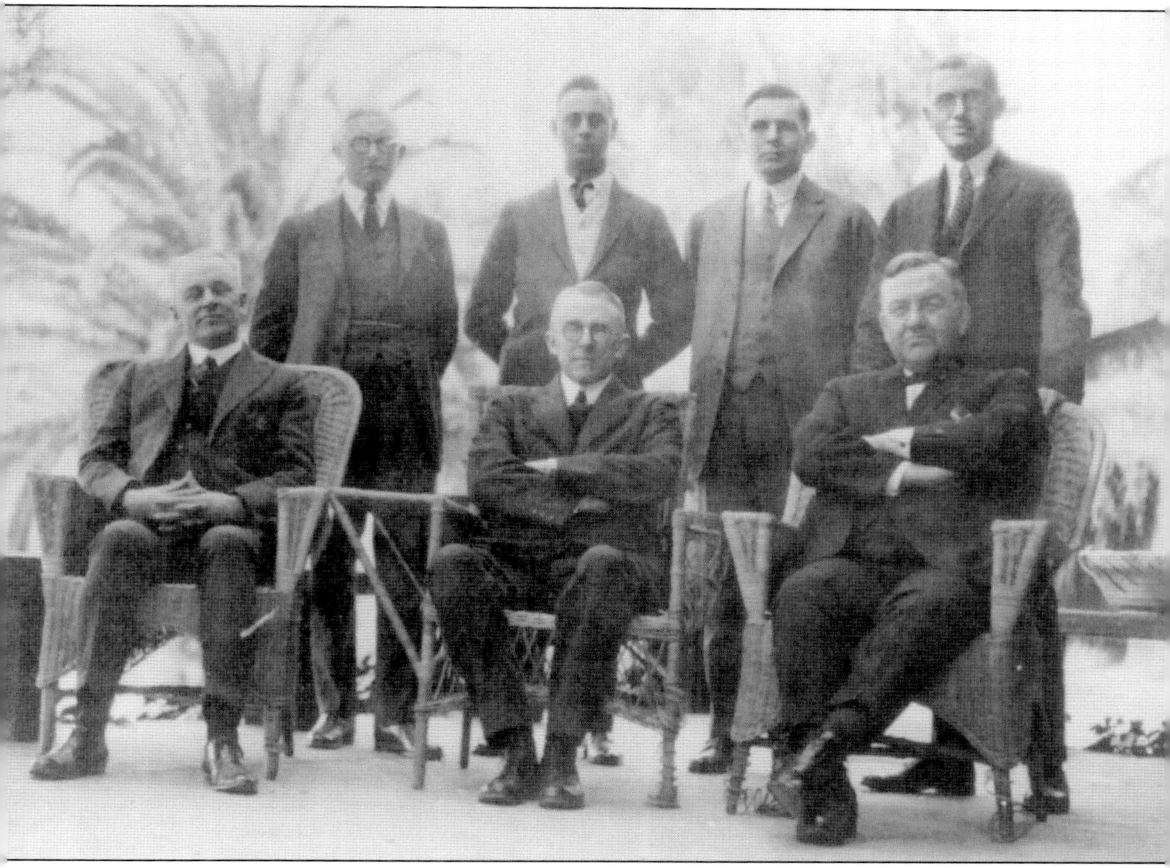

As early as 1911, Sherman Thacher entertained thoughts of incorporation. By 1924, he decided that maintaining Thacher as a viable educational and business entity would require more than just a family-management approach. He drew up articles of incorporation for The Thacher School as a nonprofit educational institution, and these documents were signed and finalized on May 24, 1924. This not only made Thacher independent of any individual, but also made it possible for the corporation to accept gifts and donations and provided for an independent board of trustees to select subsequent headmasters and oversee the operations. The first board, shown above, consisted of, from left to right, (seated) Dr. R.A. Millikan, Sherman Thacher, and George E. Farrand; (standing) F. Barreda Sherman, Richard Bard, H. Clifford Allen Jr., and Morgan Barnes.

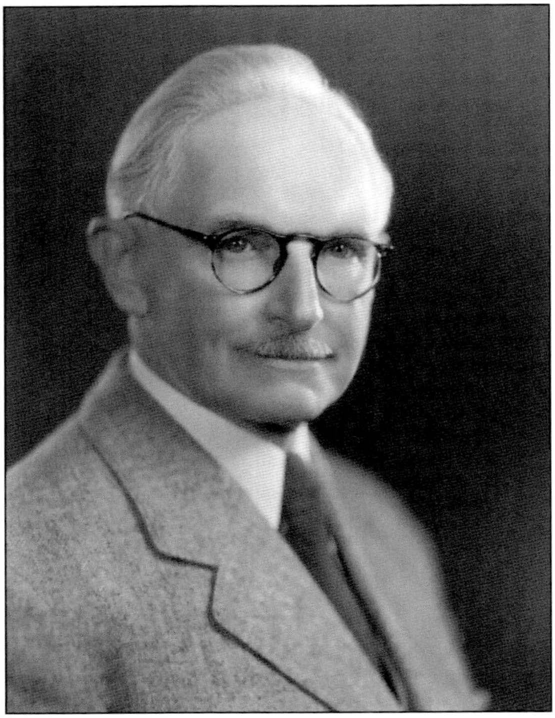

In June 1931, Sherman Thacher, 69 years old and in failing health, turned over leadership of The Thacher School to his friend, fellow faculty member, and member of the board of trustees, Morgan Barnes (left). Barnes had joined the Thacher faculty in 1903, teaching Latin, German, French, and Spanish. He was an avid horseman and camper and served as headmaster from 1931 to 1936. Under his oversight and guidance, enrollment grew to 65 and several new buildings were added. In 1936, Anson Stiles Thacher (below), son of the founder, took over as headmaster. Anson was a member of Thacher's class of 1923 and a graduate of Yale. He had previously taught at Groton and the Catalina Island School before joining the Thacher faculty in 1931. He served as headmaster from 1936 until 1949 and remained on the faculty until 1970.

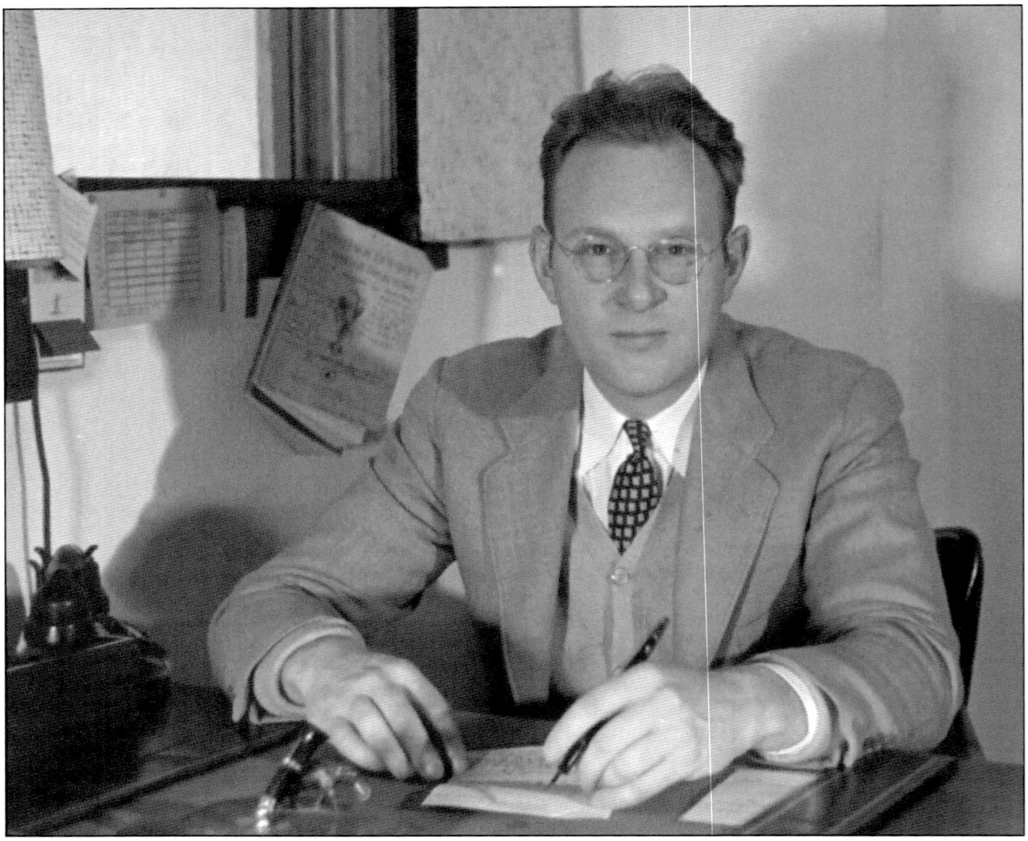

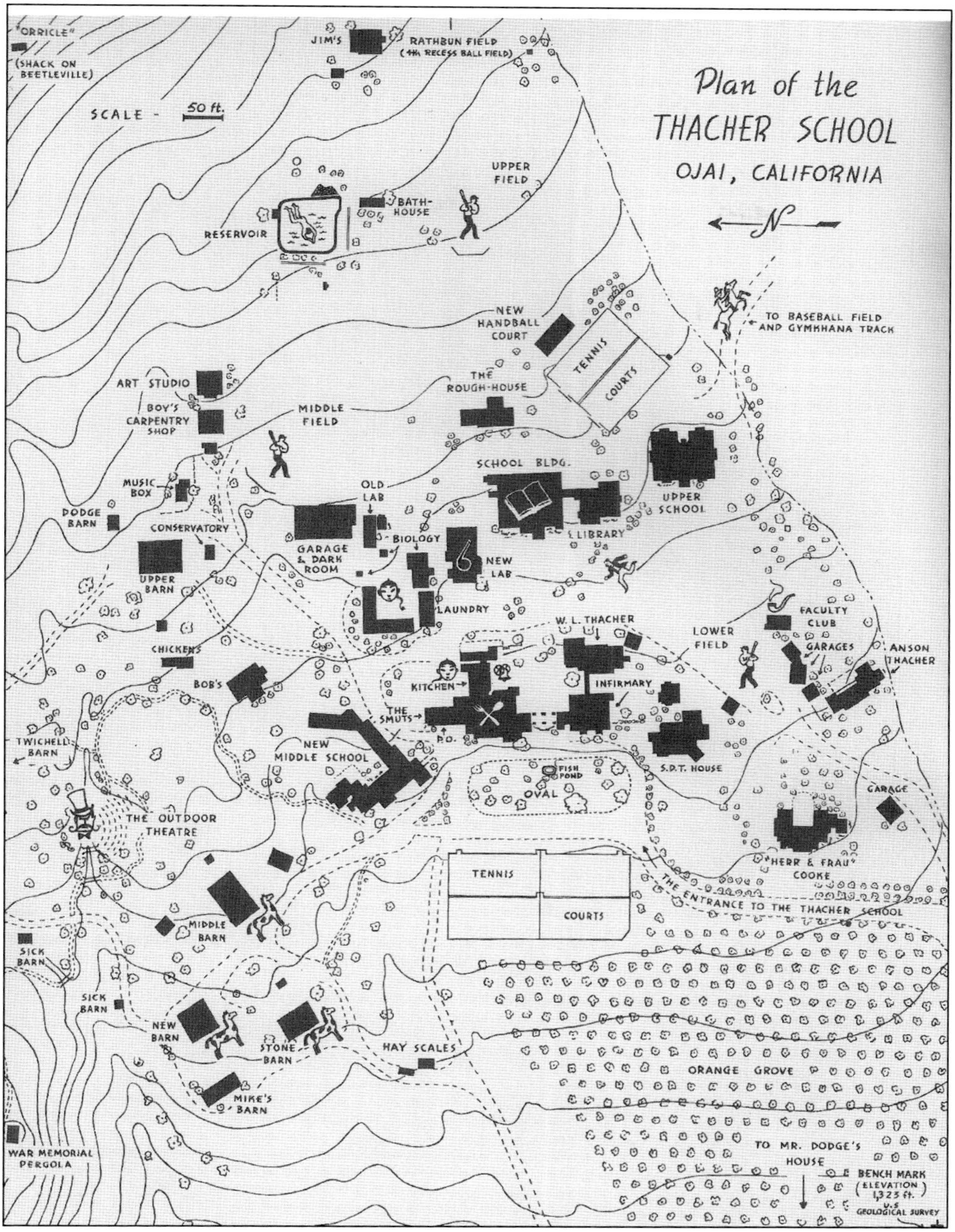

This diagram of The Thacher School in 1939 shows the buildings and facilities. Note the icons representing features such as the Chinese staff quarters, the recess baseball fields, the library, the stable area, the Faculty Club, the Outdoor Theatre, and the reservoir/swimming pool. The new laboratory, donated by Howard Hughes's father and serving as a predecessor to the Mudd Science Building; the Rough-House, an iconic landmark for nearly 100 years; and the shacks on Beadleville Hill (sometimes rendered as Beetleville Hill) are also noted. This diagram also shows a feature that has helped to condition Thacher students from the outset—it is built on a rather steep hill. Very few of the daily journeys that every student takes (class to class, dorm to dining hall, dining hall to stables) do not involve going uphill for some distance.

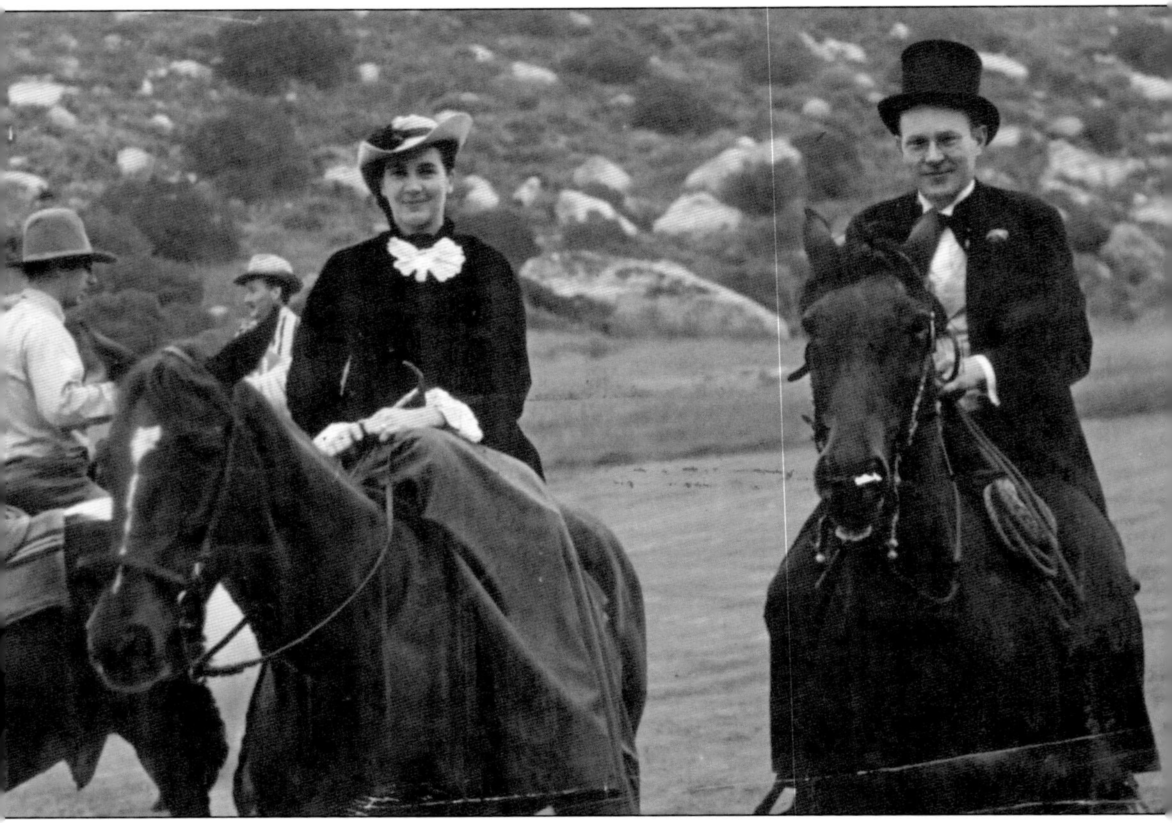

As The Thacher School emerged from the postwar period, Anson Thacher stepped down after 13 years as its head. Enrollment was strong at 94 boys, and the faculty included 16 teachers, each of whom had been carefully selected for his academic strength and enthusiasm for education and the outdoors. The infrastructure included nearly 50 buildings, and Thacher was financially secure. Anson, his wife, Peggy, and their children continued as integral members of The Thacher School family. They are shown here on horseback at the gymkhana field during the celebration of the 50th anniversary of The Thacher School in 1939. Anson died in March 1994 and Peggy in December 1995, thus ending a century of direct day-to-day participation of the Thacher family in the operation and activities of Thacher.

Two

Coming of Age

Anson Thacher turned over leadership of The Thacher School to Newton Chase in the fall of 1949 and remained on the faculty until 1970 as a mathematics teacher. Thacher had proven its worth and sustainability as it entered its seventh decade.

The 1950s were a time of relative tranquility, both at Thacher and across the country. Although the Korean War was costly and the Cold War concerning, by and large the Eisenhower years were much less turbulent than the previous decades, which had been marked by the two world wars and the Great Depression.

The 1960s began quietly enough, but by the end of the decade, the national debate over the Vietnam War and the dawning of the drug culture had impacted the entire nation. Headmasters David Twichell and Edgar Sanford were faced with heretofore unforeseen issues and challenges, and Thacher's core values suddenly were called into question by students and faculty alike. These challenges notwithstanding, Thacher weathered the storm and, by the mid-1970s, was back on an even keel. The enrollment was increased with a corresponding increase in faculty, facilities, and activities. By the time Willard G. Wyman became headmaster in 1975, enrollment had increased to 189.

One of the major tasks facing Thacher's administration was upgrading facilities. Many of the buildings dated back to the earliest days and were badly in need of repair or even outright replacement. Chase, Twichell, Sanford, and Wyman, with the guidance and support of the board of trustees, began to plan and implement these upgrades.

Perhaps the most significant course change in the history of The Thacher School was made in 1977, during Wyman's tenure as headmaster, when the board of trustees made the decision to admit girls as full-time boarding students. For the first time in nearly 90 years, Thacher was not just a boys' school, and the decision was greeted by both cheers and tears from alumni, friends, and faculty. Wyman was faced with implementing the decision. He also orchestrated the celebration of Thacher's 100th anniversary.

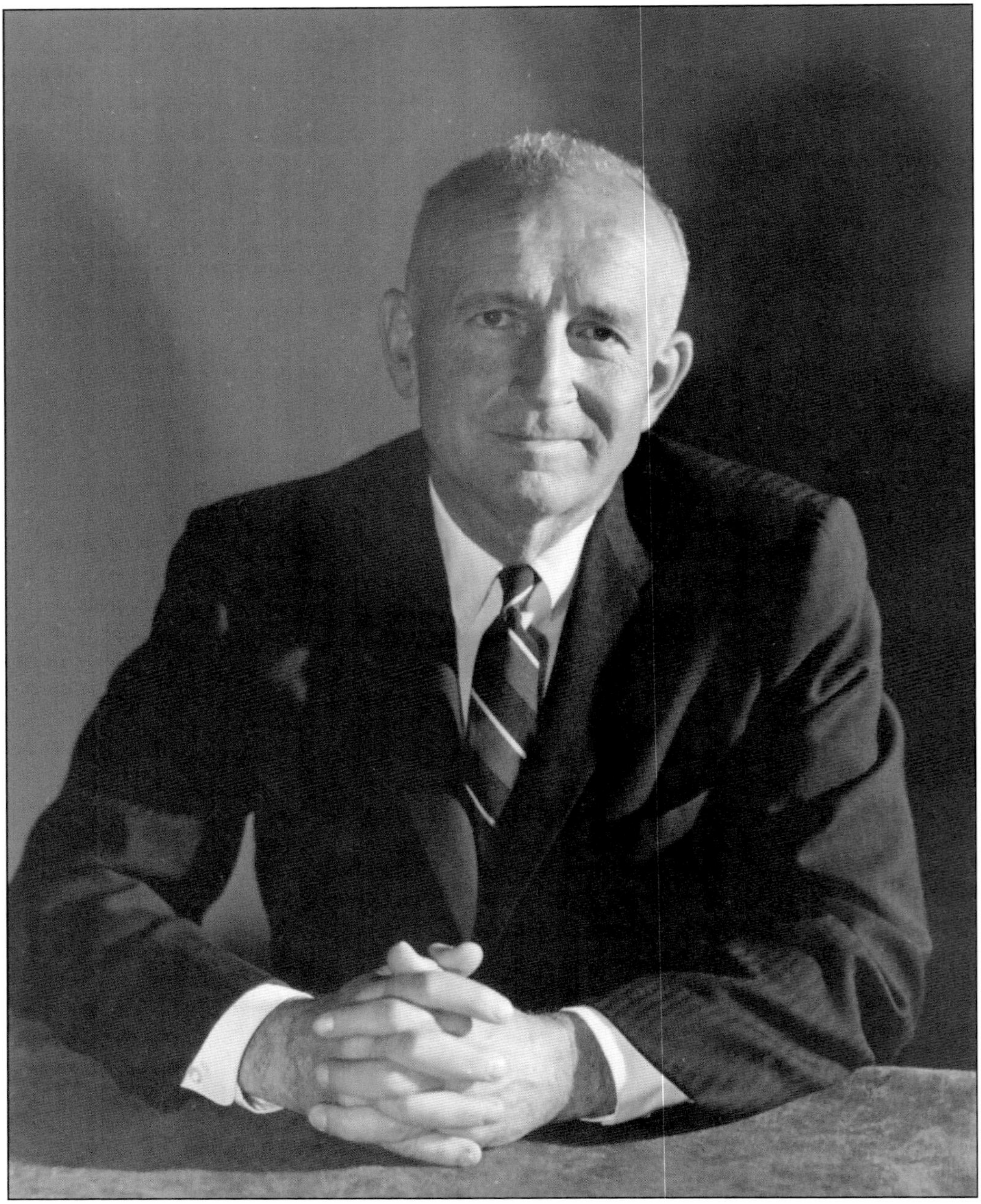

Newton Chase, headmaster from 1949 to 1963, was born in Maine and graduated from Bowdoin College. He had experienced the Depression firsthand when the school where he was teaching went bankrupt. This experience colored his view of finances, especially on the expenditure side of the ledger. In fact, Jack Huyler opined that Chase "squeezed a nickel until the buffalo bellowed." After leaving Thacher in 1963, Chase took a stab at California politics, running unsuccessfully for state senate. When his immediate successor, David Twichell, resigned in 1968 before the board of trustees had an opportunity to identify a replacement, Chase stepped into the breach and served as interim headmaster for the 1968–1969 school year. For much of his tenure, his wife, Betty, was Thacher's nurse, and it was through her efforts that a new infirmary was designed and built.

Austen Pierpont, an architect and member of Thacher's class of 1909, designed an auditorium that served Thacher for the latter half of the 20th century. Completed in 1959, it was later remodeled as the Frederick Stymetz Lamb Auditorium in honor of history teacher and tennis coach Fred Lamb. The Lamb Auditorium was razed in 2004 and replaced by the Thacher Commons and the Milligan Center for the Performing Arts.

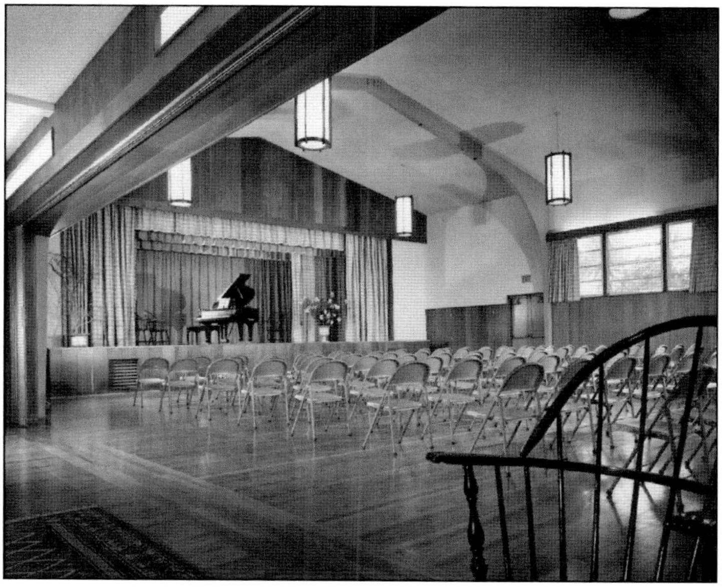

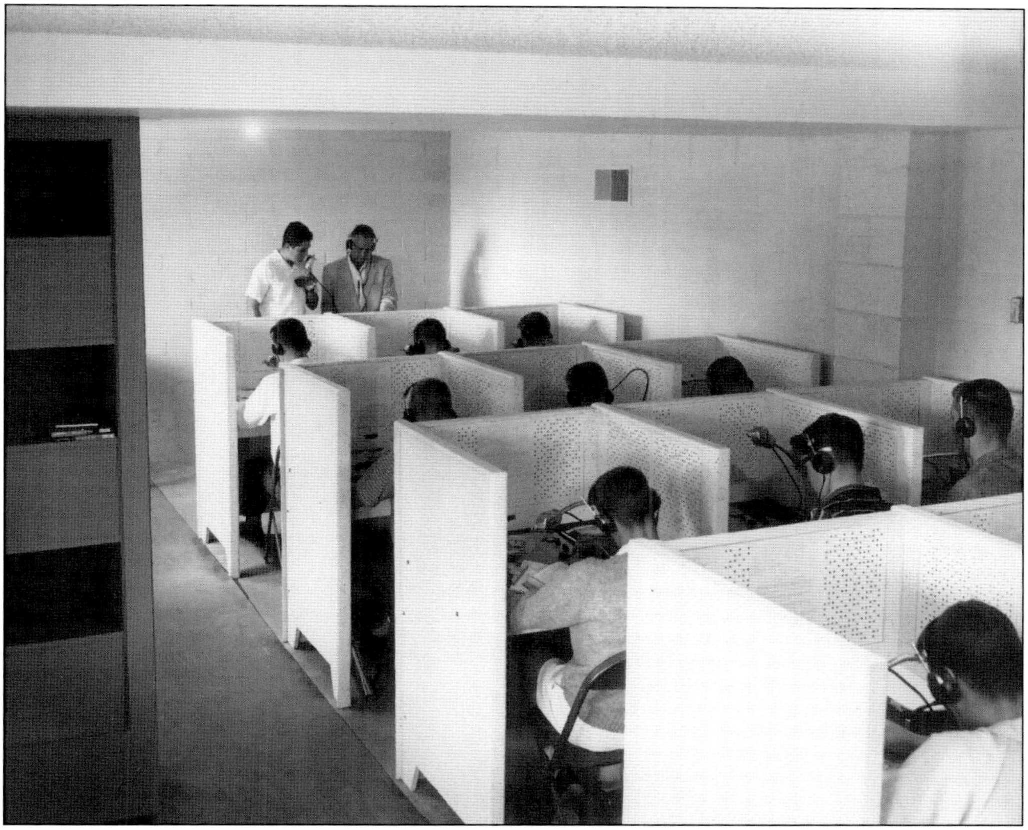

In addition to providing facilities for lectures, concerts, and social events, the Lamb Auditorium included a language laboratory. This facility, located on the lower level of the auditorium, was state of the art for the 1960s and serves as an excellent example of Thacher's efforts to use innovative approaches to education. Shown here is Bob Miller directing an audio lesson for one of his Spanish classes in the language lab.

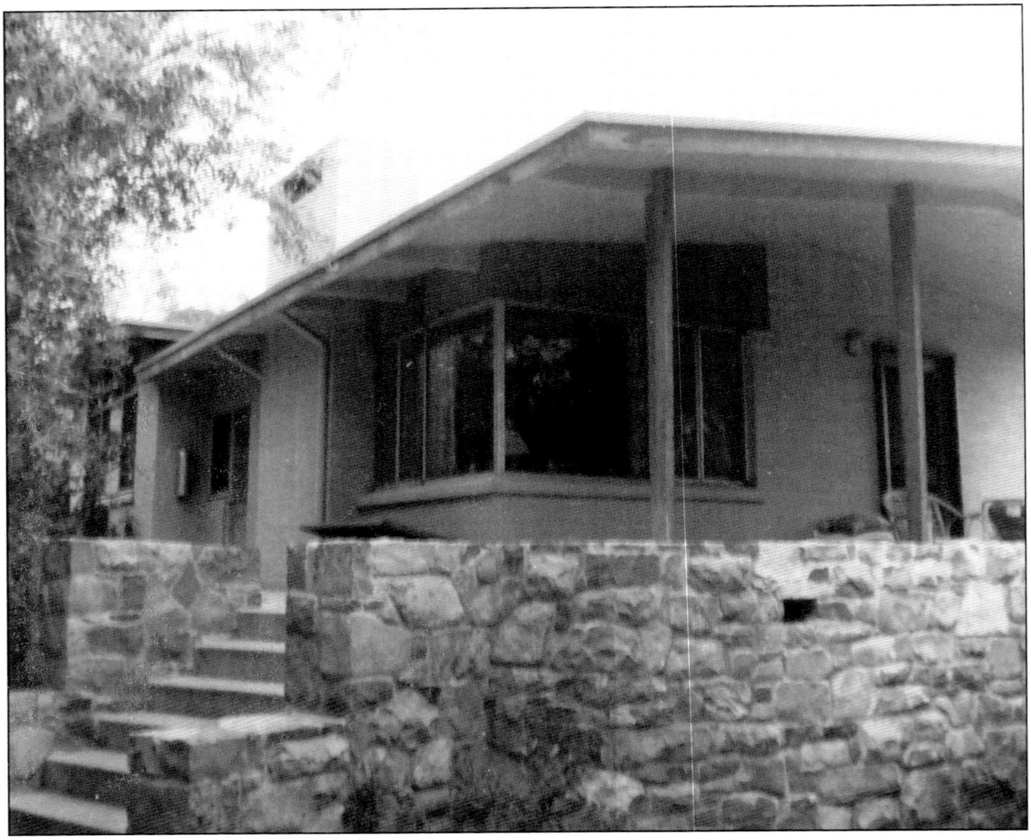

Another facility that was badly in need of upgrading was the infirmary. Under the leadership of Betty Chase—the headmaster's wife and Thacher's nurse—a new facility (above) was designed and constructed in 1954 at the foot of the Upper School Field. This building was replaced by the present Health Center in the former Chinese staff quarters when the Milligan Center for the Performing Arts was built in 2006. A new freshman dormitory named Casa de Piedra (shown below after the 2012 renovation) was built in time for the 1964-1965 school year just down the hill from the 1949-vintage Lower School.

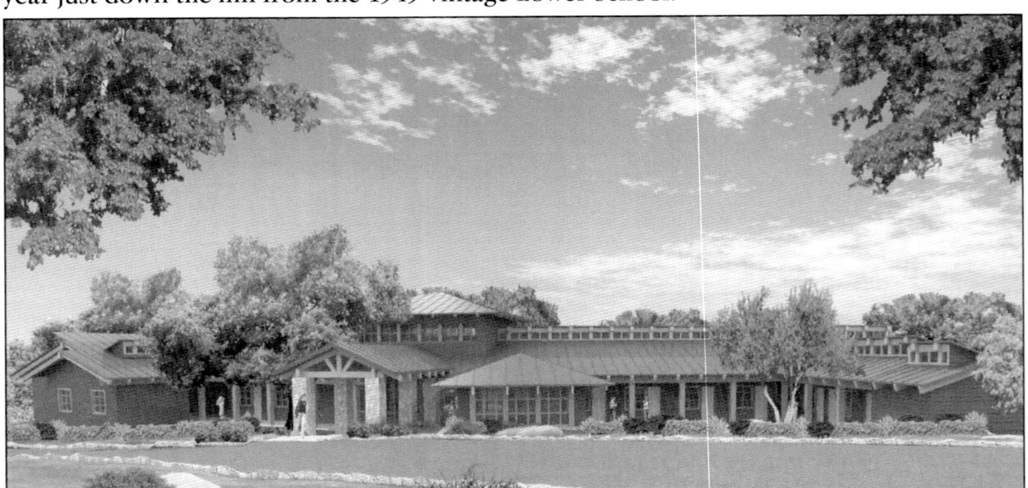

David Twichell, Thacher's headmaster from 1963 to 1968, had strong ties to Thacher. He had graduated in the class of 1936, and his father had taught at Thacher. Additionally, Twichell himself had taught at Thacher in 1946 after serving as a pilot in World War II. He returned to Thacher after a long stint as the headmaster of the Pomfret School in Connecticut. Twichell was an educational innovator and an unabashed supporter of all things outdoors. He made a number of curricular and operational changes (introducing variable class schedules, senior projects, and trimesters and eliminating the marks system) and insisted that all new boys ride their horses at least three days a week and participate in athletics on the remaining two days.

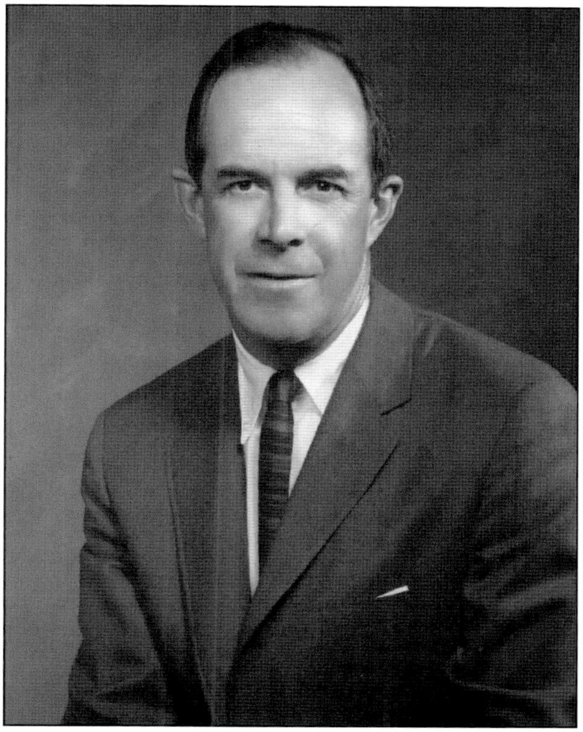

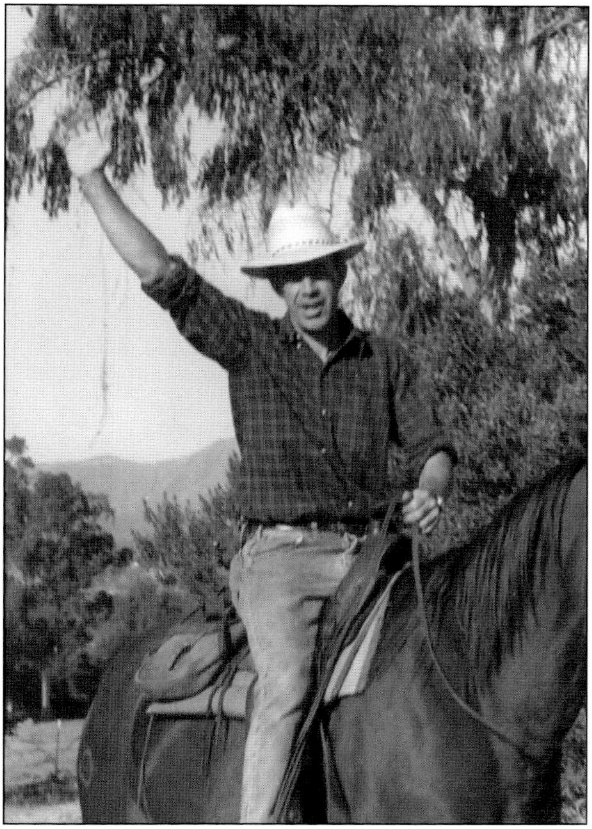

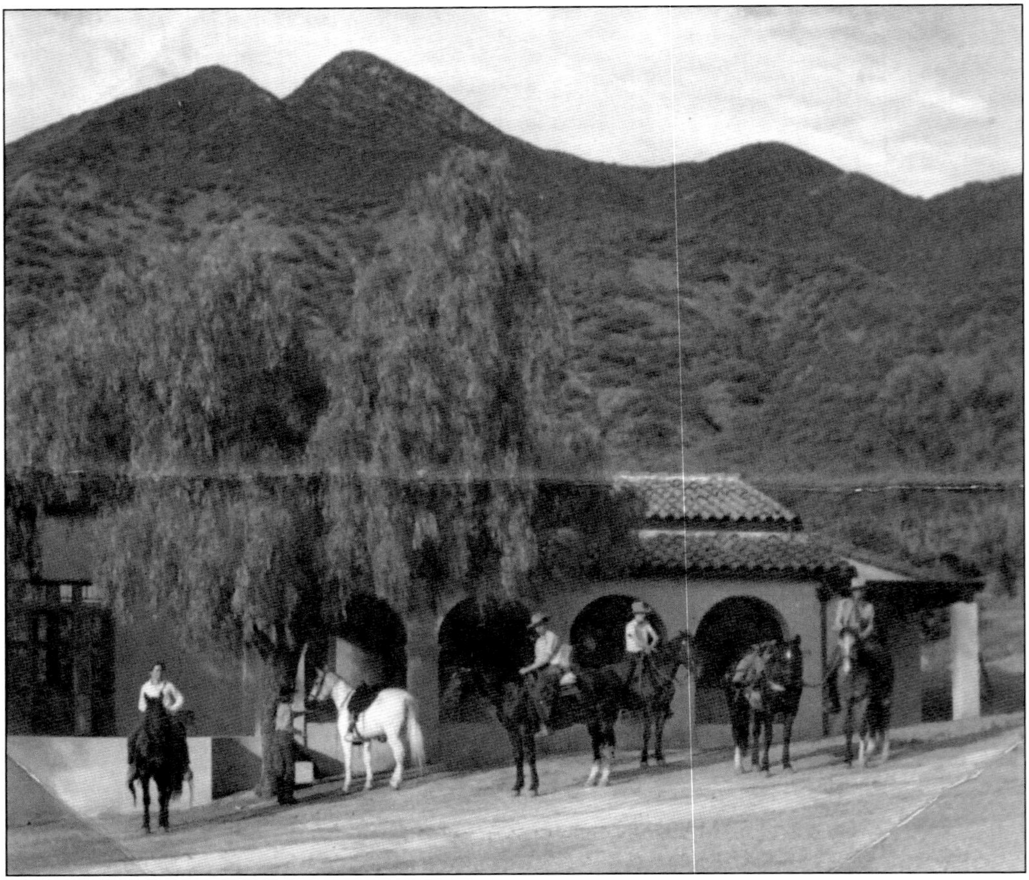

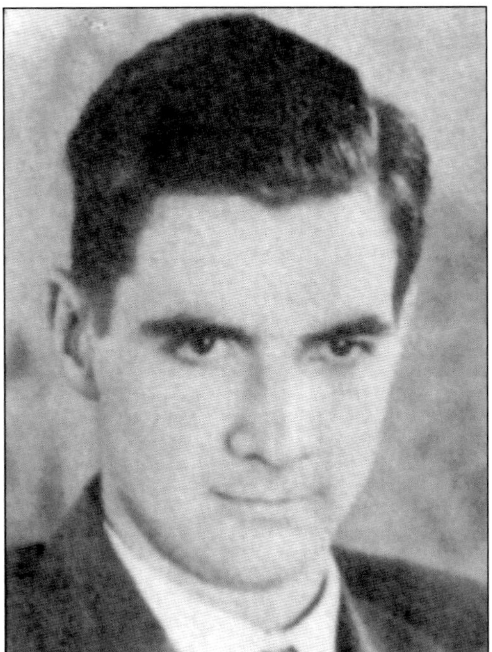

For the first five decades of The Thacher School, science was taught in standard classrooms. The first dedicated science building (shown above in the late 1930s) was donated by the father of Howard Hughes (shown at left), the famed hermit aviator who had spent one of his high school years at Thacher as a member of the class of 1923. This structure had been used for biology, chemistry, and physics for more than 25 years when David Twichell became headmaster. However, it had become obsolete, so a new facility was designed and constructed just north of the original using money from the Seeley G. Mudd Fund.

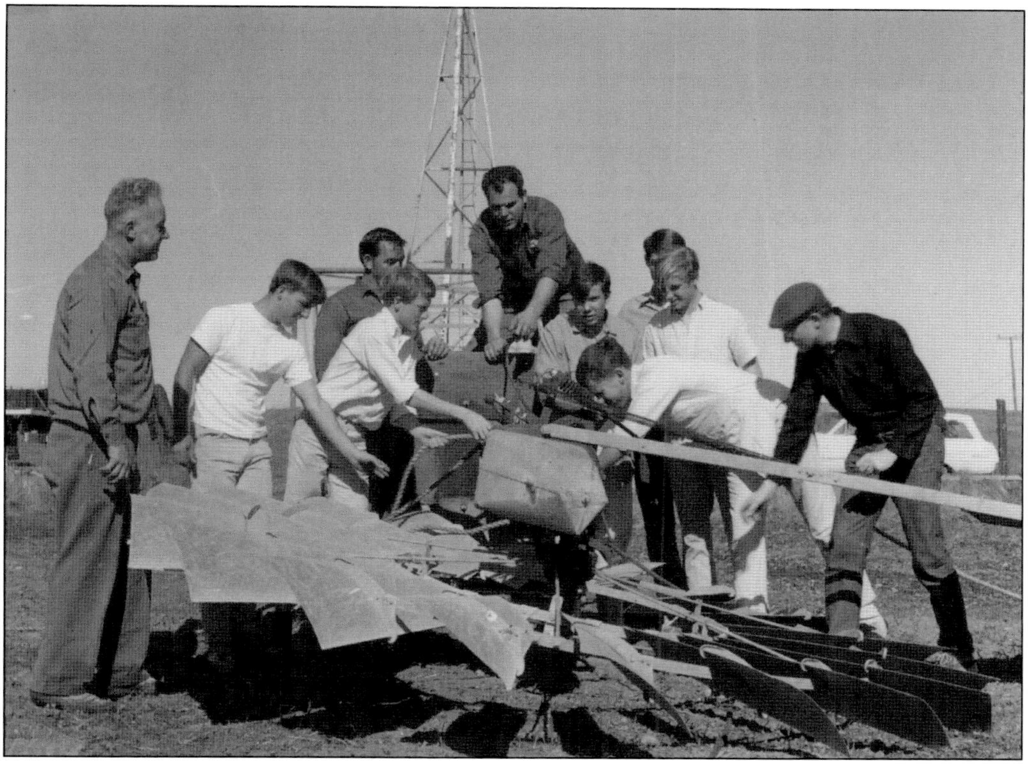

Thacher has always been closely connected to the Ojai community. Local residents are invited to plays and lectures, and Thacher has been a major contributor to and sponsor of the famed Ojai Tennis Tournament (founded by William L. Thacher), first played in 1893. However, formal community outreach beyond the local area had not been initiated until David Twichell began the community service program in 1966. Marvin Shagam (above, far right with hat) and a group of students are shown above raising a windmill to supply water to a village in Baja California in 1967. This outreach has continued with various community support programs, including cleanup of beaches, student tutoring, visits to local elder care facilities, and caring for animals at the Ojai Valley Humane Society.

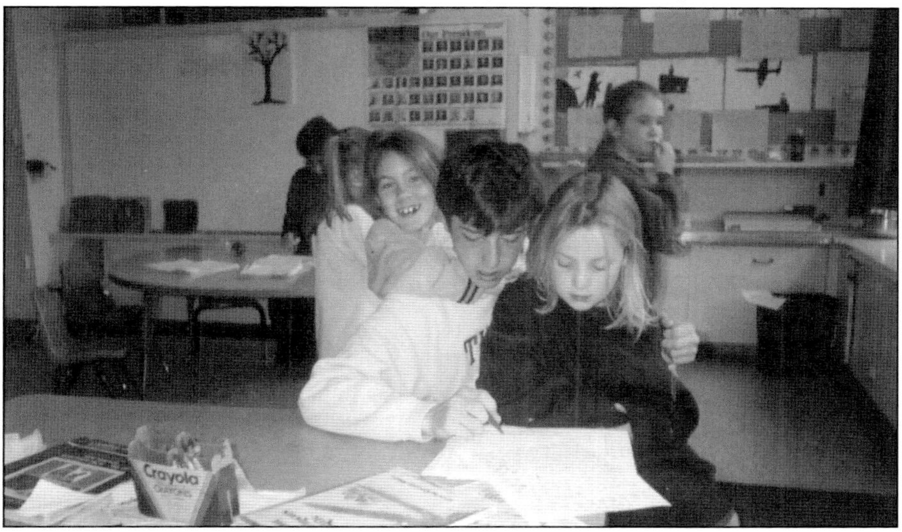

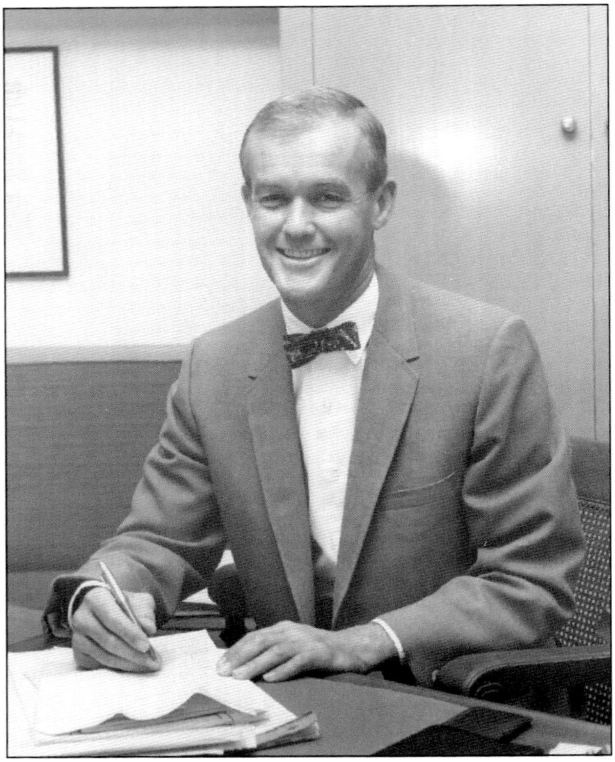

When Twichell left in the spring of 1968, the search committee had not yet identified a replacement, so Newt Chase came out of retirement to serve as interim headmaster until Edgar Sanford (left) was selected as a permanent replacement. Sanford came to Thacher from the Charles Wright Academy in Tacoma, Washington, where he had been headmaster since 1959. He headed Thacher from 1969 to 1975.

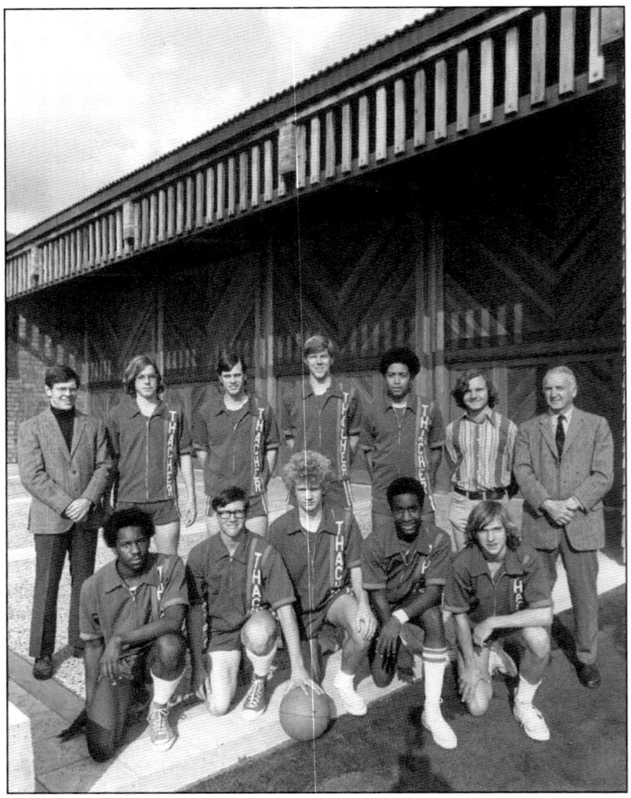

Radical hairstyles, rebellious music, and a surging drug culture confronted school administrators across the country, including at Thacher. The board gave Sanford a strong directive: "Rid the School of drugs!" Based on a student survey, it was concluded that a significant part of the problem was the lack of facilities for organized activities during the winter, so Sanford was given permission to install grass athletic fields and build a gymnasium.

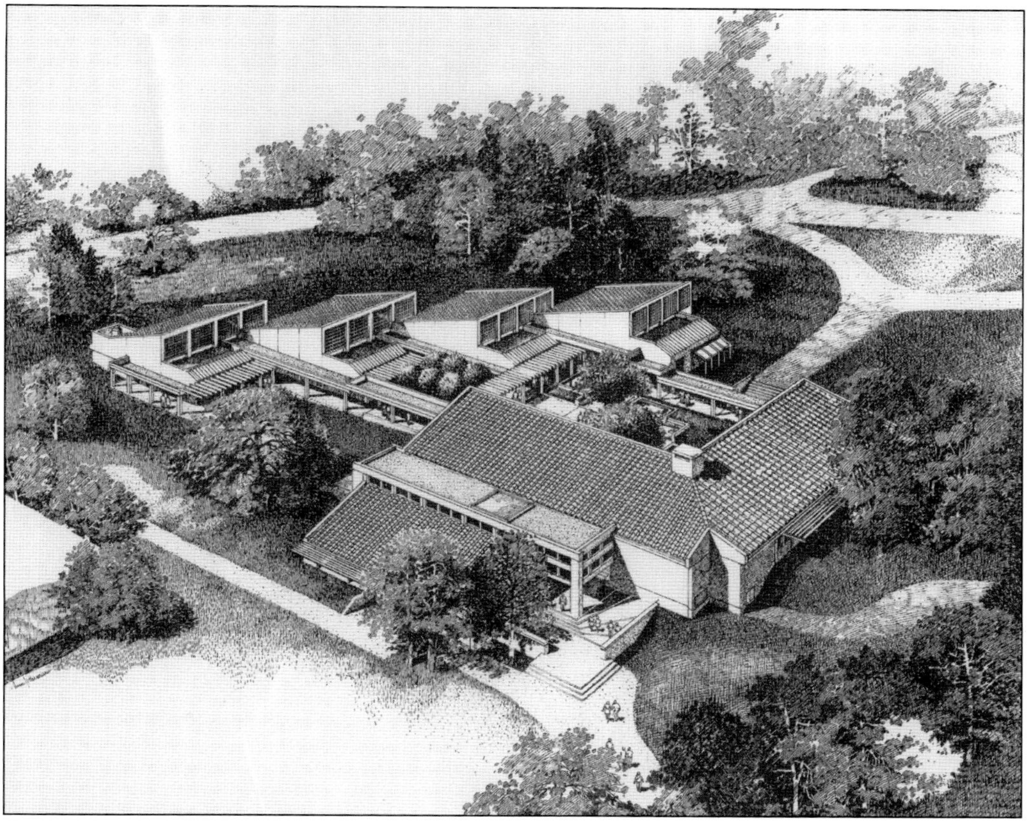

The new science building was also upgraded in 1975 under Sanford's oversight using another generous grant from the Seeley G. Mudd Fund. The upgrades included additional state-of-the-art laboratory and classroom space while retaining the Spanish architecture that characterizes many structures at Thacher. With the introduction of computers in 1968 and the new science facilities, Thacher was once again pushing the technology revolution as implemented in secondary education.

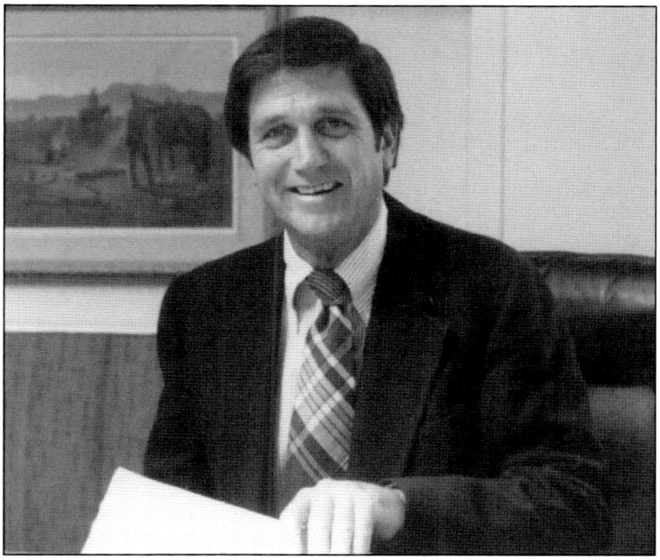

The board of trustees hired Willard G. Wyman as Thacher's seventh headmaster when Edgar Sanford announced his resignation in 1975. Wyman came from Colby College, where he was dean of students and professor of English literature. Prior to that, he had been dean of students and special assistant to the president of Stanford University. Under his oversight, Thacher would undergo the largest paradigm shift in its storied history—coeducation.

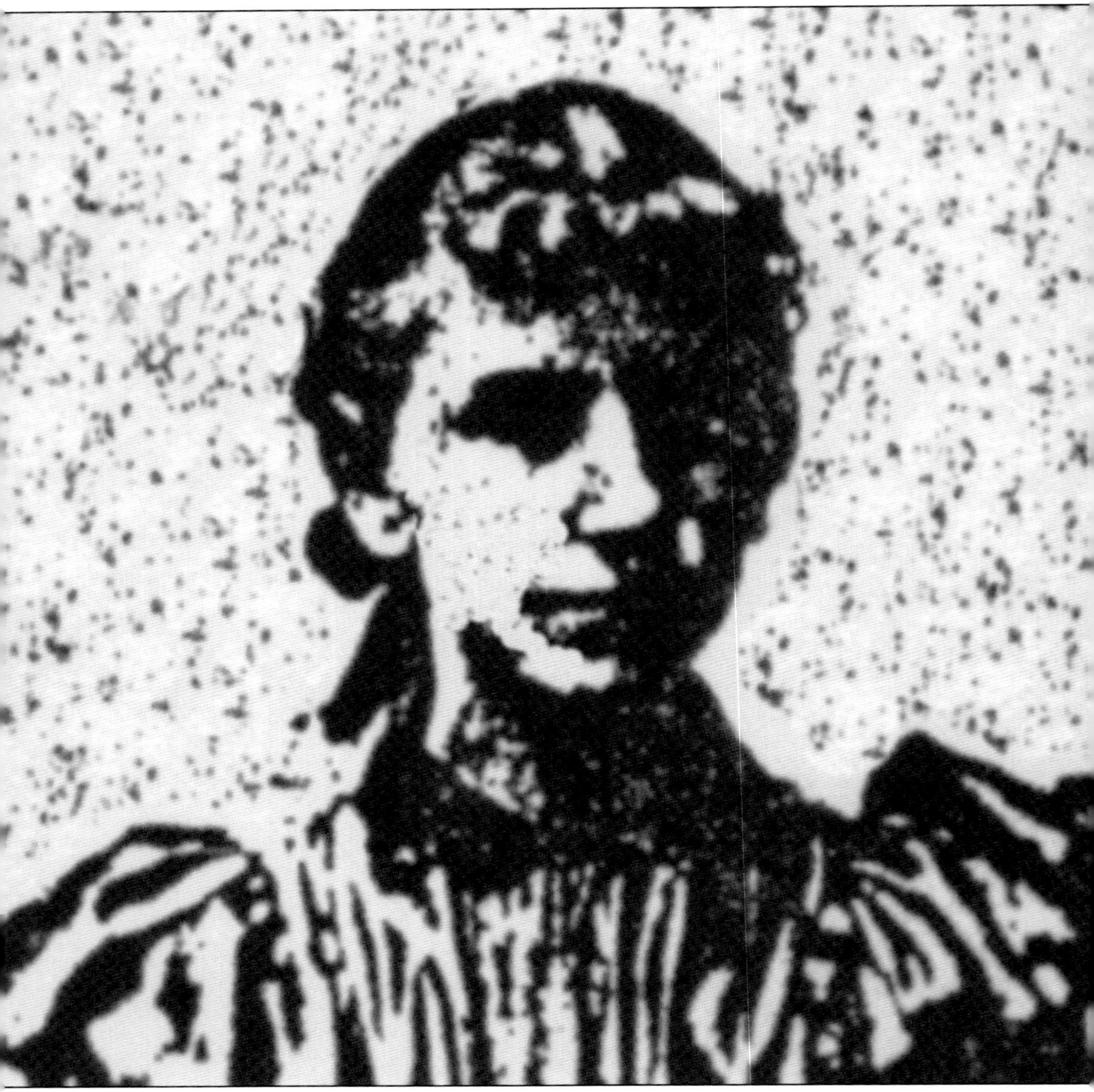

The fall of 1977 was not the first time that females had shared the classrooms and activities at The Thacher School. In fact, in 1893, Sherman Thacher advertised that "classes for girls in geometry, physics, and English have been arranged at the Casa de Piedra Ranch School for which the nominal charge of 25 cents apiece for each lesson will be made to residents of the valley." Three girls— Alice Baker (above), Gertrude Hobart, and Jacqueline Newton—took advantage of the offer and enrolled as day students. In 1968, David Twichell struck a deal with Leonard Richardson, headmaster of the Katharine Branson School in Ross, California, for a weeklong exchange to take place in the spring of 1969. A few Katharine Branson girls would attend classes and participate in activities at Thacher, while some Thacher boys would do the same at Katharine Branson. Although there was some trepidation on the part of the Thacher faculty, then being led by Newt Chase, the "cultural exchange" was characterized by some as more of a "house party" that raised morale. (Courtesy of Craig Thacher.)

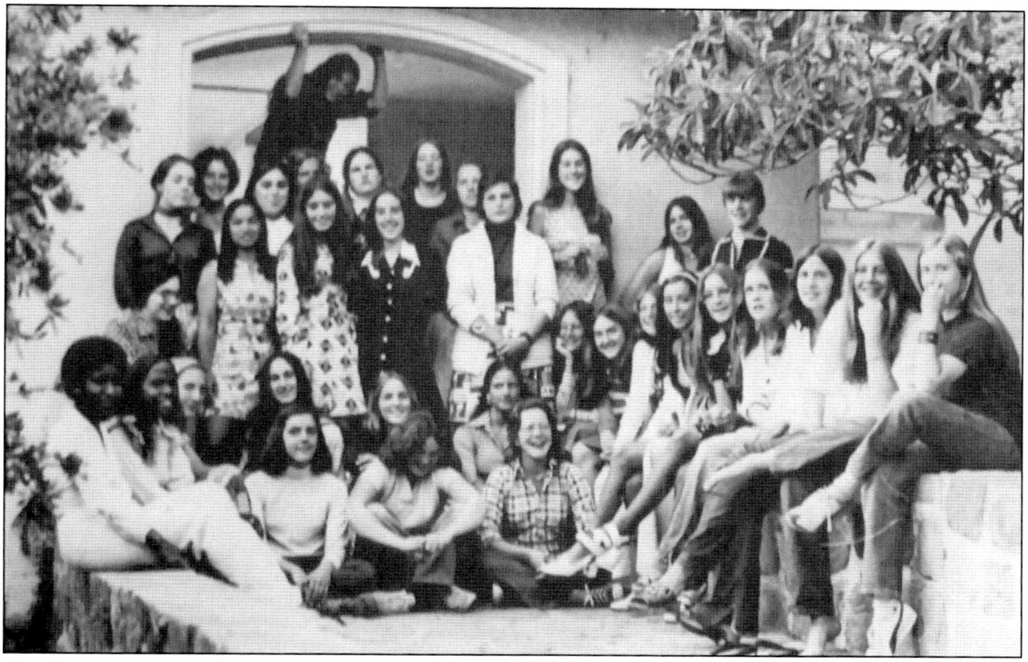

Coeducation resurfaced in 1974, this time with the Emma Willard School in Troy, New York. The arrangement was that Thacher juniors could spend their spring term at Emma Willard, with Emma Willard juniors spending their spring term in Ojai. This was felt to be a reasonable evaluation of coeducation without "taking the irreversible plunge." The first group of Emma Willard "Thacher girls" is shown above in the spring of 1974.

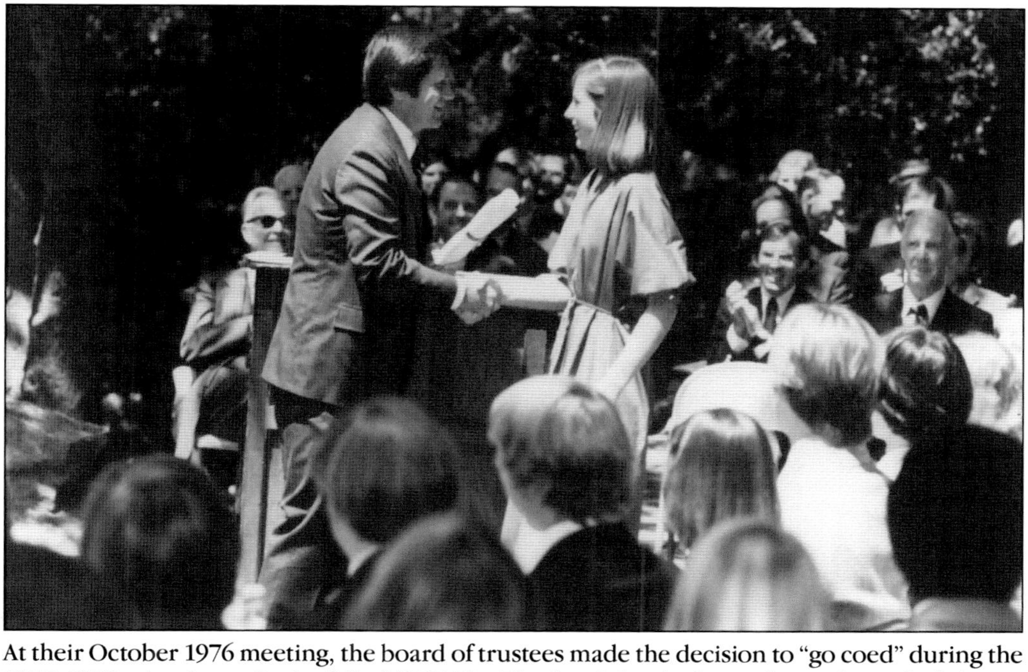

At their October 1976 meeting, the board of trustees made the decision to "go coed" during the 1977–1978 school year. In the fall of 1977, The Thacher School admitted 53 girls (and 167 boys). The first girl to walk across the stage and receive a Thacher diploma was Janet Miller, daughter of longtime Thacher teacher Bob Miller and his wife, Thacher librarian Denise Miller.

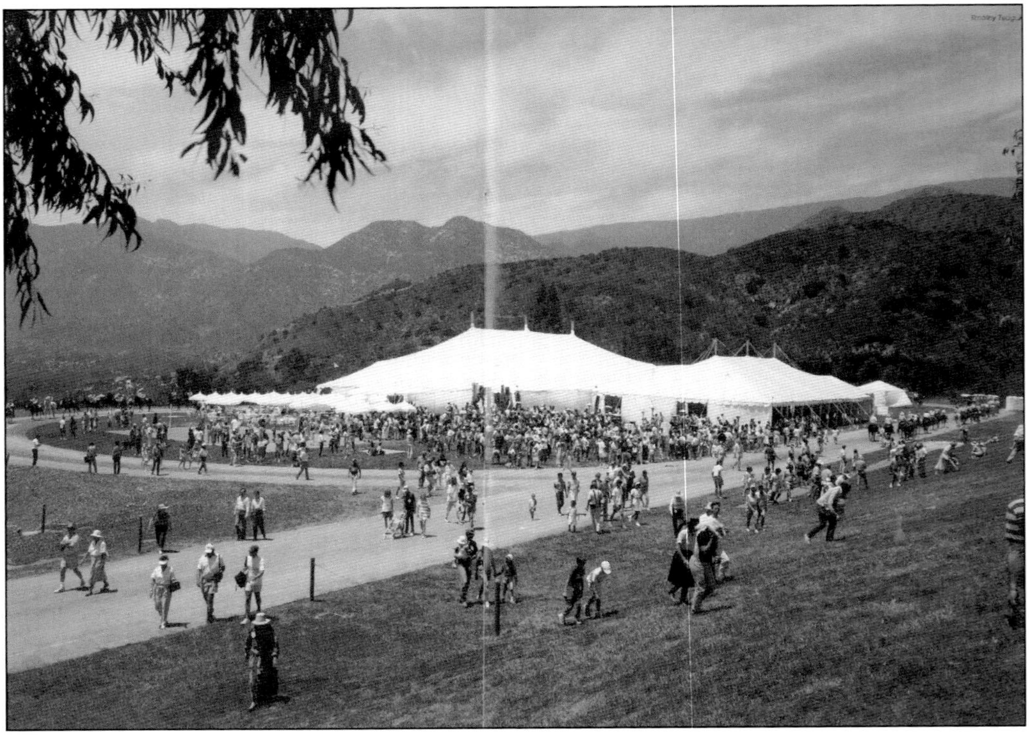

In 1989, under the direction of Willard Wyman, The Thacher School celebrated 100 years of educational excellence. A century of existence and success is a landmark for any institution, and Thacher set out to celebrate in style. Alumni returned from all over the country and from across the globe for a weekend of sports, gymkhana, reunion, and fellowship. A huge tent complex was set up on the Upper Field to accommodate the crowds and to serve the anniversary meal. A special quilt that now hangs in the development office was made by Ann Johnston, sister of longtime history teacher David Johnston. A fund drive, designated as the Centennial Campaign and initiated in 1983, ended in 1989 with over $18 million raised.

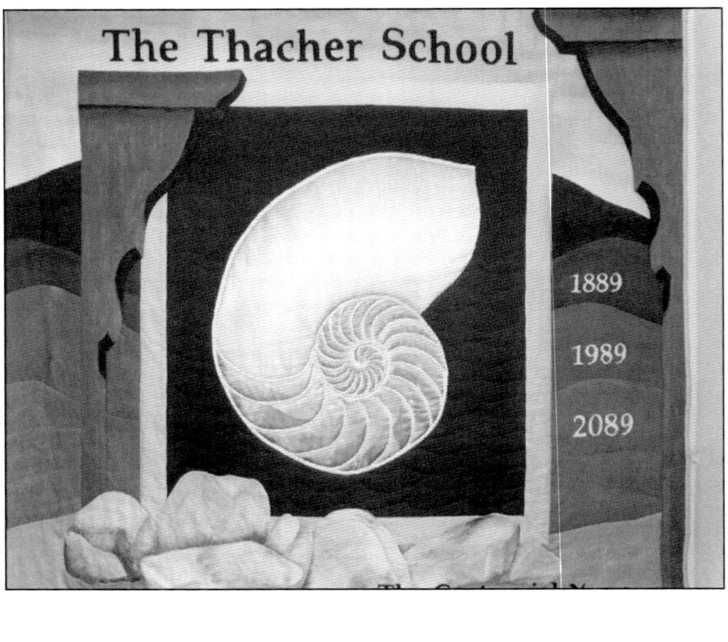

Three

A New Paradigm

Michael Mulligan took up the reins of The Thacher School in 1993 and initiated a number of major activities. Significant among these was development of plans to guide Thacher into the 21st century. These included a series of strategic plans and the *Master Plan 2020*. Core elements of the strategic plans were their statements of philosophy and mission:

> The philosophy of The Thacher School is rooted in the wisdom and work of its founder, Sherman Day Thacher, who embraced the extraordinary natural venue of his school and sought above all else to train his students 'in the art of living for their own greatest good and for the good of their fellow citizens.' He believed the most worthwhile education combined a vigorous academic life with rugged outdoor activities that engendered self-reliance, concern for others, and fidelity to four principles: honor, fairness, kindness, and truth.
>
> The mission of The Thacher School is to train young men and women in the art of living for their own greatest good and for the greatest good of their fellow citizens in a diverse and changing world. To that end, the School augments its highly challenging academic program with profound lessons learned from the care of a horse, regular chores around the School, teamwork on playing fields, outstanding instruction in the arts, the give and take of everyday life with schoolmates and teachers, and adventures shared in the wilderness. The aim is to inspire and encourage hard work, integrity, self-reliance, a lifelong love of learning and truth, self-knowledge, and a deep concern for the world in which we live.

Mulligan, now the second-longest-serving headmaster in the history of Thacher, has focused his efforts in four main areas—ensuring the sustainability of Thacher's infrastructure, facilities, and financial security; investing in faculty compensation, housing, and professional development; adapting curriculum to meet the demanding and evolving admission requirements of today's colleges and universities; and increasing the diversity of the Thacher family, both in the student body and the faculty.

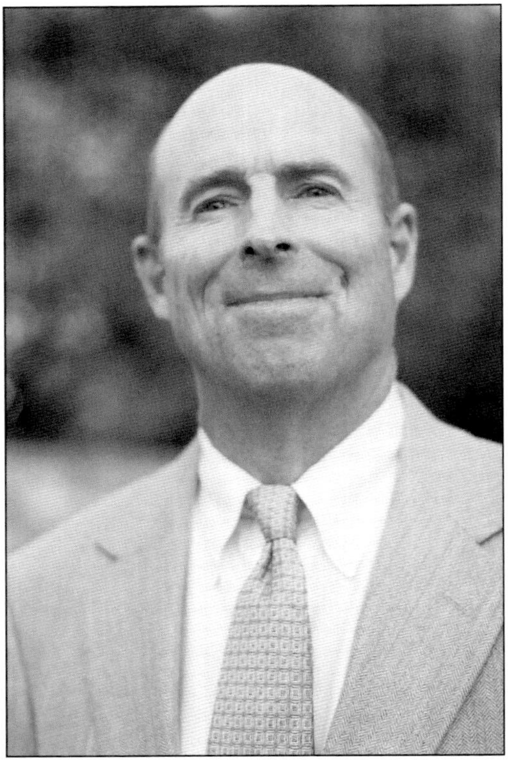

Michael Mulligan graduated from Middlebury College and received master's degrees from both Middlebury and Harvard. After spending a few years in the corporate world, he returned to his alma mater, the Governor Dummer Academy (now the Governor's Academy), where he taught history and English and coached soccer, lacrosse, and wrestling. Mulligan and his wife, Joy Sawyer-Mulligan, came to Thacher in 1986. He served in a number of administrative capacities at Thacher before being selected as The Thacher School's eighth headmaster in 1993. Joy is a teacher in the English department, and both Mike and Joy are avid supporters of the outdoor programs that are so unique to Thacher.

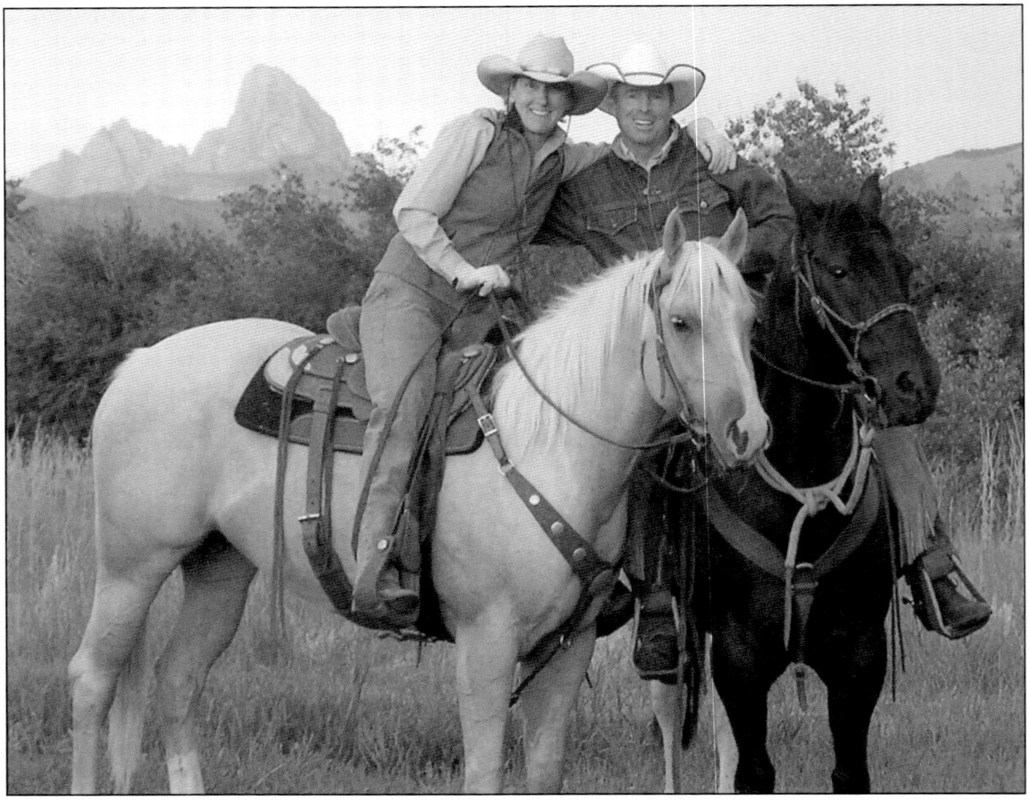

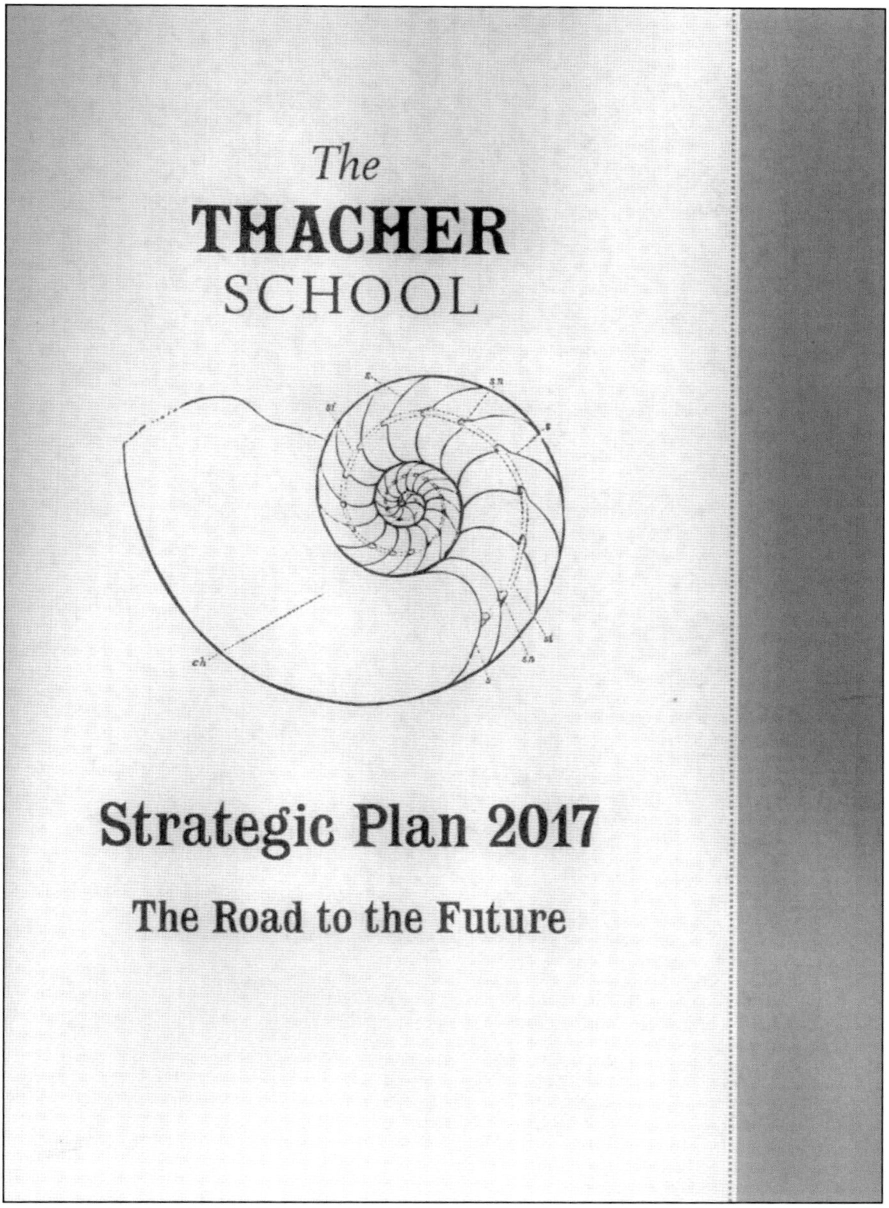

Mulligan realized the importance of formalizing the planning process. Thacher's fifth headmaster, David Twichell, had formed a long-range planning committee in the mid-1960s, but Thacher's first formal strategic plan was not published until 1997, with an update in 2004. This plan was put together "with a huge effort on the part of faculty, administration, trustees, parents, and 13 different professional consultants who helped examine every area of this School." A new plan (cover shown above) was issued in 2012. This plan "offers definitive statements about the purpose of a Thacher education and how we will measure our progress in the next ten years. In it, we also map out the critical goals relative to the unending work of all schools: plans, for example, of ensuring that Thacher hires and retains the best faculty possible; objectives for increasing our ability to enroll diverse and talented applicants from all socio-economic quarters; goals for continuing to improve the School's grounds and facilities; and models to ensure Thacher's long-term viability and financial strength."

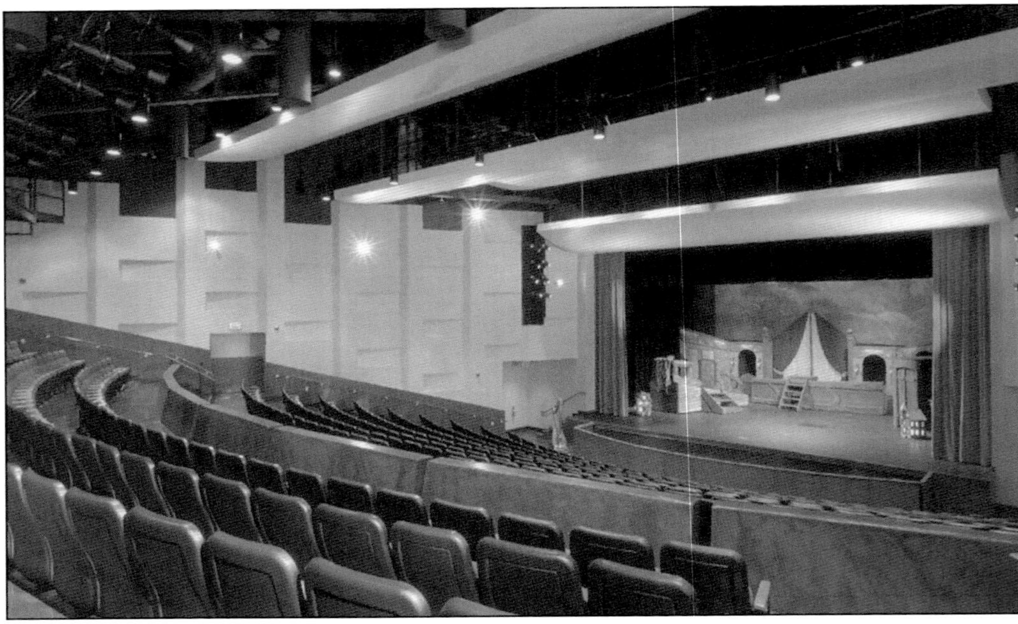

Three infrastructure priorities during the Mulligan administration have been the construction of the Milligan Center for the Performing Arts, the construction of the Thacher Commons building, and the continued enhancement of Thacher's integration into the wireless world. The 450-seat performing arts center (above) was completed in 2006, and the Thacher Commons (below), which includes a game room, meeting rooms, and the student store, was dedicated on October 7, 2005, on the site of the former Lamb Auditorium.

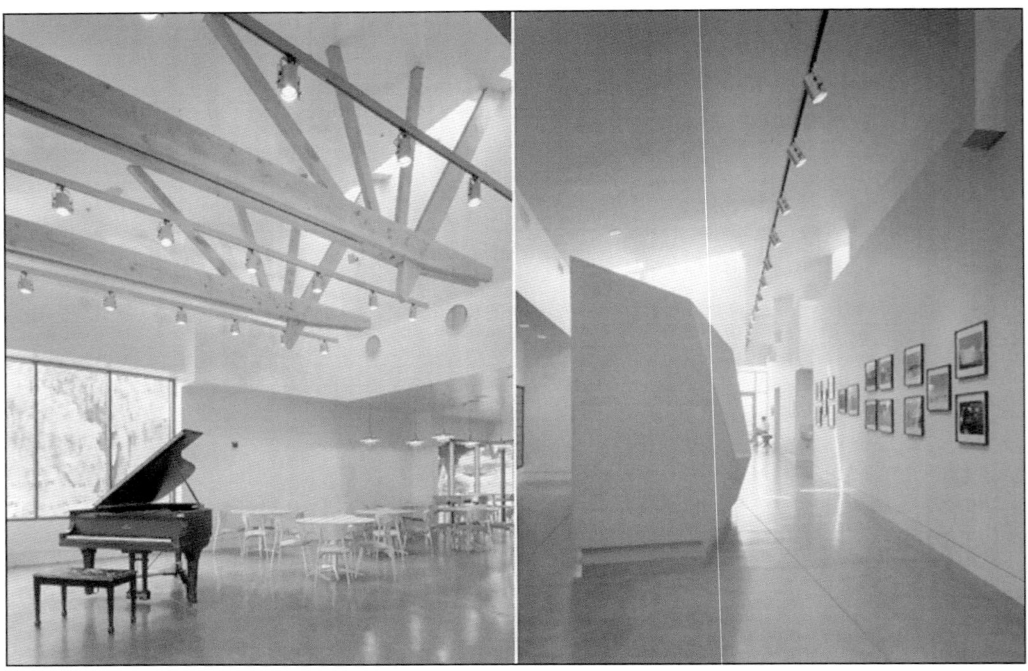

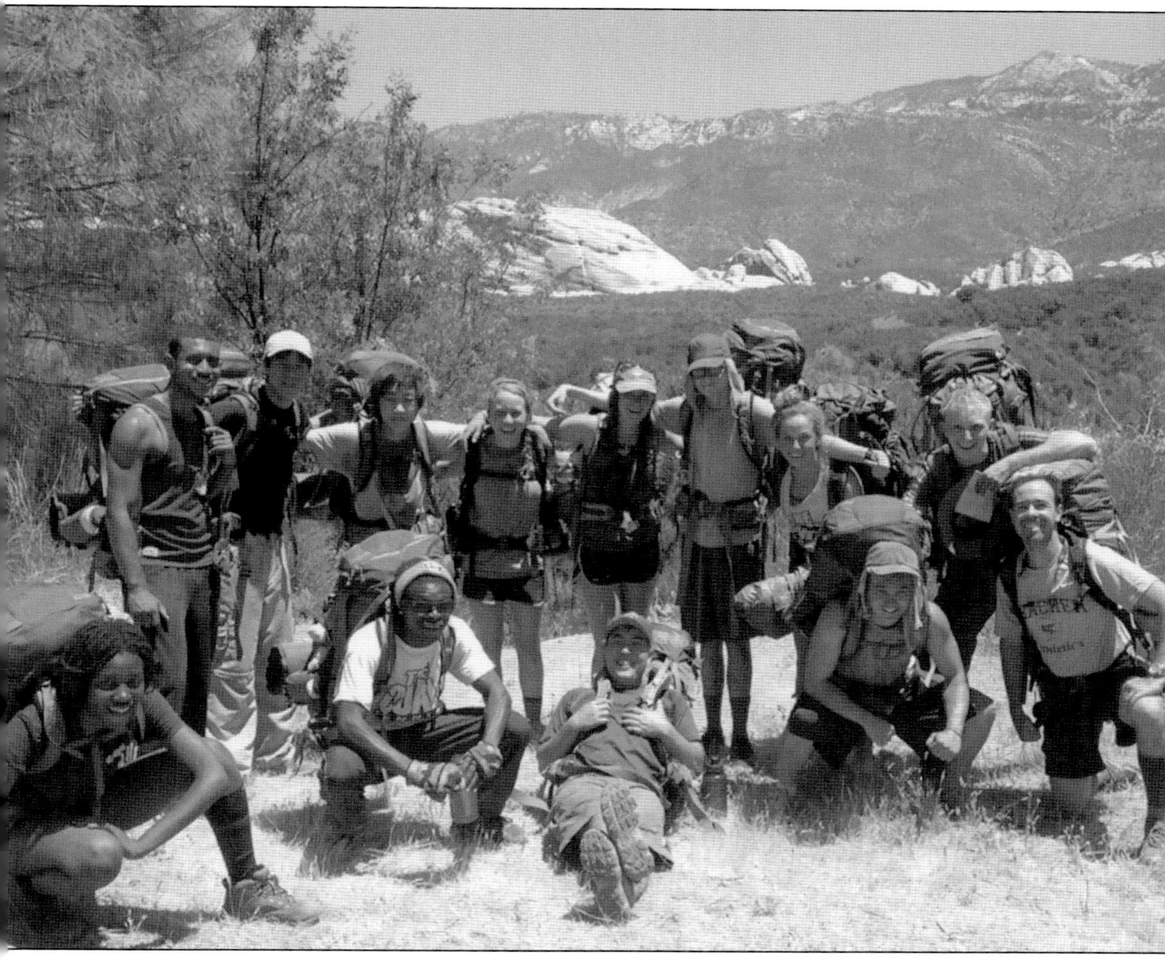

An important aspect of Thacher's student body is its diversity. As late as the middle of the 20th century, Thacher was a bastion of white males from California. Today, Thacher is coeducational, 12 percent of the enrollees for the 2012–2013 school year were international students (representing 11 countries), and 36 percent were students of color. In addition, The Thacher School provides a significant scholarship outreach to students who meet the stringent entrance requirements but may not have the personal financial resources to attend. In fact, 27 percent of incoming students receive some form of financial aid. In the early years, a majority of the students came from California. Now, nearly half are from other states.

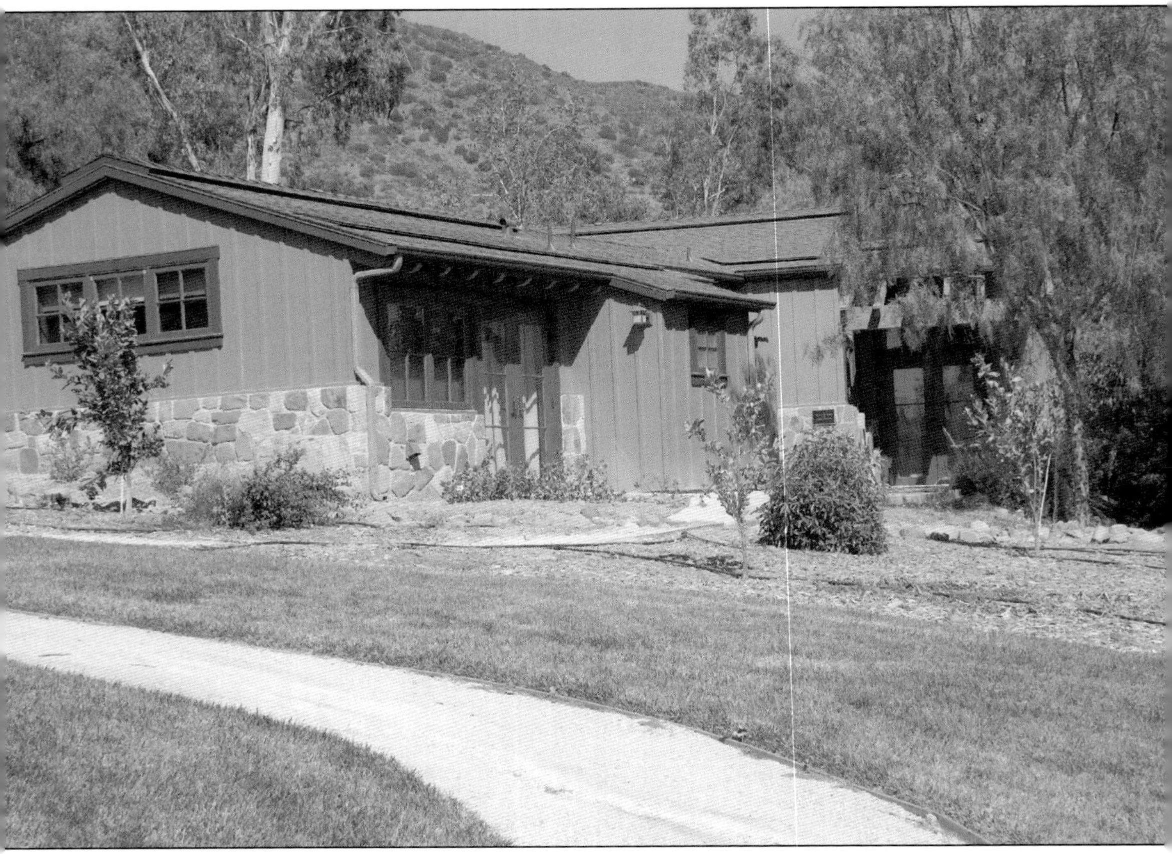

Teaching at a boarding school, especially Thacher with its extensive outdoor programs, provides very different challenges than those of a standard public school. Teachers are essentially "on duty" 24 hours a day, 7 days a week and are expected to be full participants in both classroom and outdoor activities. Mulligan set about improving living conditions for his faculty by providing better housing and by increasing compensation. In the early days, most faculty members lived in apartments built into the dormitories. This arrangement provided for excellent oversight of student behavior but little or no privacy for the teachers and their families. Although conditions had improved considerably over the years, Mulligan realized that adequate (or perhaps even better than adequate) housing would make Thacher a much more attractive place for the high-quality faculty he wanted to draw. Although some faculty members still live in dormitory complexes, their accommodations are much improved over those of their predecessors. Shown here is the faculty home for the Anacapa Fellowship visiting scholar.

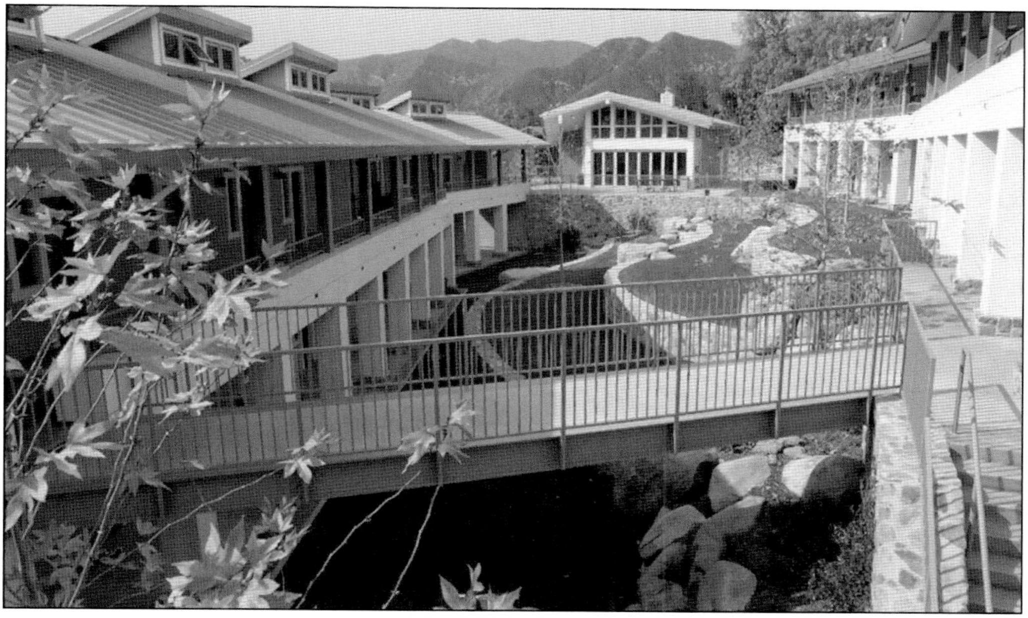

Mulligan's ability to improve faculty residences, increase teacher compensation, and continue the ambitious facility and infrastructure upgrade program was greatly enhanced by the addition of $82 million from the successful "Campaign for Thacher." The modern Hill Dormitory (above), the Los Padres Dormitory, and a new Lower School (below, replacing the 1949 structure); refurbishment of the Upper School and the Casa Dormitory; and remodeling of the William Larned Thacher Admissions Office were also completed during his tenure. Both the Hill Dormitory and the new Lower School, with their unique incorporation of open space, were designed and constructed by MATT Construction Corporation of Santa Fe Springs, California.

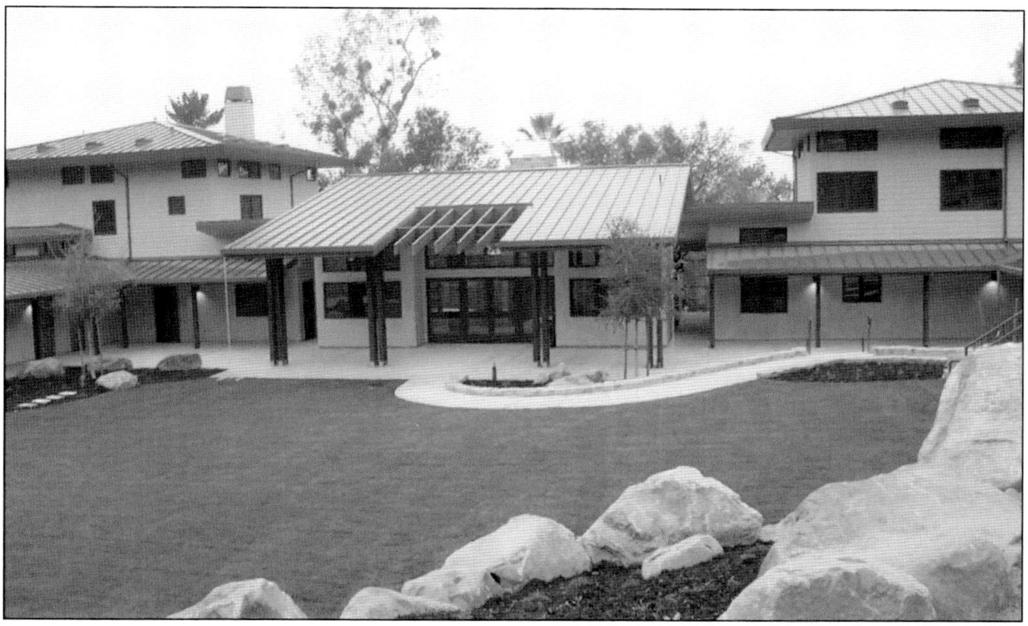

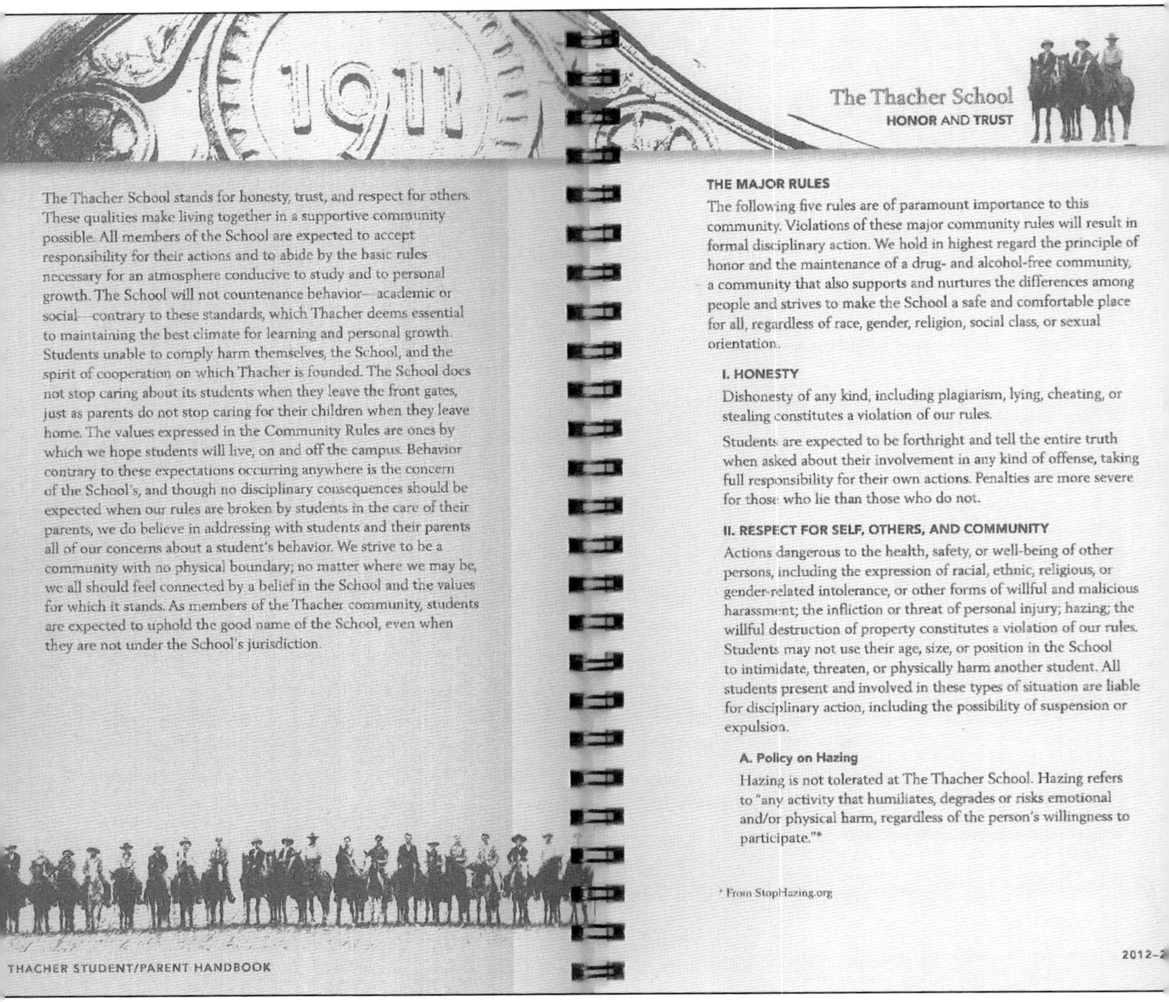

The Thacher School stands for honesty, trust, and respect for others. These qualities make living together in a supportive community possible. All members of the School are expected to accept responsibility for their actions and to abide by the basic rules necessary for an atmosphere conducive to study and to personal growth. The School will not countenance behavior—academic or social—contrary to these standards, which Thacher deems essential to maintaining the best climate for learning and personal growth. Students unable to comply harm themselves, the School, and the spirit of cooperation on which Thacher is founded. The School does not stop caring about its students when they leave the front gates, just as parents do not stop caring for their children when they leave home. The values expressed in the Community Rules are ones by which we hope students will live, on and off the campus. Behavior contrary to these expectations occurring anywhere is the concern of the School's, and though no disciplinary consequences should be expected when our rules are broken by students in the care of their parents, we do believe in addressing with students and their parents all of our concerns about a student's behavior. We strive to be a community with no physical boundary; no matter where we may be, we all should feel connected by a belief in the School and the values for which it stands. As members of the Thacher community, students are expected to uphold the good name of the School, even when they are not under the School's jurisdiction.

THACHER STUDENT/PARENT HANDBOOK

The Thacher School
HONOR AND TRUST

THE MAJOR RULES

The following five rules are of paramount importance to this community. Violations of these major community rules will result in formal disciplinary action. We hold in highest regard the principle of honor and the maintenance of a drug- and alcohol-free community, a community that also supports and nurtures the differences among people and strives to make the School a safe and comfortable place for all, regardless of race, gender, religion, social class, or sexual orientation.

I. HONESTY

Dishonesty of any kind, including plagiarism, lying, cheating, or stealing constitutes a violation of our rules.

Students are expected to be forthright and tell the entire truth when asked about their involvement in any kind of offense, taking full responsibility for their own actions. Penalties are more severe for those who lie than those who do not.

II. RESPECT FOR SELF, OTHERS, AND COMMUNITY

Actions dangerous to the health, safety, or well-being of other persons, including the expression of racial, ethnic, religious, or gender-related intolerance, or other forms of willful and malicious harassment; the infliction or threat of personal injury; hazing; the willful destruction of property constitutes a violation of our rules. Students may not use their age, size, or position in the School to intimidate, threaten, or physically harm another student. All students present and involved in these types of situation are liable for disciplinary action, including the possibility of suspension or expulsion.

A. Policy on Hazing

Hazing is not tolerated at The Thacher School. Hazing refers to "any activity that humiliates, degrades or risks emotional and/or physical harm, regardless of the person's willingness to participate."*

* From StopHazing.org

2012–2

Despite the many improvements in infrastructure and physical plant, perhaps the most important aspect of the Mulligan administration, as with previous administrations, is its emphasis on the honor code. This concept has its roots in Sherman Thacher's original goal of instilling in each of his students a commitment to honor, fairness, kindness, and truth. The expectation, as stated in the *Student-Parent Handbook* shown above, is that "all students will be honest, forthright, kind, and respectful in all of their dealings, thereby supporting in actions and in words the fundamental principle of honor behind the Rules and Regulations." The Honor Code is not just about academic performance—dorm rooms are not locked, and students simply sign out materials from the library without formal supervision. As Jack Huyler noted, "If you ask Thacher students, past or present, about the three top elements that make Thacher the place it is, they will, without hesitation, name the Honor Code as one."

Four

A DAY IN THE LIFE

This section will follow a day in the life of a typical Thacher student, with an emphasis on "the good old days" and the "great new days." Fair warning—there will be some bouncing back and forth between past and present.

The rhythms of day-to-day life at Thacher were and are announced by the dining hall bell, although the regimen is less structured now than in the early days. The academic day runs from 8:30 a.m. to 3:15 p.m., and both breakfast and lunch are served buffet style. Daily activities are overseen by a formalized chain of command. The first level of management is a set of prefects who are appointed by the faculty and who are responsible for mentoring their charges as well as enforcing basic cleanliness, timeliness, and discipline. Early in Thacher's history, a group of upper classmen known as School Prefects, mentored, supported, and guided the prefects. Then and now, the senior member of the student body is the chair, elected by a vote of the students.

In addition to the formal structure, there are organizations to monitor various aspects of Thacher life. For example, the gymkhana teams assist the director of the horse program by inspecting horses, corrals, and stalls, tasks formerly assigned to the Outdoor Committee. The Indoor Committee arranges for events such as dances, concerts, lectures, and recitals. In general, senior student leaders fulfill administrative functions that were formerly assigned to these and other committees.

Individual students assume a great deal of personal responsibility from the moment they arrive at Thacher. They must arrange their personal schedules to fit meals around their classes and to accommodate their athletic or equestrian activities. This is very much in keeping with Sherman Thacher's goal of instilling in his charges "accurate, thorough, and self-reliant habits of thought and study."

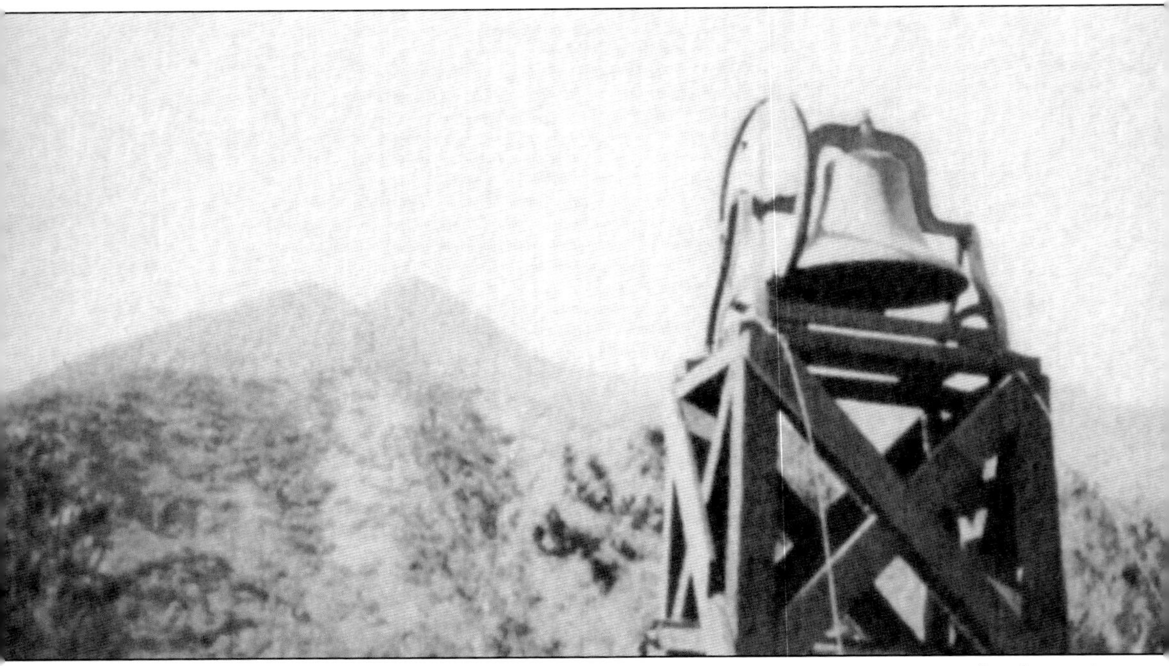

In the early days, Thacher needed a way to let everyone know when it was time for the major events of the day, such as meals, assemblies, and recess. This was accomplished by means of a large bell installed atop the dining room and rung by the kitchen staff. Each meal was preceded by a 20-bell (ie: 20 minutes before mealtime), a 10-bell, and a walker (or 5-bell), so named because, when heard, students were expected to be walking to the dining hall. As individual timekeeping came into vogue, Thacher kept the tradition of the bells for meals and recess lunch and then dropped all bells except those for dinner. The bells could be heard as far away as Jameson Field and on many of the nearby trails, although if students were still on a trail or at the field at the 20-bell, they would really have to hustle to make it to dinner after a shower (and in a coat and tie, per regulation).

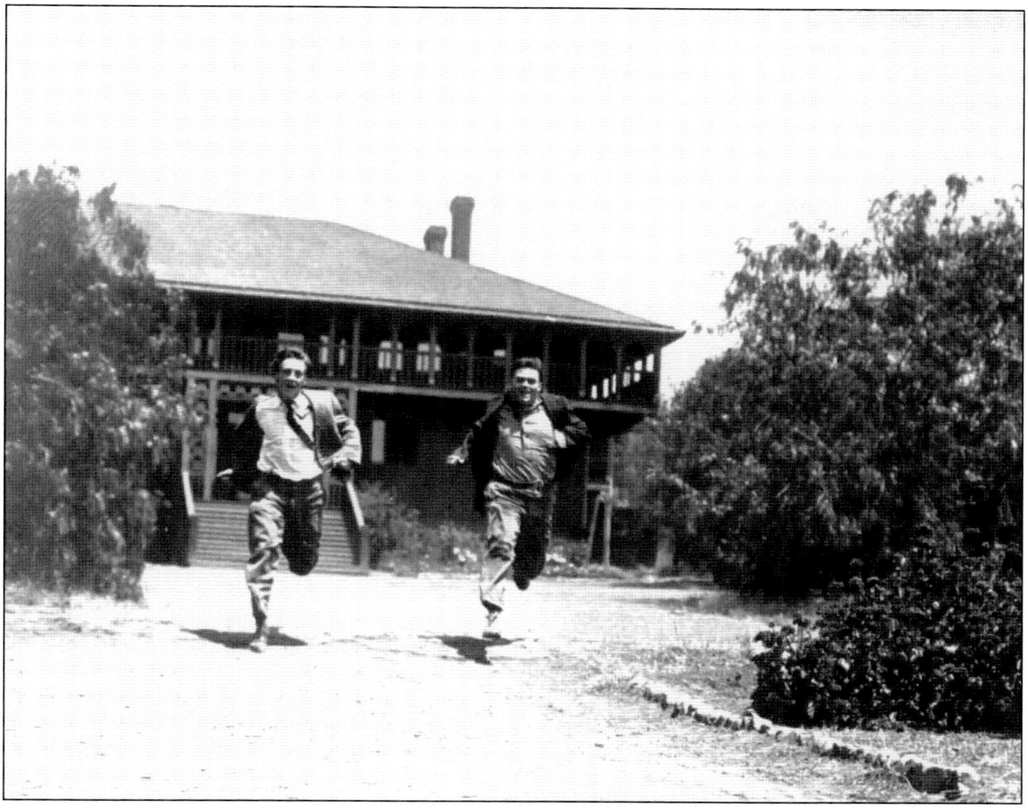

A Thacher day begins early. Rising to the sound of the dining hall bells, students and faculty used to head for breakfast at 7:00 a.m. Originally, they would have had to stop briefly to grab a coat and tie (usually a neckerchief or bolo) before entering the dining room, but this is no longer a requirement for breakfast or lunch. Some students procrastinated to the point that they had to jump out of bed and sprint to the dining room at the sound of the walker to avoid a lateness mark. After breakfast, which is now buffet style and begins at 6:30, students with horses head for the barns to feed and clean their horses, check their water, and muck out corrals and stalls. Members of the horse faculty and gymkhana teams check the corrals and horses (tasks formerly performed by the Outdoor Committee), noting any cleanliness or health issues that need to be addressed.

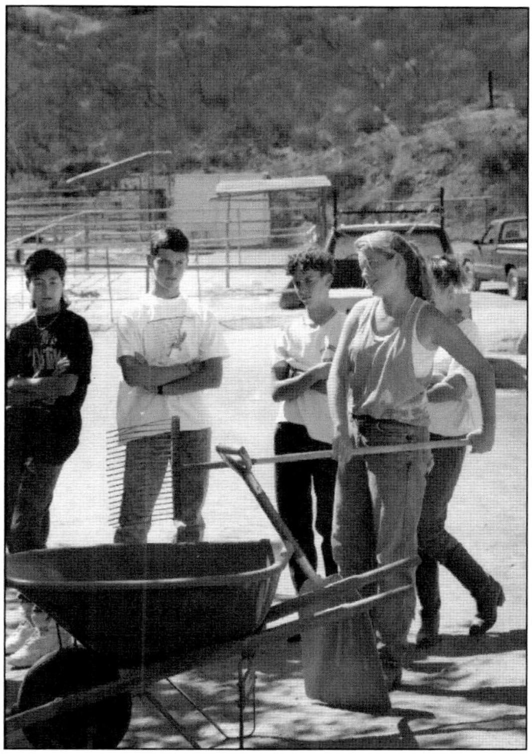

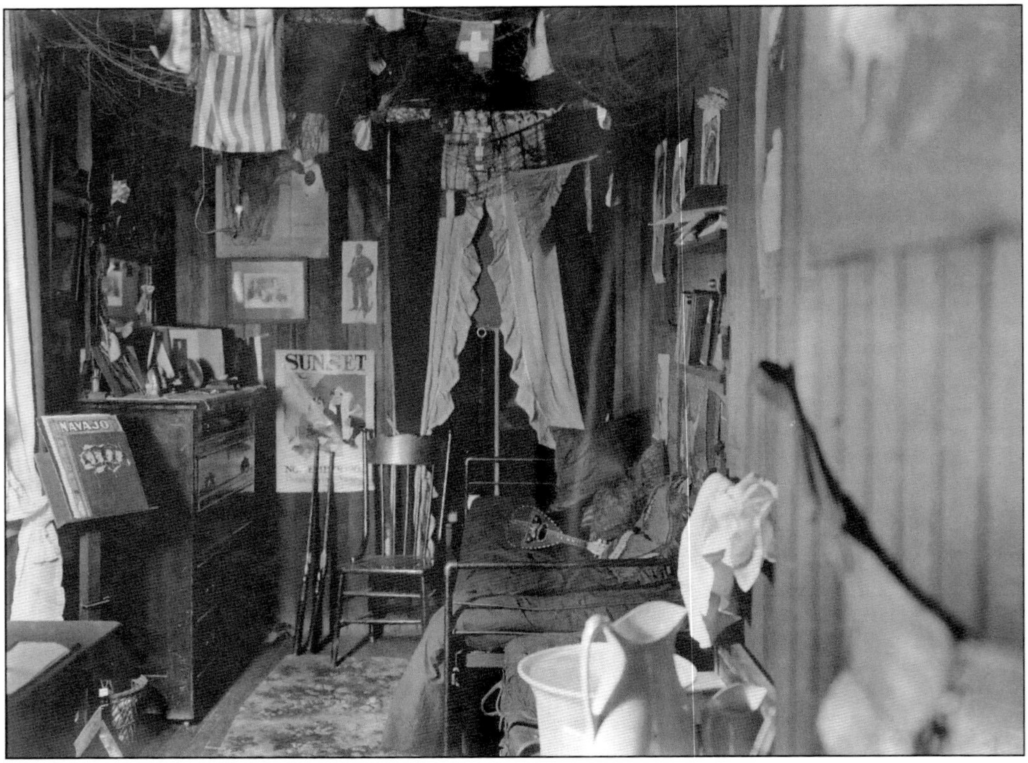

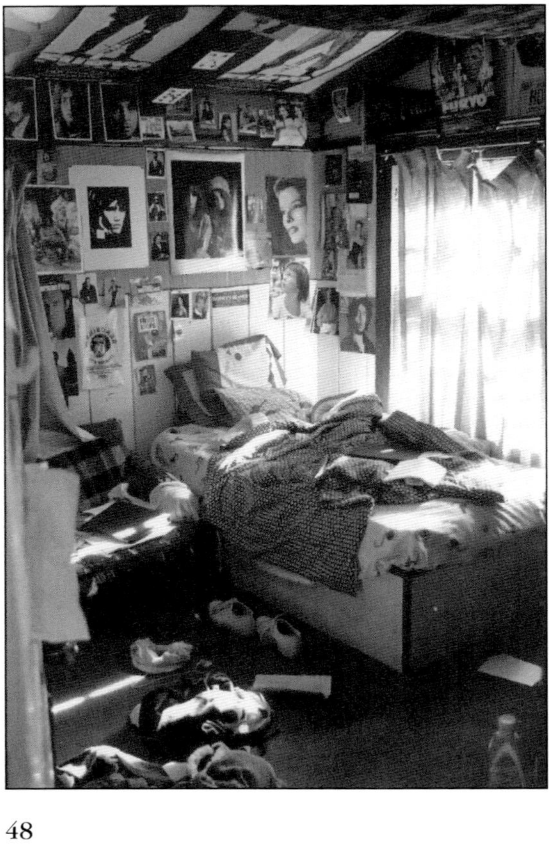

After taking care of their horses, students return to their dormitories to make their beds and clean the rooms and common areas. Those who do not have horses or who rose early enough to have cleaned their room beforehand may sneak a few minutes of studying or reviewing for the quiz in their first period class. In the early days of Thacher (shown above), rooms were cleaned and beds were made by members of the Chinese staff, who also manned the dining hall. (Note the guns leaning against the wall—this was permitted in the early days.) The 1980s photograph at left shows a more typical room before cleaning. Once the rooms are clean, the prefect or dorm faculty member inspects the room, noting deficiencies that need to be corrected.

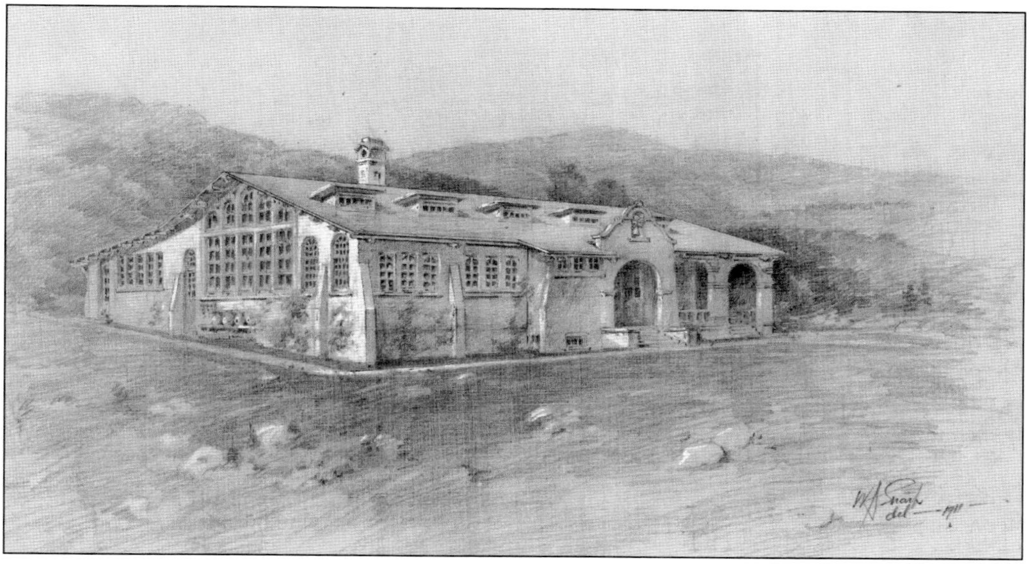

The academic day has always begun between 8:00 and 8:30 a.m. Before Thacher outgrew it, the morning began with an assembly in the Study Hall, also known as the Main School Building. Freshman and sophomores (then lower and middle schoolers) sat in individual desks in the center of the room. Upperclassmen sat on benches that lined the outside of the room, starting with the chair (who sat just to the right of the dais in the front) and moving counterclockwise through the prefects, upper uppers, and lower uppers. The faculty sat to the left of the dais, and the headmaster (now head of school) sat at a table on the dais.

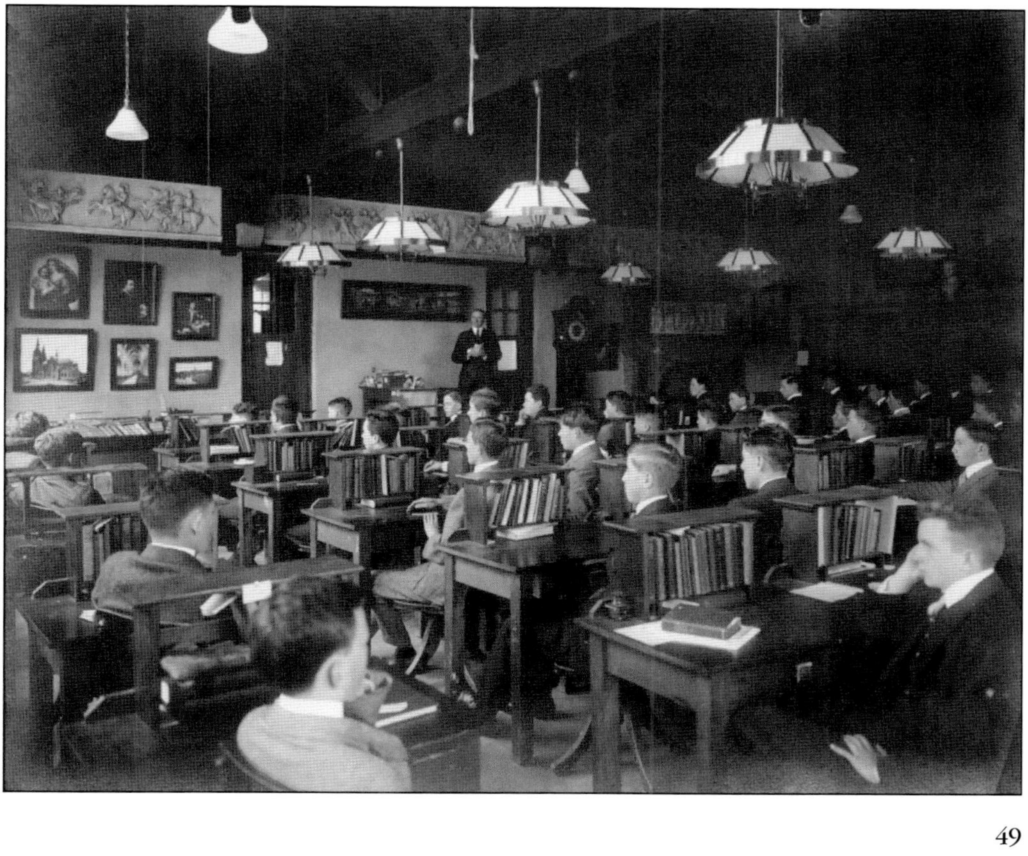

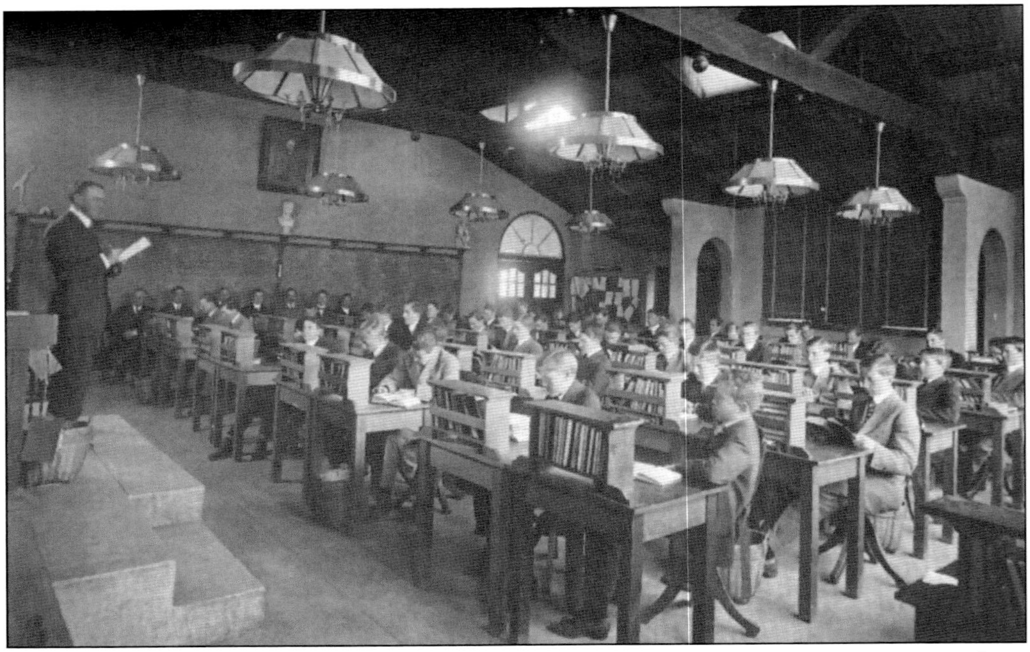

Students began to migrate toward the Study Hall as soon as room inspection was complete. The building hummed with a gentle murmur as they chatted about the day's plans or bemoaned their latest ticks on the marks board. Morning assemblies included announcements of daily activities, new opportunities, or perhaps the much-coveted school holiday. In years past, there may have been a reading by the headmaster or a faculty member. Favorites included Benet's "Golden River," a specialty of Anson Thacher; Oliver Wendell Holmes's "The Chambered Nautilus," with its stirring refrain about building more stately mansions; or Jesse Kahle telling one of his hilarious "Uncle Josh" stories (below).

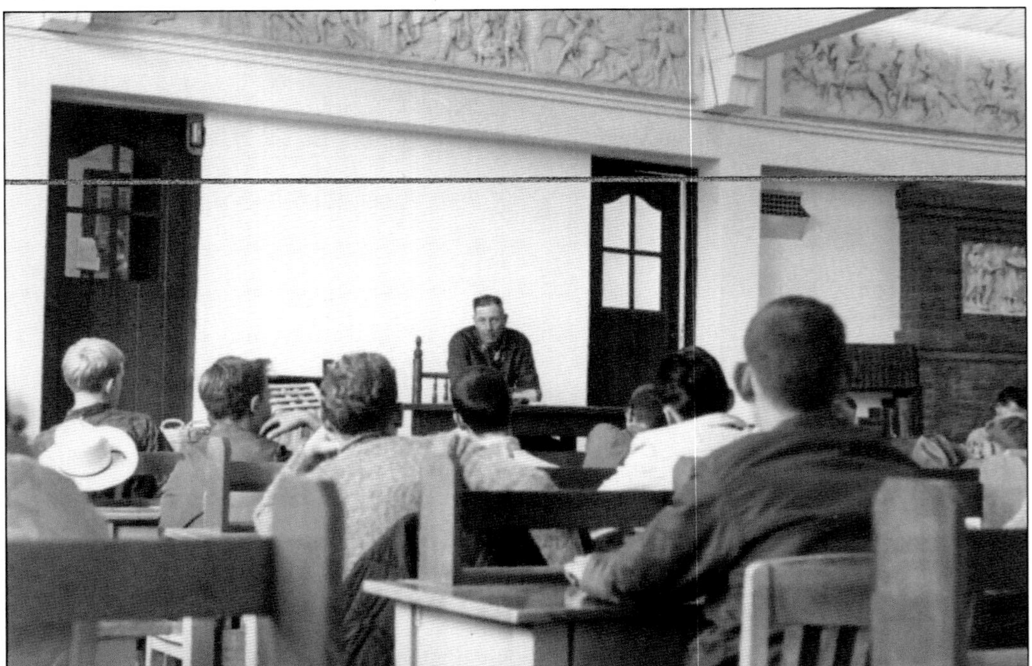

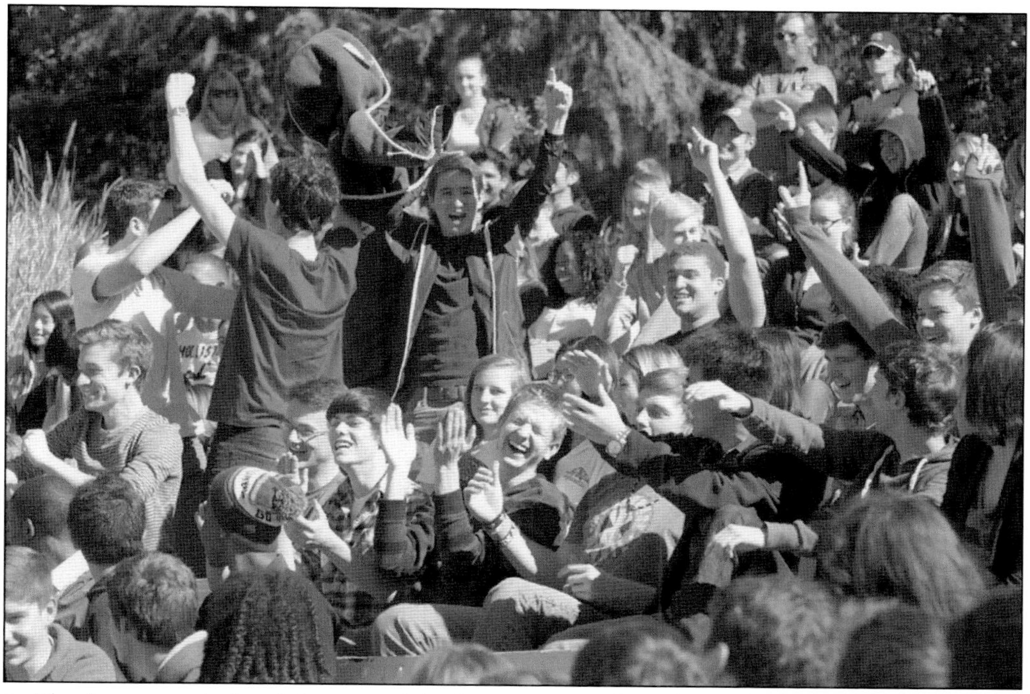

As Thacher expanded and class schedules became more flexible, the fixed 8:30 assembly in the Study Hall was changed. Since 1970, all-school assemblies have been held in the Centennial Amphitheater or on the Pergola on Mondays, Wednesdays, and Fridays. As before, there are opportunities for announcements by faculty and students, presentations of awards, and perhaps a skit, performance, song, or reading by one of the student groups.

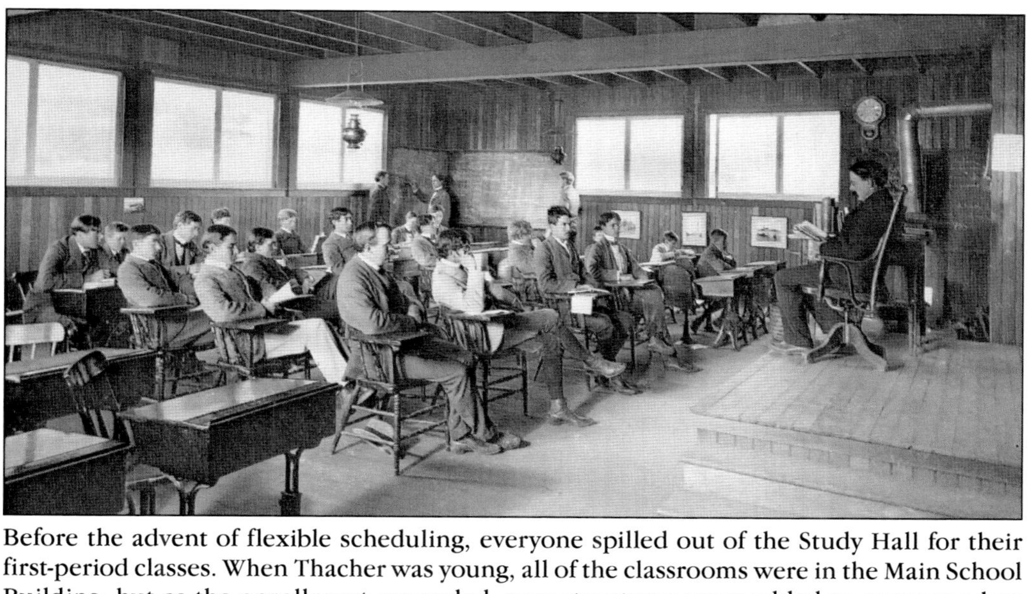

Before the advent of flexible scheduling, everyone spilled out of the Study Hall for their first-period classes. When Thacher was young, all of the classrooms were in the Main School Building, but as the enrollment expanded, new structures were added to accommodate larger numbers and a more diverse curriculum.

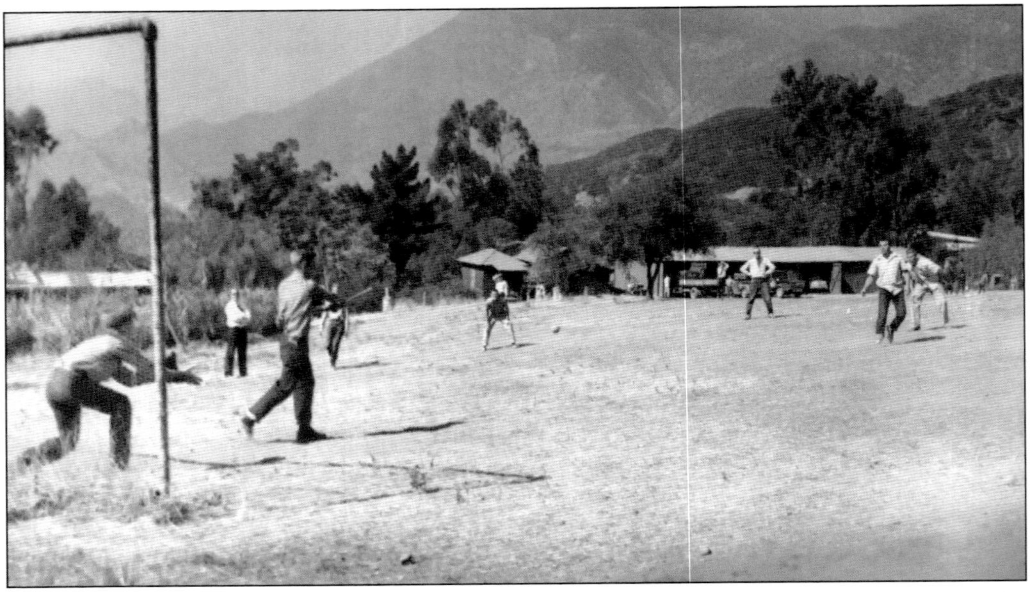

Until the mid-1960s, a 10:30 bell rang for morning recess. There was a mass exodus to the recess baseball fields. Everyone—headmaster, faculty, students, and even some staff—played energetic games of softball on teams that rotated periodically. After 20 minutes of exuberant activity, everyone congregated at the Pergola for recess lunch—milk, graham crackers, and oranges (in season). Before the age of smart phones and the Internet, this was an opportunity to catch up on the news of the day. The author has a vivid memory of crowding around a portable radio at recess lunch on a cool November morning to hear the first reports of the assassination of Pres. John F. Kennedy.

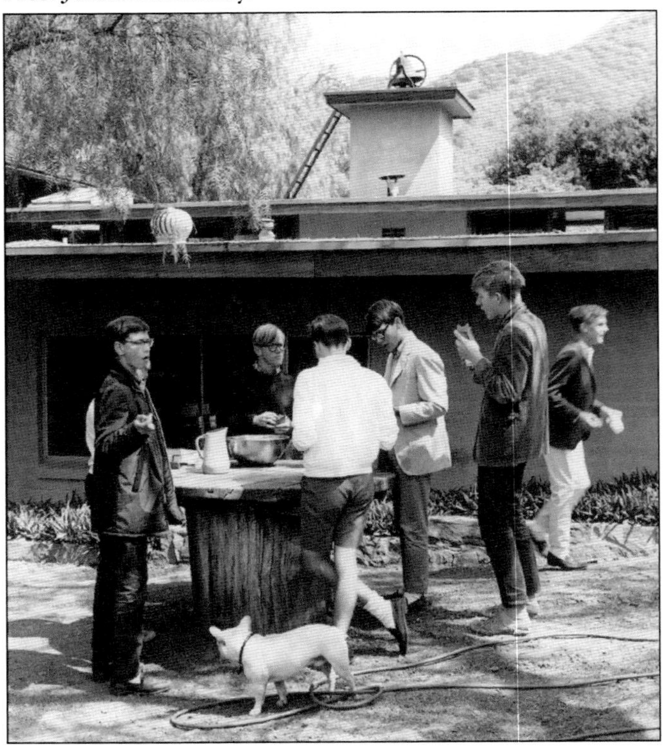

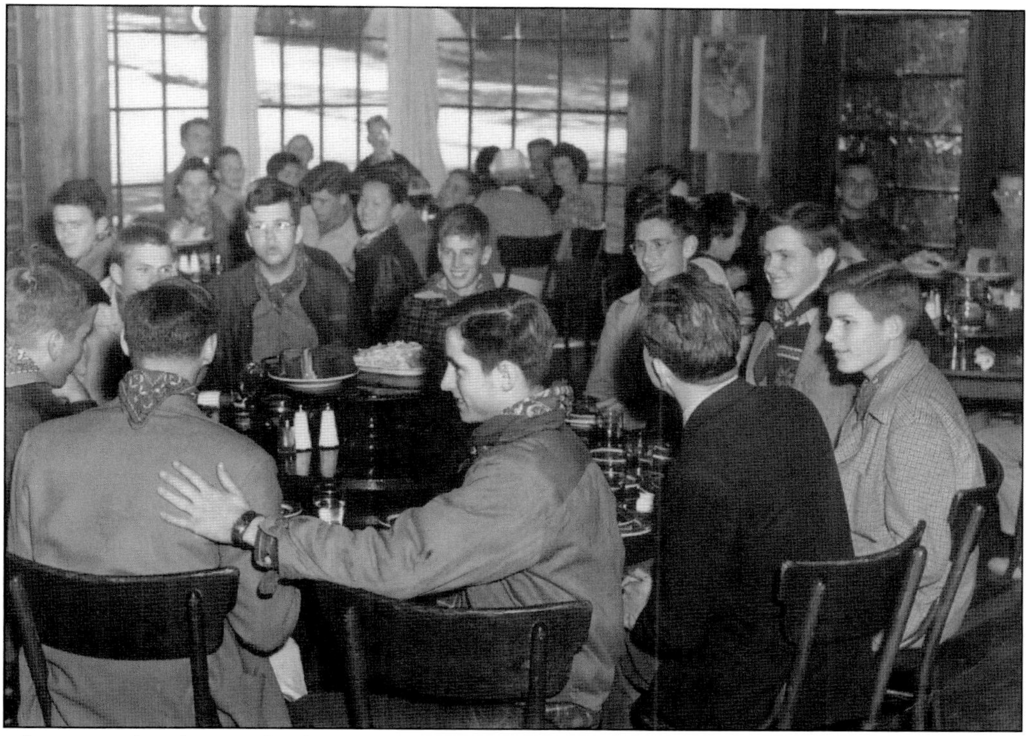

After recess lunch it was back to class until lunch. During lunch, there might be a few additional announcements or a rousing chorus of "Here's to Captain Holmgren [or whomever] and the team; raise your voices free; here's to victory!" to give a fitting send-off to an athletic team competing that afternoon. After lunch, there was a short break before classes resumed for the afternoon. With lunch now served buffet style, the announcements and team send-offs no longer raise the dining hall roof.

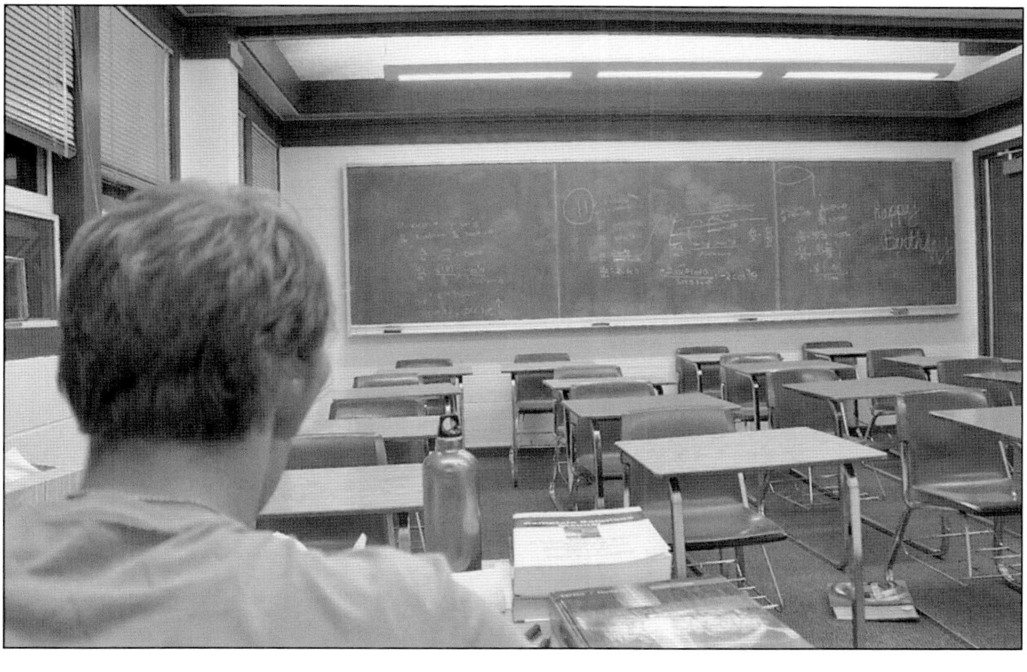

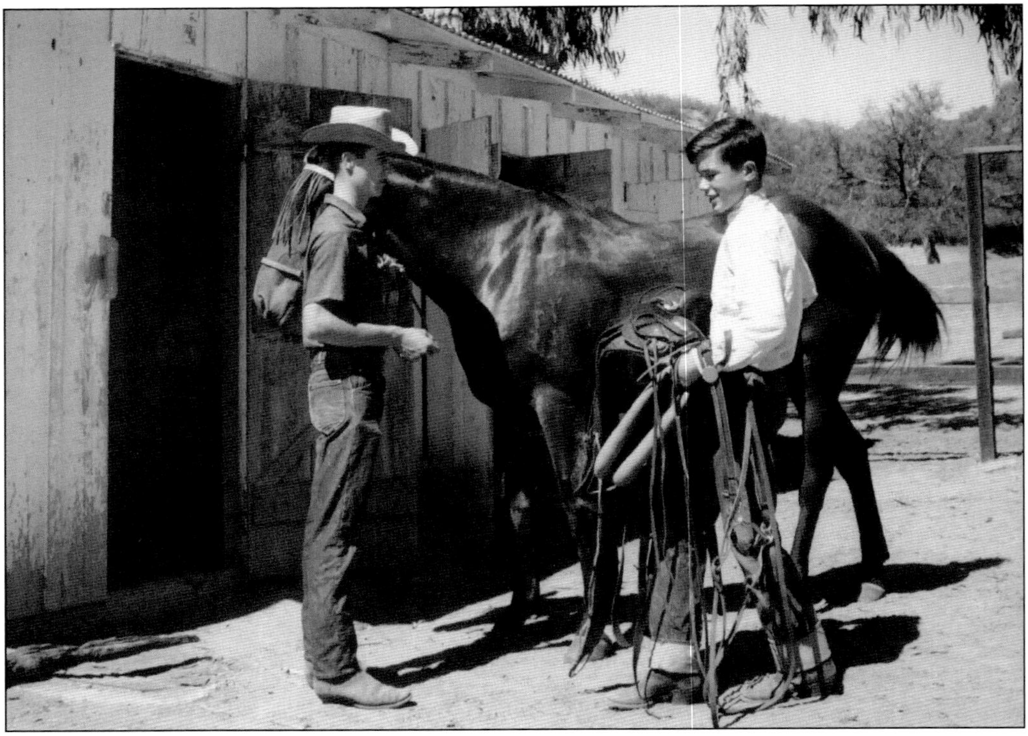

When afternoon classes are complete, a tornado of sorts strikes Thacher. Students burst out of the classrooms headed in a thousand directions. Some go straight for the barns to saddle up for an afternoon trail ride or a trip to Jameson Field for some gymkhana practice. Gymkhana is an activity that requires time and patience; the rider trains the horse, and, in the case of many veteran Thacher horses, the horse trains the rider. Whether the team of horse and rider is practicing ring spearing, trying to learn to open a gate on the trail-horse course, or penning cattle, repetition and more repetition are the order of the day.

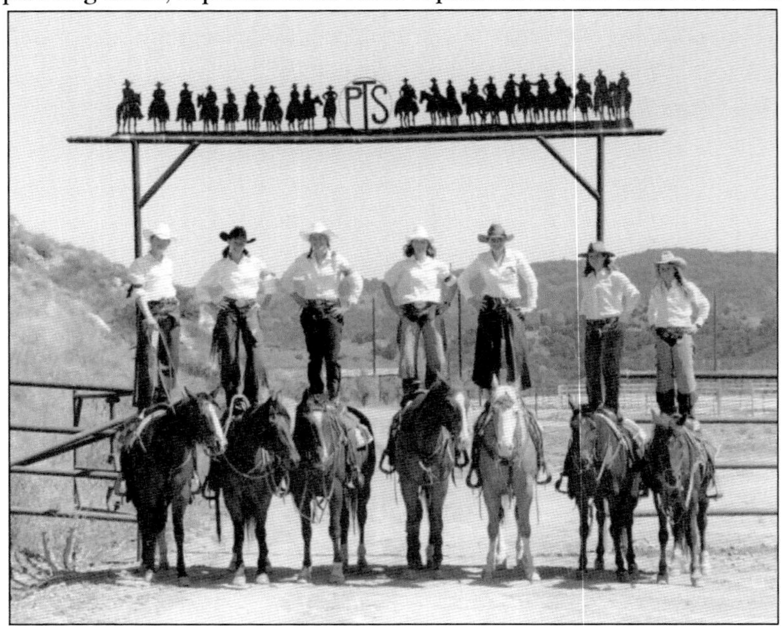

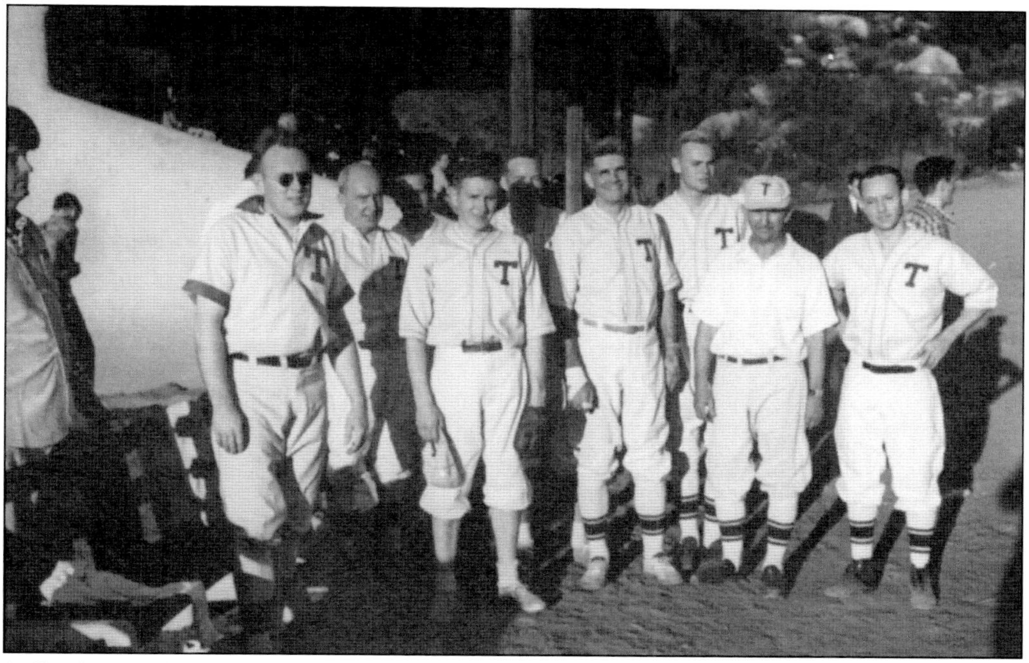

Still other students head for their rooms to gather equipment for athletic practice. Until grass fields were installed in the late 1960s, field sports were played on the dirt surfaces of Jameson Field, or the New Field, so players had to quickly change clothes and jog the mile out to the field. Occasionally, one would throw a bridle on his horse and ride to the field, hoping to fit in a quick L. Moore and Huntington trail ride on the way back to keep his horse in shape. Now the fields are closer at hand, giving the coaches more time for calisthenics and wind sprints.

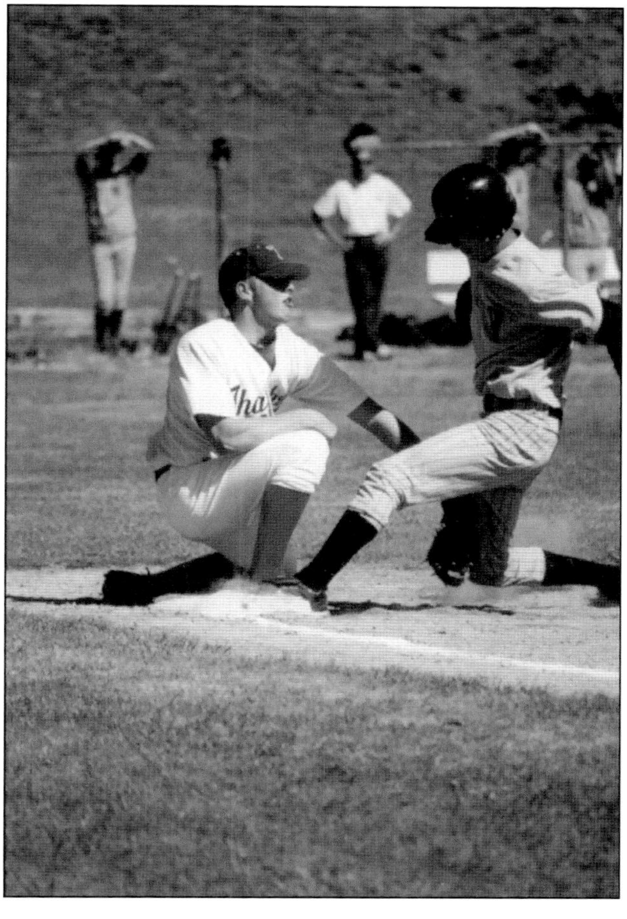

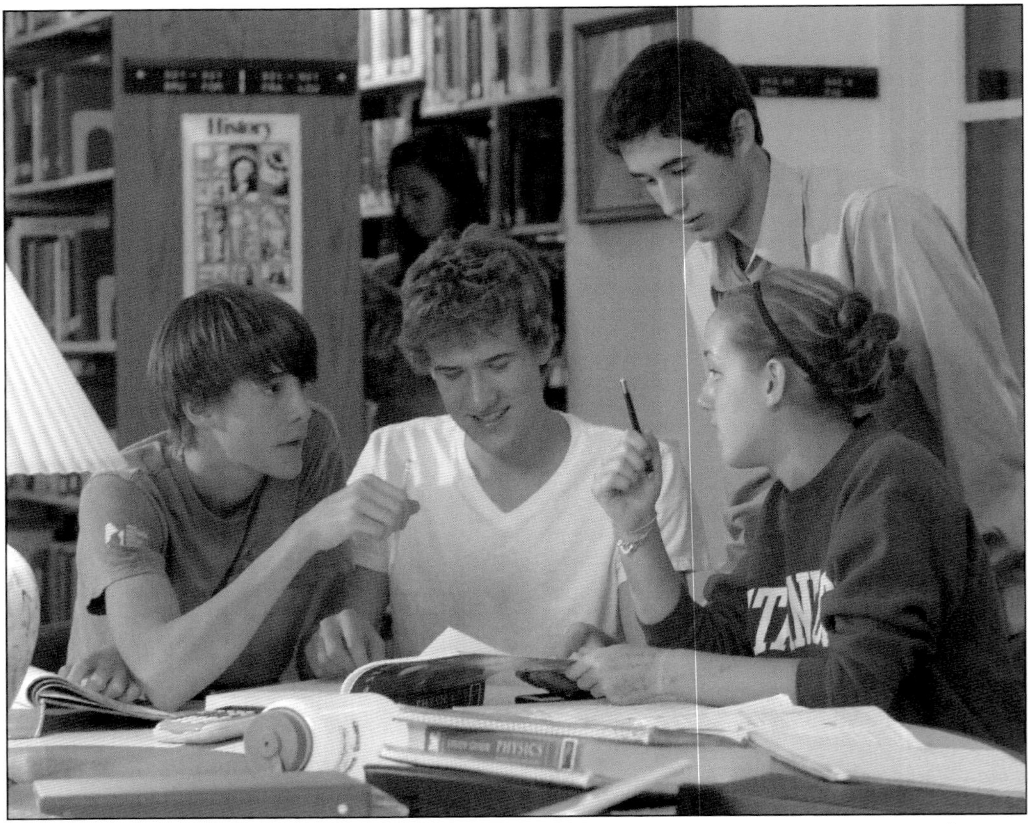

All students are required to either ride or participate on an athletic team. However, if sports or horse activities are not on this day's agenda, it is likely that the afternoon (or free periods during the day) will find students gathering in the library or their dorm rooms, surrounded by books and papers as they complete homework and prepare for upcoming assignments and tests. Others may gravitate to one of the science labs to work on an experiment. If the weather is nice, perhaps some will lounge on one of the many grassy areas to study or chat. If the weather is really nice and they have no pressing commitments (an unusual circumstance to be sure), they might find their way to the pool for some sun or to the new fitness center for a workout.

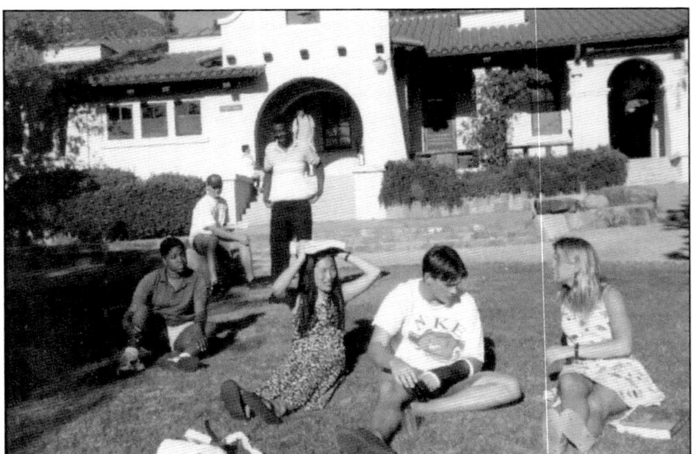

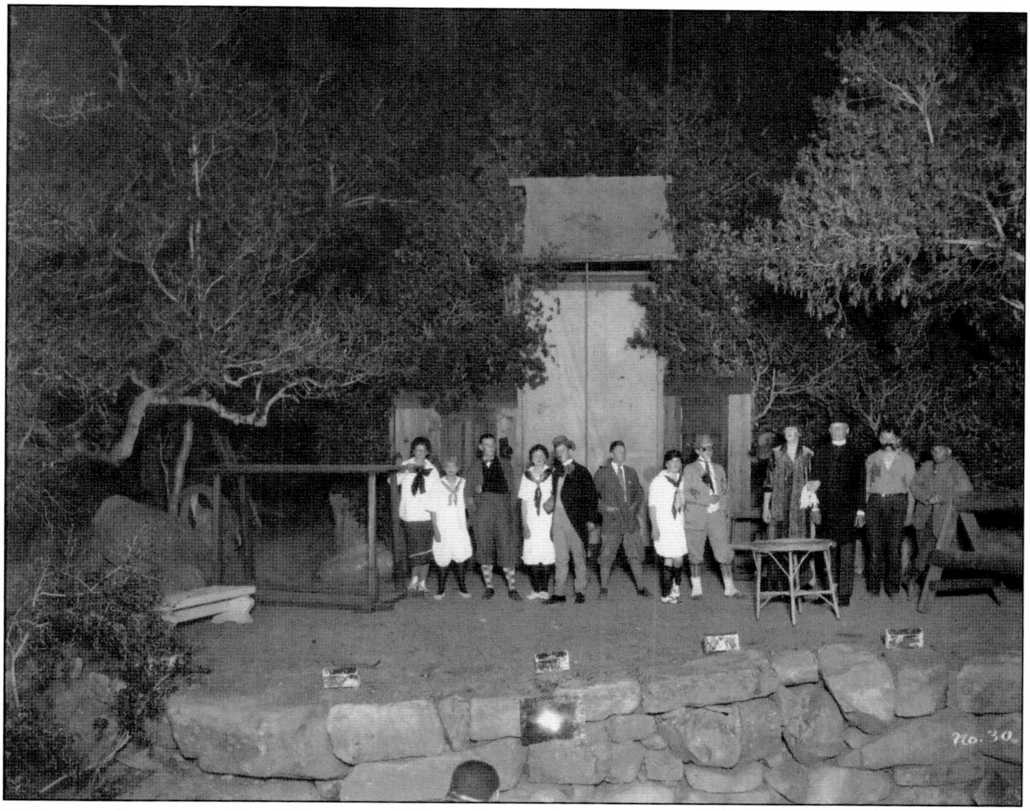

Other students may head for one of the rehearsal rooms in the Milligan Center or Thacher Commons for a private music lesson or just to practice music or dance for a scheduled recital or as a part of an independent project. Some may gather in the Outdoor Theatre to rehearse for an upcoming drama production, while others hike to one of the nearby hilltops to take photographs or to do a rough sketch for a painting. Some may gravitate to the art studio or woodshop for painting, sculpture, woodworking, or ceramics. Others may return to a classroom to practice for an upcoming debate.

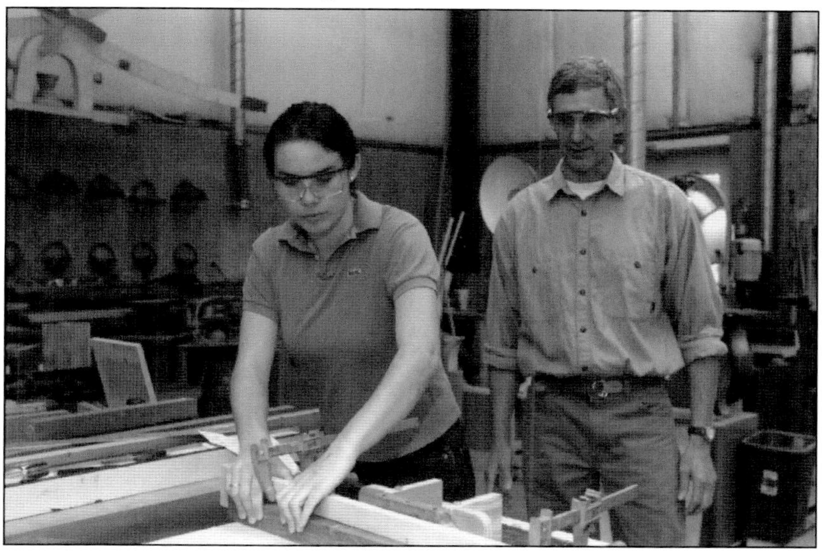

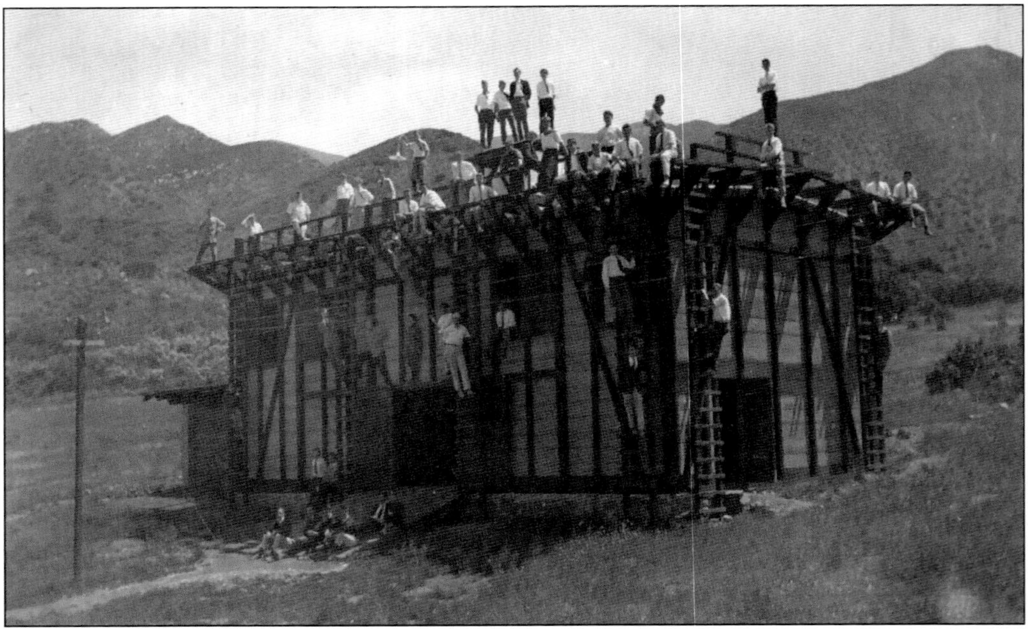

Opportunities were a bit more limited in the earlier days, so when boys needed a chance to just blow off steam in the afternoon or on weekends there was the Rough-House. This unique facility, a brainchild of Sherman Thacher, was a multilevel, barn-like building located right behind the Study Hall. It had hanging ropes, wooden slides, and a sawdust-covered floor.

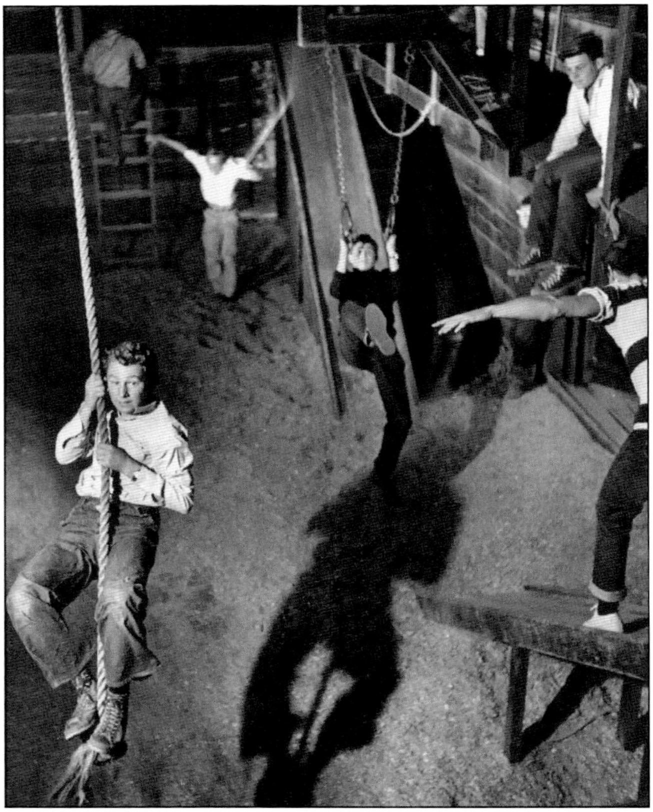

It was, perhaps, remarkable that the only Rough-House casualties were an occasional splinter from a wooden slide and one or two broken arms (including one by Robert F. Kennedy during a visit to Thacher). However, in the summer of 1973, during a period of safety consciousness and liability concern, it was torn down, much to the dismay of boys returning for the fall term. It is a shame that current and future generations cannot dare their friends to swing from one high balcony across to the other, a feat known as the Great Grand Swing.

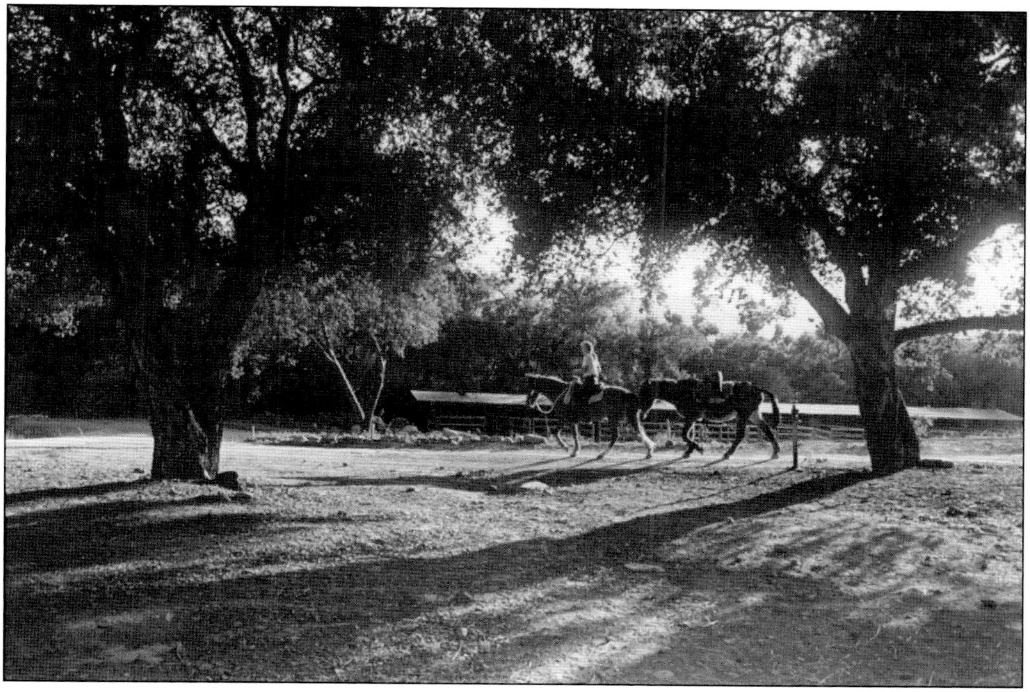

As shadows lengthen and the afternoon draws to a close, the dorms become active with athletes and riders cleaning up and dressing for dinner. The image below shows the original shower facility somewhere near the Upper School. Members of the gymkhana team make a quick pass through the barns to make sure that horses are properly fed and taken care of, and everyone heads for the dining hall as the walker sounds. Some students may attend advisor-hosted dinners in faculty homes or in a restaurant in Ojai instead of eating in the dining hall. (Above, courtesy of The Thacher School Archives; below, courtesy of the Louisa Hagen collection.)

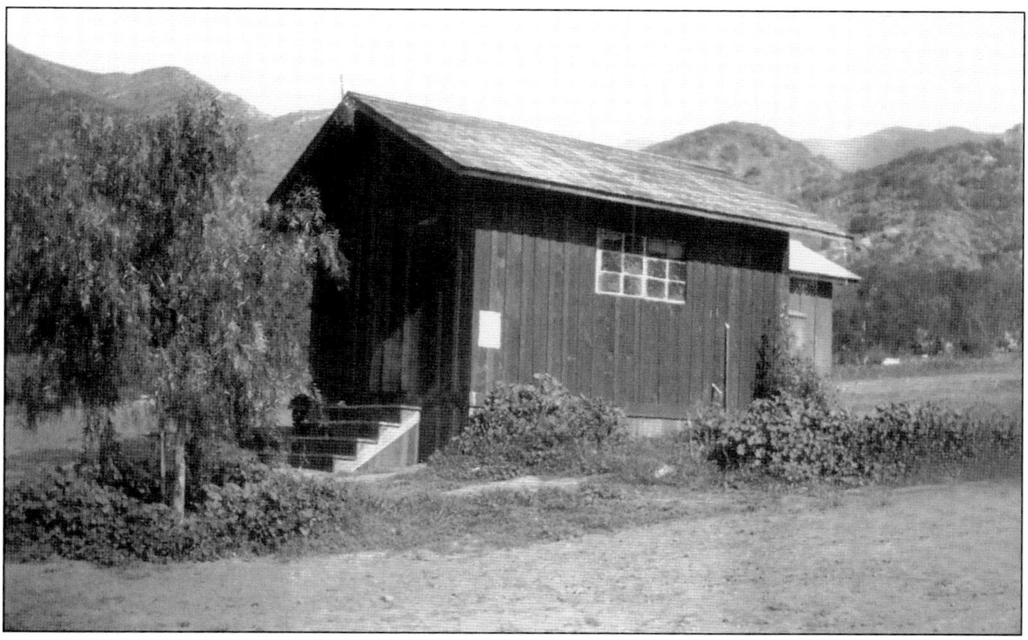

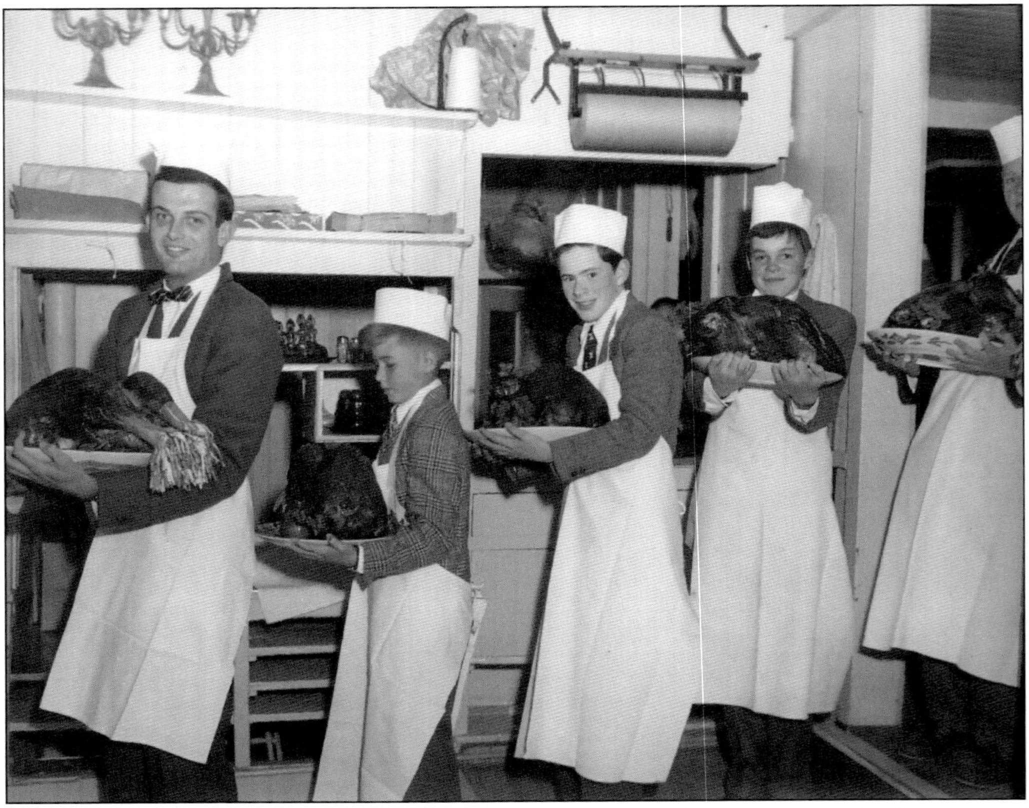

Formal dinner in the dining hall (coat and tie for men, dresses for women) used to be required every night but is now held only on Monday, Tuesday, Thursday, and Sunday. Evening meals are preceded by grace or, formerly, by singing "Domine" or the "Banquet Song." Then the assigned student-waiter at each table brings the food, and the meal begins. This image shows student-waiters at a Thanksgiving banquet in the 1940s.

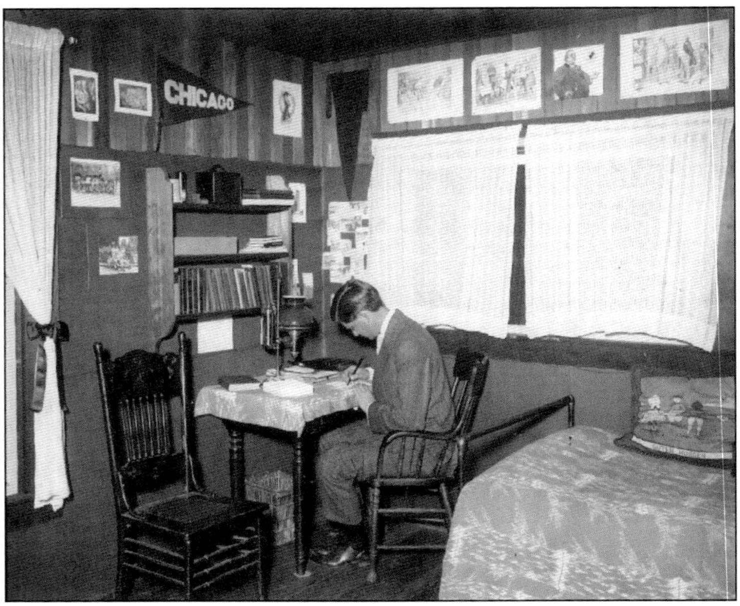

After dinner, there may be lectures, special seminars, or class get-togethers at a faculty home. And there is always homework and studying. Some students study in their rooms (note the kerosene lamp and the lack of computers in this photograph from the days before electricity); others may choose the library. But regardless of the location, everyone realizes that he or she is at Thacher to learn.

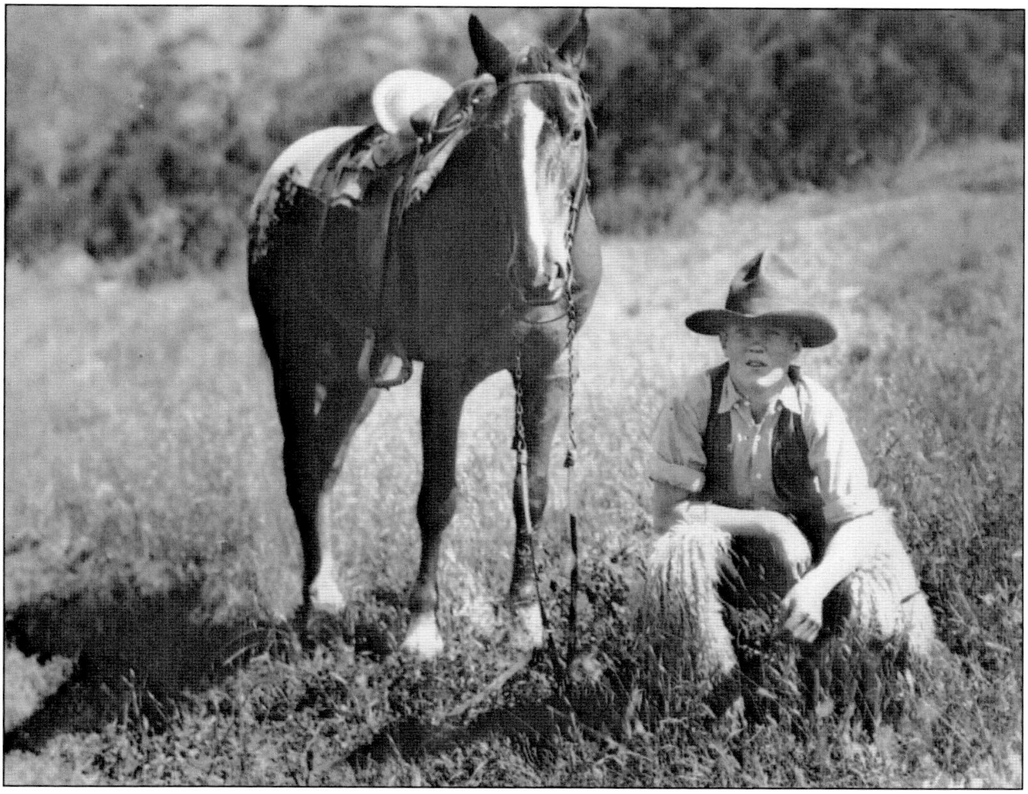

Weekends have a somewhat different rhythm at Thacher, although the same themes of friends, teammates, horses, music, and study, study, study still prevail. Some campers may have received permission to leave at noon on Thursday, others gather at Camp Supply early Saturday morning to pack their horses for a quick trip over the ridge to Ladybug or Middle Lion, and still others pick up day-trip lunches while they debate between a ride to the Pines or Twin Peaks. Teams assemble in the parking lot to board buses for trips to Cate, Midland, or one of the other competing schools. Other athletes head to one of the athletic fields to warm up for a home contest. Meanwhile, members of the Indoor Committee might be decorating Thacher Commons for a dance.

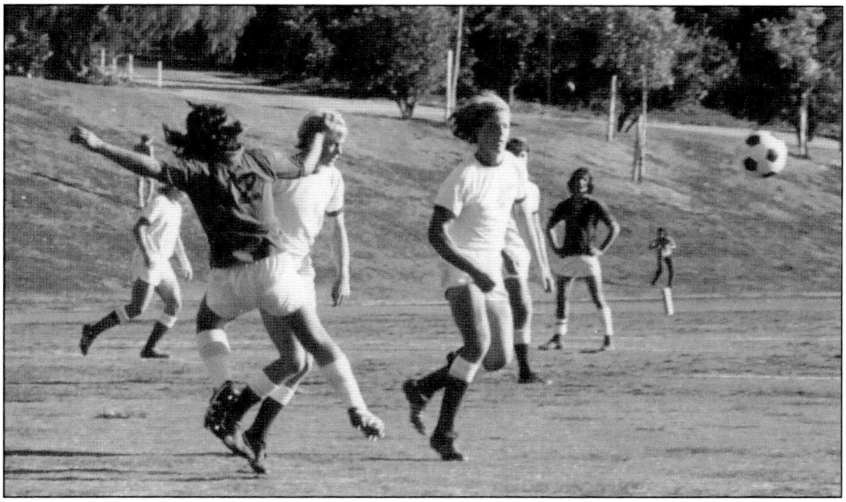

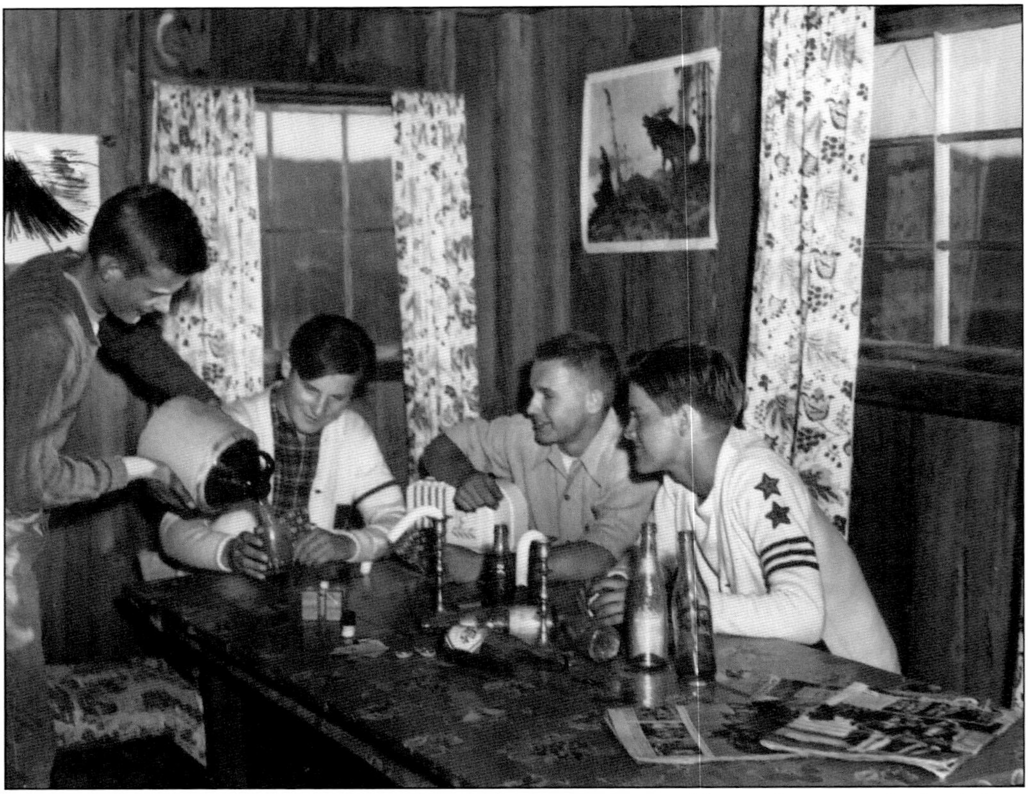

In the early days, weekends might have included a party at one of the student-owned "shacks" on Beadleville Hill (also rendered Beetleville Hill). These five emporia—Beadleville, Erectheum, Oracle, Parthenon, and Wingless Victory—were owned by groups of students and passed down from student group to student group. They were a place where the "owners" could get away from it all and "kick back." Sundays might also include another trail ride or a friendly (but always competitive) tennis match. Some may choose to attend church services in Ojai (on horseback in the days before automobiles) or to attend a nondenominational service in the Outdoor Chapel with its spectacular view of the valley.

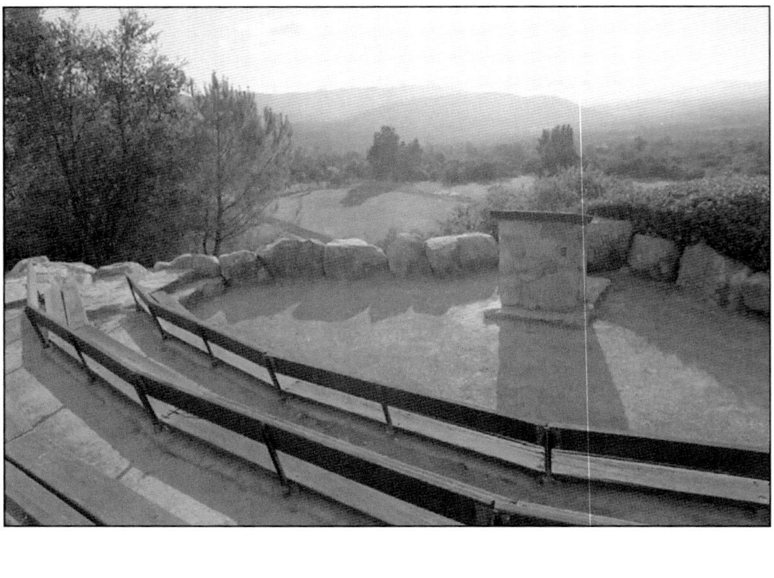

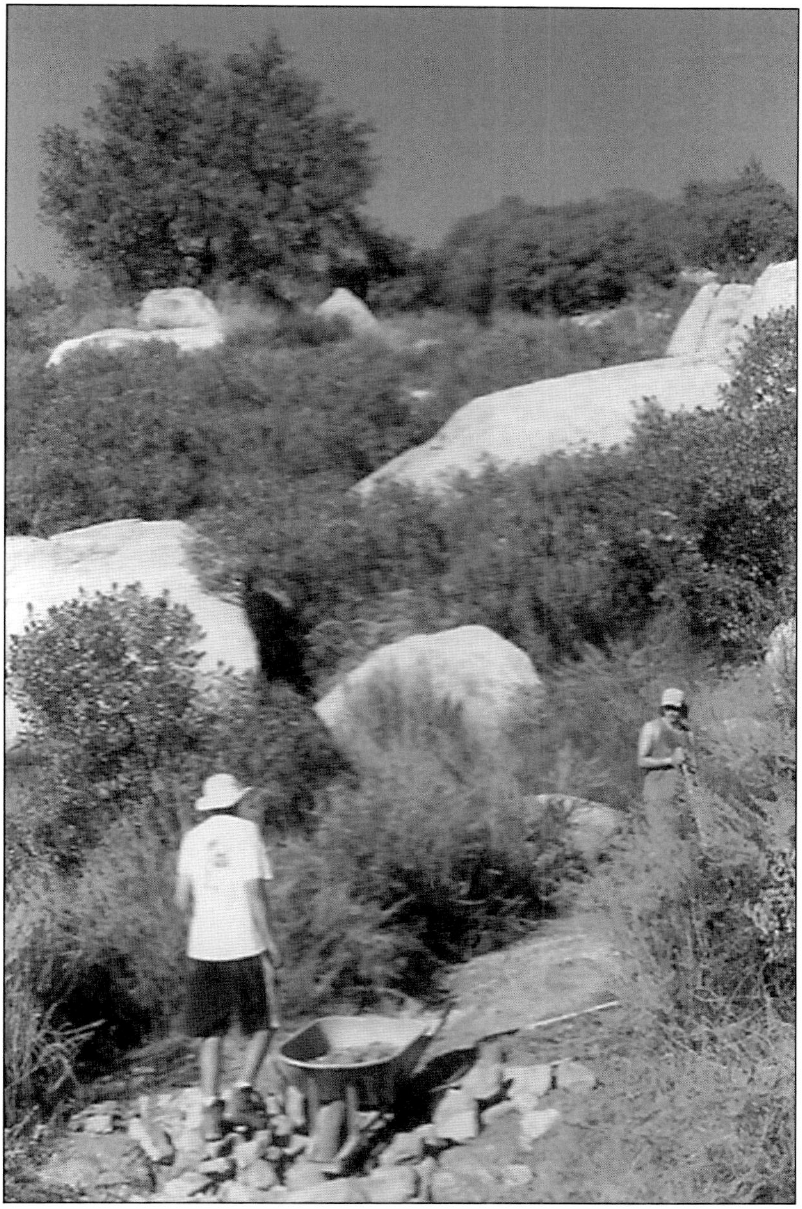

Each individual, from prefect to faculty member, enforces Thacher's expectations, rules, and guidelines. Until 1966, this process was accomplished using the marks system—a student received a cleanliness mark for an untidy room or a dirty stall; a lateness mark for being late to a meal, class, or scheduled event; or a misconduct mark (equal to two of the others) for any of the aberrant behaviors that frequently characterize teenage boys. Accumulation of six marks in a week meant that the "miscreant" was assigned penalty work, perhaps running laps or maintaining trails with a mattock or brush hook. (Note that the photograph above shows students volunteering to do trail work as a part of a senior project, not for disciplinary reasons.) Accumulation of 12 or more marks in two weeks meant that the student was "campused;" they were not allowed to leave Thacher or participate in special activities such as games or dances. Today, the process is less formal and relies more on counseling and discussion than on the humiliation of the very public marks board.

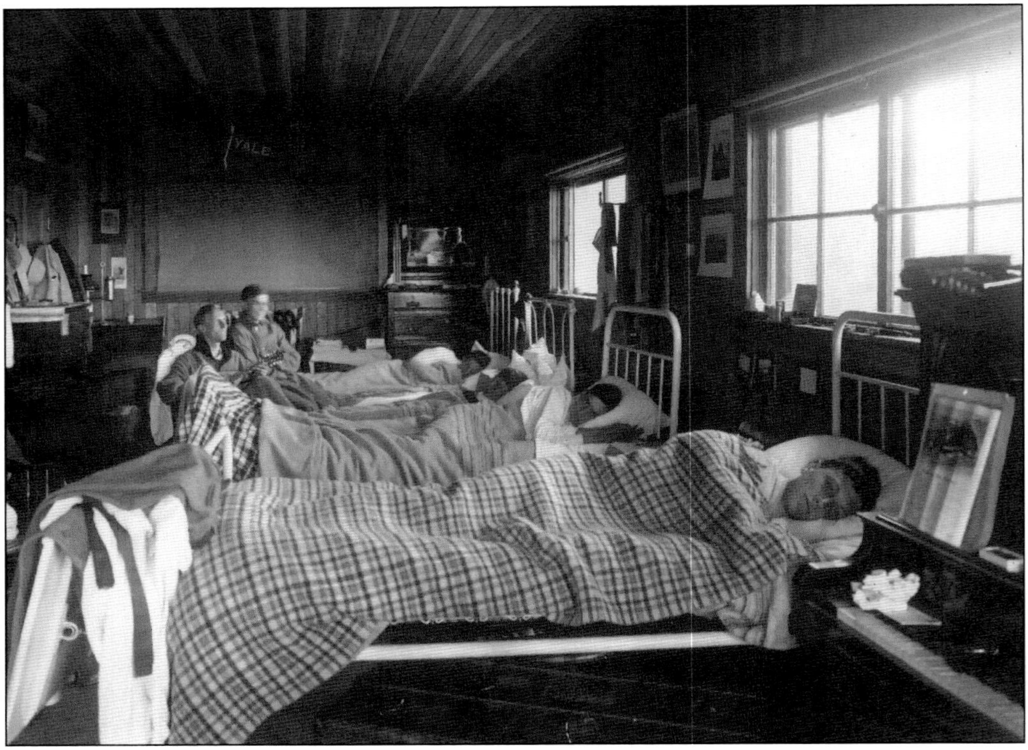

In the original dormitory, lower and middle schoolers slept on a sleeping porch. Lights out for lower schoolers (now freshmen) is 10:30, and for middle schoolers (now sophomores) it is 11:00. Prefects checking on their charges will occasionally see the glimmer of a flashlight under the bedspread as someone tries to get one more chapter finished, but most of the students are only too happy to call it a day. Upper schoolers may have more freedom relative to bedtime, but they, too, are generally ready for a good night's sleep, knowing that tomorrow will be another busy day. (Above, courtesy of The Thacher School Archives; below, courtesy of Ojai Valley Inn & Spa.)

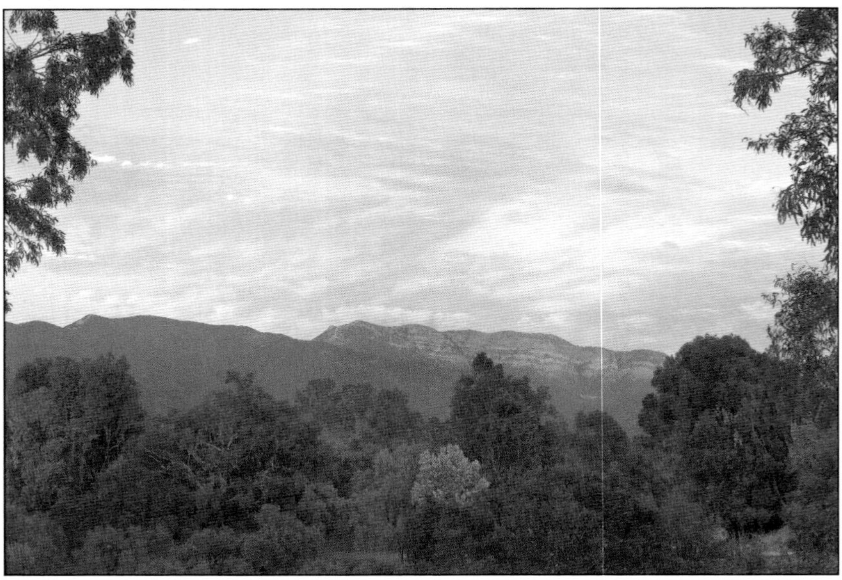

Five

Academics

Since its founding, Thacher's students have been instructed by several hundred different *classroom* teachers. Notice the emphasis here on "classroom," since each member of the staff, from the administration to the facilities and maintenance crews, is an integral part of Thacher's educational process.

Thacher's earliest academic offerings were "sciences, modern languages, manual training, music, and physical development." These have evolved and morphed over the century and a quarter to today's offerings, which include, among others, physics, chemistry, biology, environmental science, psychology, astronomy, veterinary science, English, Chinese, French, Latin, Spanish, world history, Middle Eastern history, US history, art, and music. Many of these are offered at the Advanced Placement (AP) level.

An important academic innovation of the Mulligan administration is the senior exhibition program. As a requirement for graduation, each senior identifies a topic of personal interest and works one-on-one with an advisor and an exhibition coach before making a public presentation of his or her findings. Exhibitions take place during a weekend in the spring; students become the teachers, and the entire campus community, joined by many proud friends and relatives of seniors, shares in the fruits of sustained intellectual inquiry. In 2012, the senior exhibition program was the focus of an Edward E. Ford Foundation Leadership Grant that was awarded to Thacher to support a Thacher-led forum designed to help other schools develop and improve their senior capstone projects.

Every Thacher student, from the youngest freshman to the soon-to-graduate senior, realizes that while he or she is at Thacher, academics are job one. No matter what his or her athletic, artistic, or equine prowess may be, classroom work must come first. As a Thacher senior, quoted by Jack Huyler, put it, "Friendships you make, sports and camping you're involved in, academic and social responsibility and in-depth faculty contacts are how it all ties together."

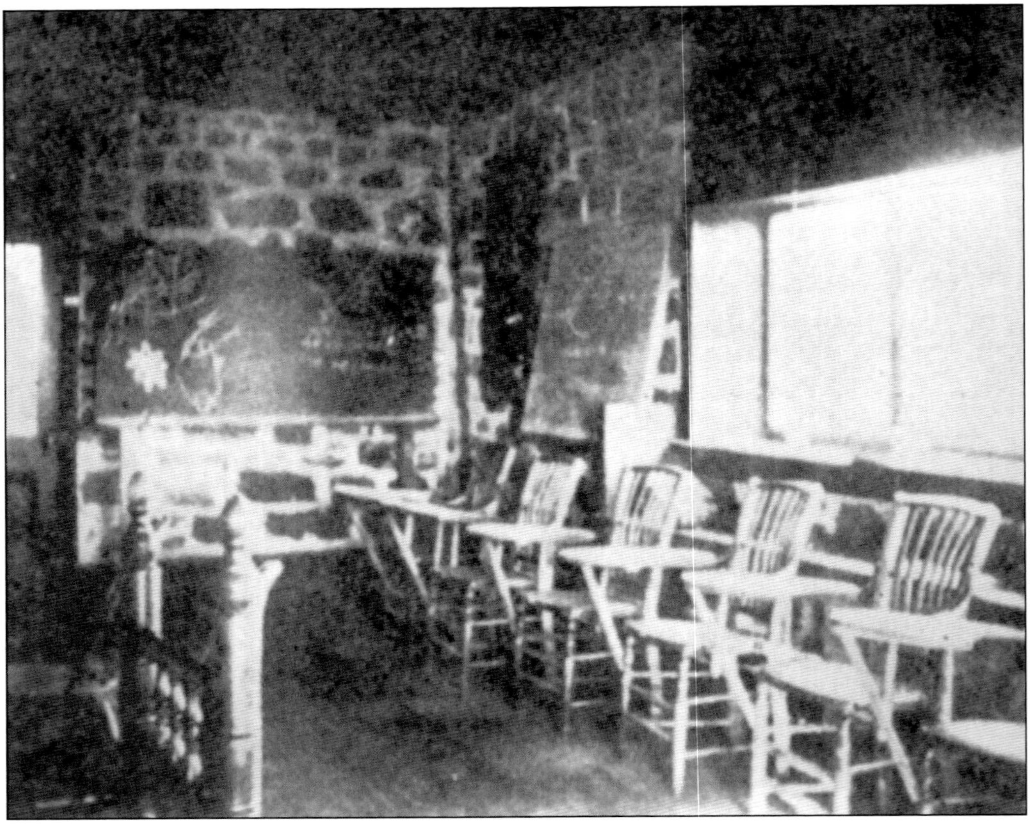

Academics, although initially in a very different setting from eastern preparatory schools, have been the core of the institution ever since Sherman Thacher named it the Casa de Piedra Ranch School in 1889. The first classroom in the stone house is shown above. With a relatively small enrollment, this could suffice. However, after the fires of 1895 and 1910 and the increase in enrollment, the previous school structures were replaced in 1911 with the new Main School Building, where assemblies and classes were held. This building, shown as an isolated entity in the pre-1919 postcard below, now houses state-of-the-art English classrooms, the Alumni Development Office, and the Study Hall recently refurbished to the glory of its early days.

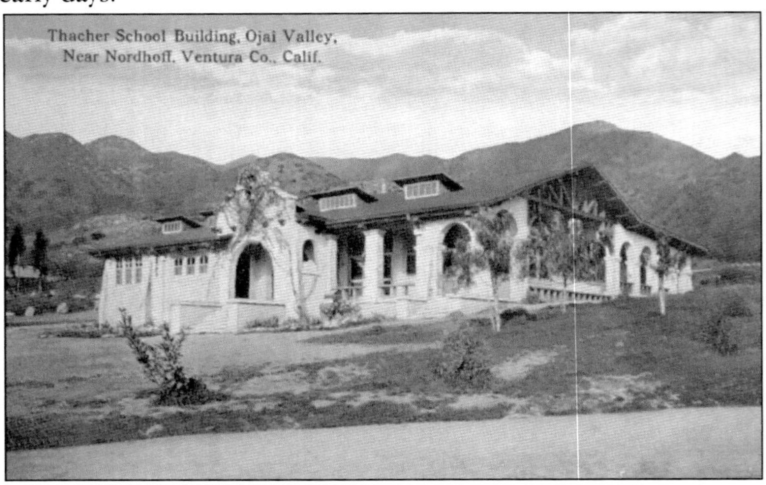

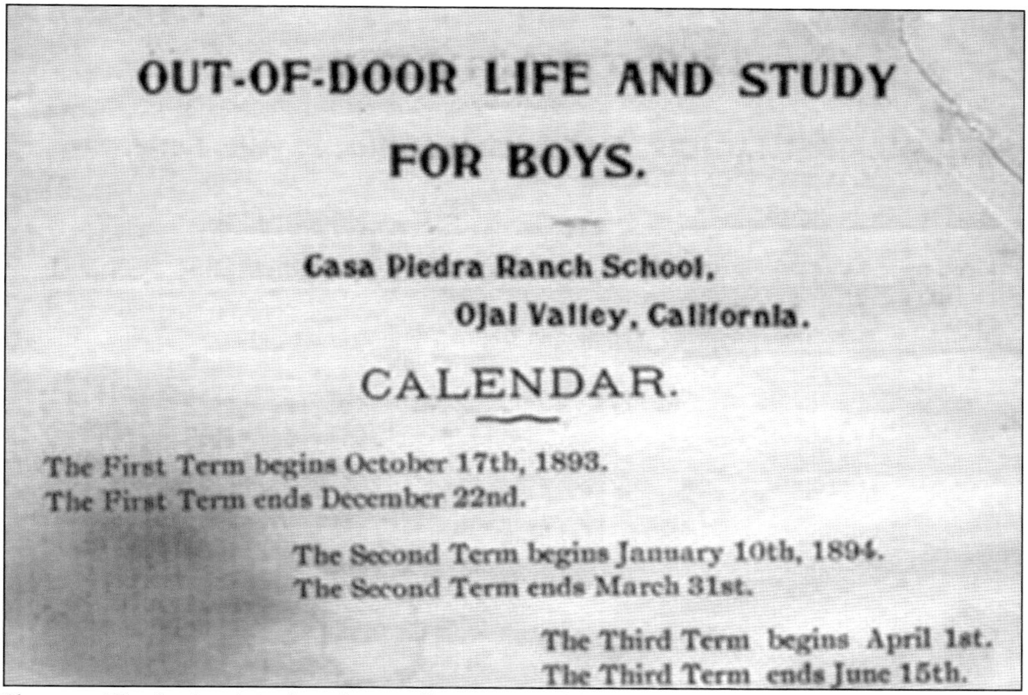
OUT-OF-DOOR LIFE AND STUDY

FOR BOYS.

Casa Piedra Ranch School,

Ojai Valley, California.

CALENDAR.

The First Term begins October 17th, 1893.
The First Term ends December 22nd.

The Second Term begins January 10th, 1894.
The Second Term ends March 31st.

The Third Term begins April 1st.
The Third Term ends June 15th.

Sherman Thacher's original academic offerings, as published in a number of eastern newspapers, were sciences, modern languages, manual training, music, and physical development. Students were required to take English, Latin, and Greek and had the opportunity to choose French or German. Science emphasized physics, based around a core of mathematics. With a relatively small faculty (shown below in 1897, with Sherman Thacher on the far left), this meant that instructors had to be multidisciplinary. In addition, they had to be (or quickly to become) proficient in Thacher's outdoor programs. Today's academic programs are divided into six departments—English, mathematics, languages, science, history, and fine arts.

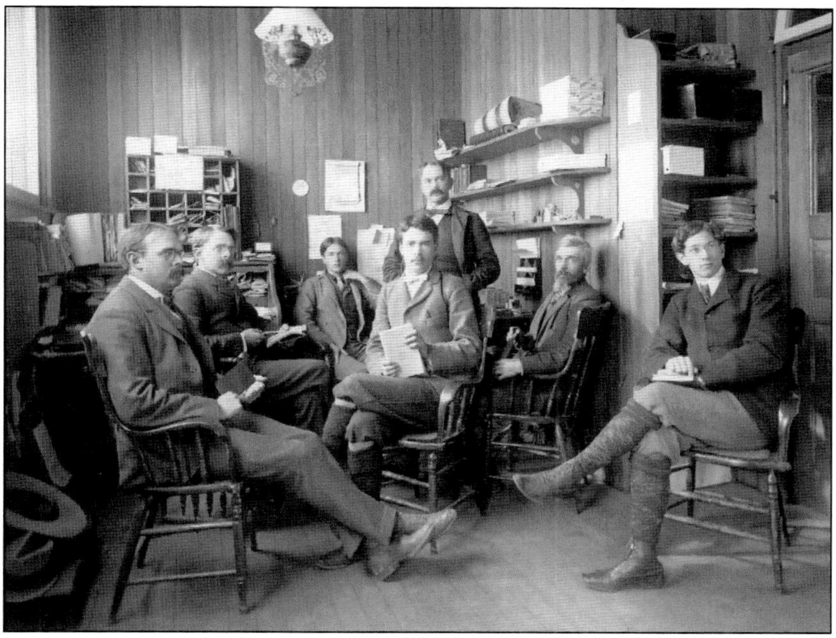

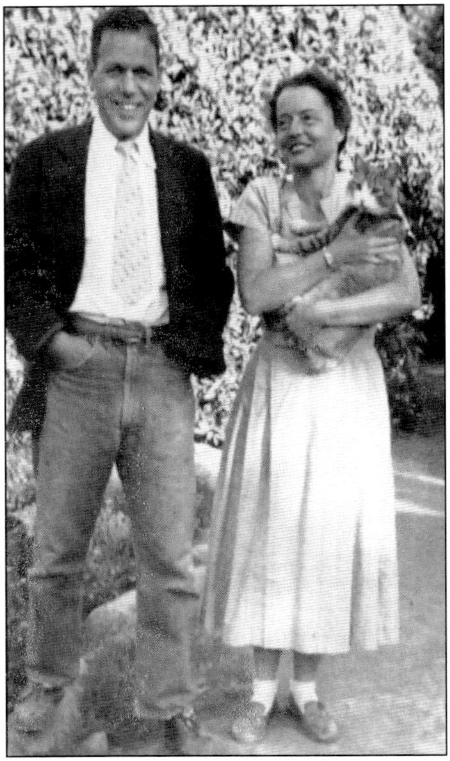

Oliver Wendell Holmes once said, "Language is the blood of the soul into which thoughts run and out of which they grow." This could be a motto for Thacher's English programs. Since the beginnings of The Thacher School, students have been required to take four years of English, taught by luminaries such as David Lavender, renowned Western author and historian (shown at left with his wife, Brookie, who was Thacher's librarian). There are few alumni from Jack Huyler's era who can forget the challenge of his annual English IV assignment to write a 25-page (minimum) paper on "The Political, Historical, Religious, and Moral Allegory of Edmund Spenser's *Faerie Queene*." Today's English curriculum carries on that tradition of building critical reading, writing, and thinking skills through the study of a diverse body of literature.

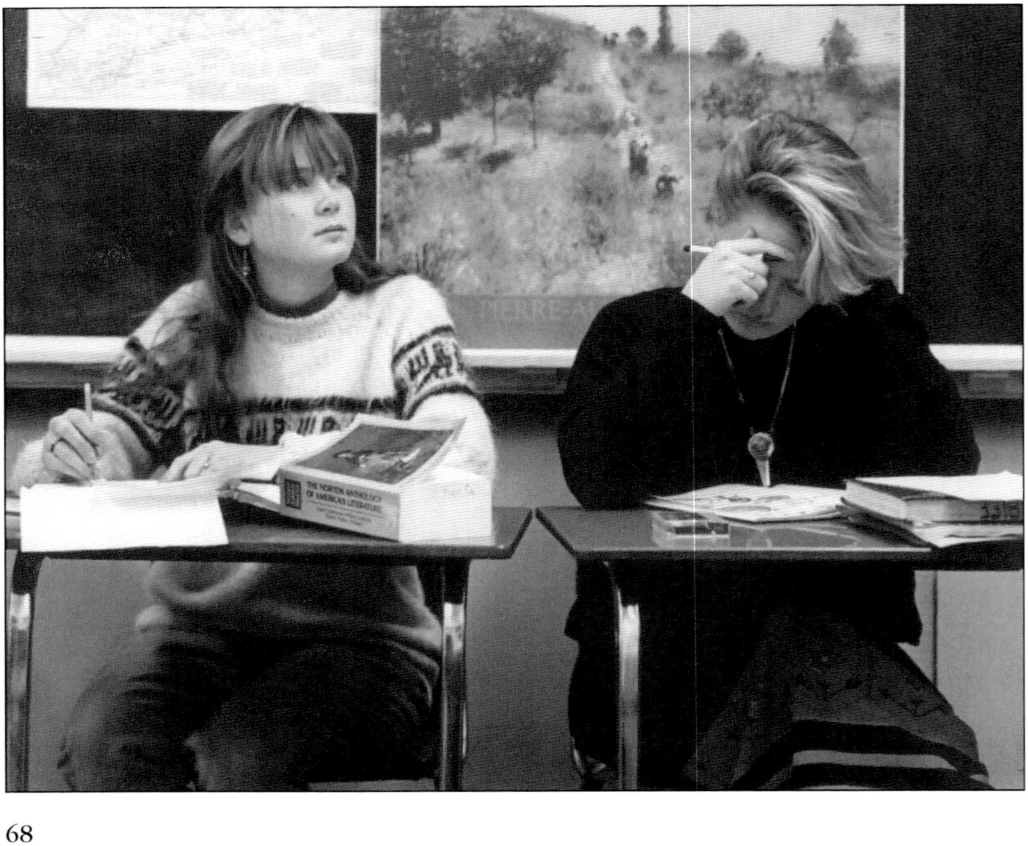

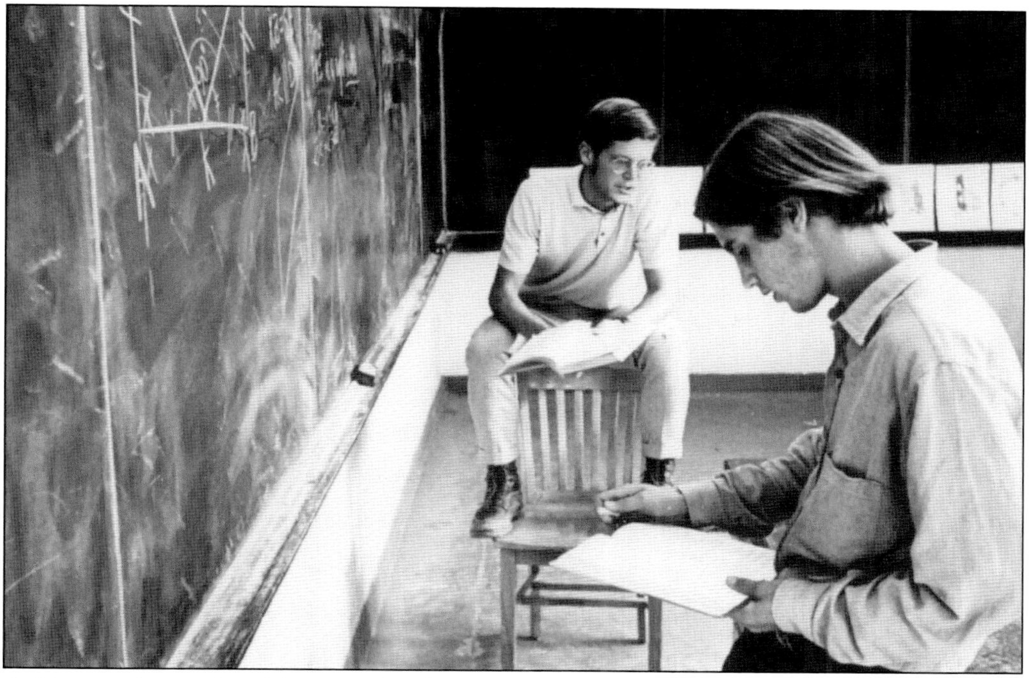

Galileo professed that "the great book of nature can be read only by those who know the language in which it was written. And that language is mathematics." Thacher has always recognized the importance of mathematics as a foundational part of a well-rounded education. In today's world of science and technology, a solid understanding of basic mathematics is essential. Many Thacher students aspire to careers in engineering, medicine, or technology, so more advanced math, including calculus, is provided. Some of Thacher's prominent math teachers include Anson Thacher (son of the founder), Clem Taylor (father of the author), and Gallia Vickery (shown below).

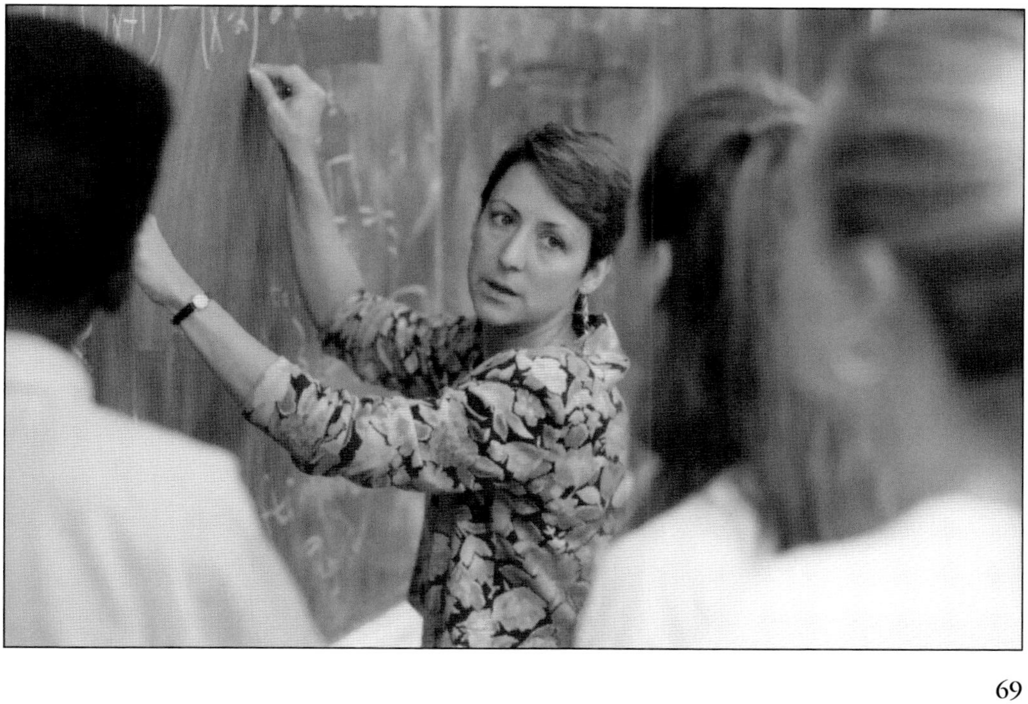

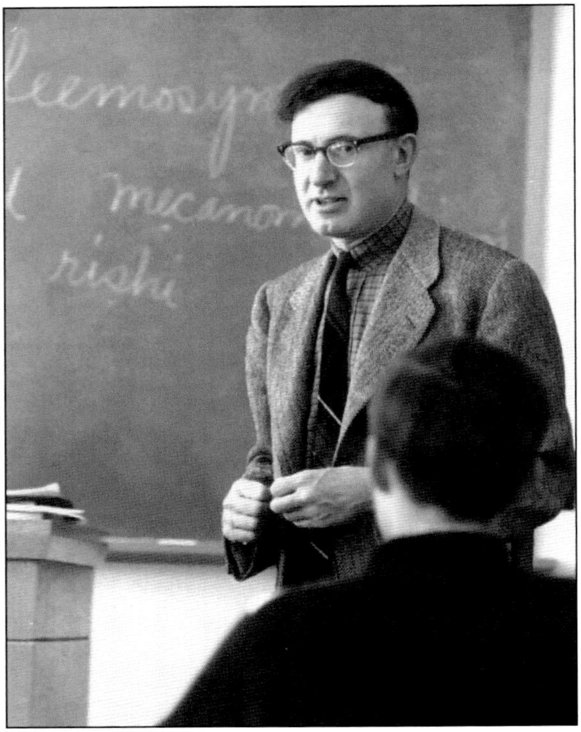

In the late 19th and early 20th centuries, French was the language of cultured society, German was the language of science, and Latin and Greek were considered critical elements of learning to speak and write acceptable English and were also taught simply as part and parcel of the studies of a well-educated citizen. Marvin Shagam (at left) taught Latin, including courses that required translation of Virgil's *Aeneid* and Caesar's *Commentaries on the Gallic War*. Today, Thacher offers Latin, French, Spanish, and Mandarin (taught by Eric Shi, shown below) at the introductory through post–AP levels.

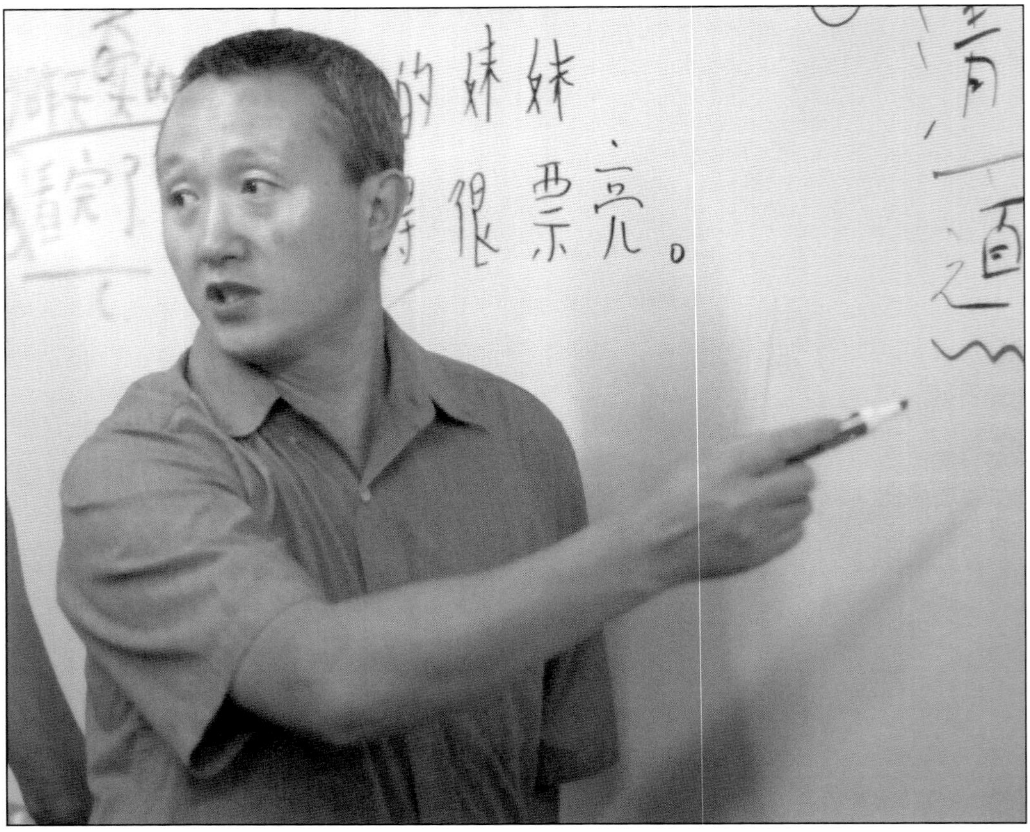

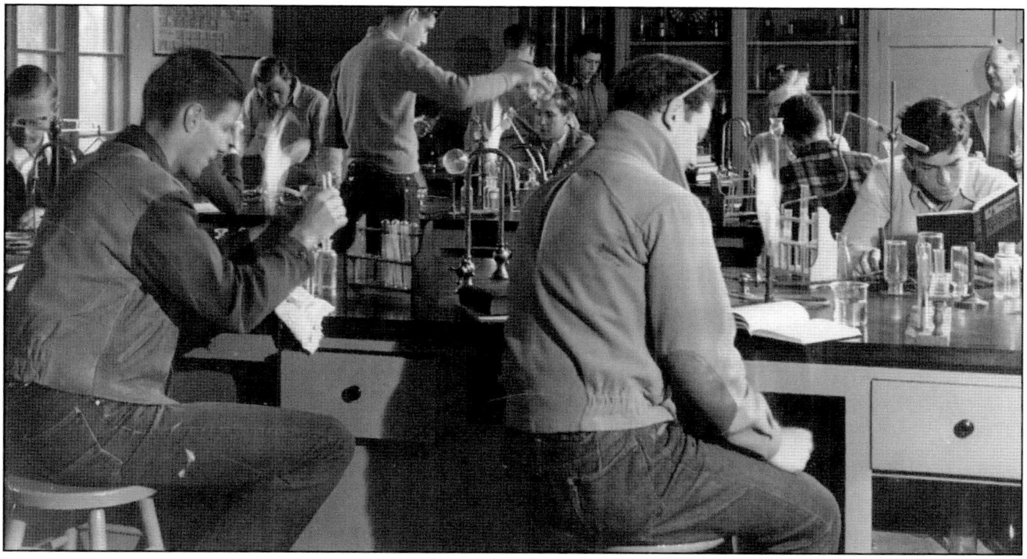

A chemistry class in 1942 is shown above, and a current class is shown below. Note the safety glasses in one and not the other. Sherman Thacher required a study of the sciences, especially physics, for all students, regardless of their intended university destination. This basic offering has been expanded to include introductory and AP biology; introductory, honors, and AP chemistry; AP environmental science; introductory and AP physics; AP psychology; astronomy; cellular and molecular biology; evolution; geology; human anatomy and physiology; marine biology; science and society seminar; and veterinary medicine. Students are required to take at least three years of science.

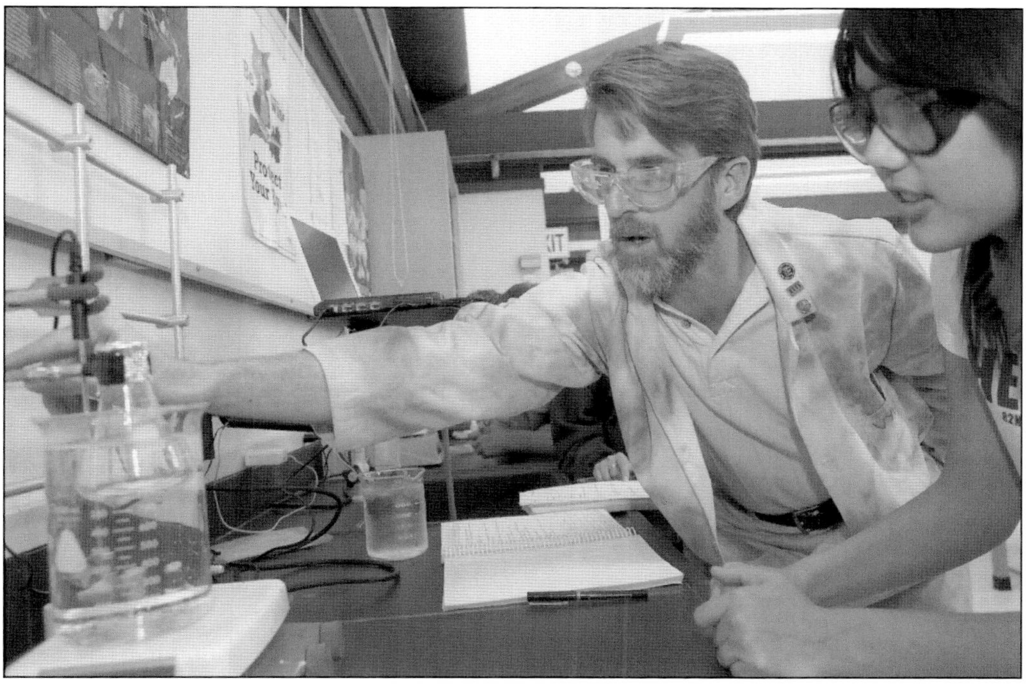

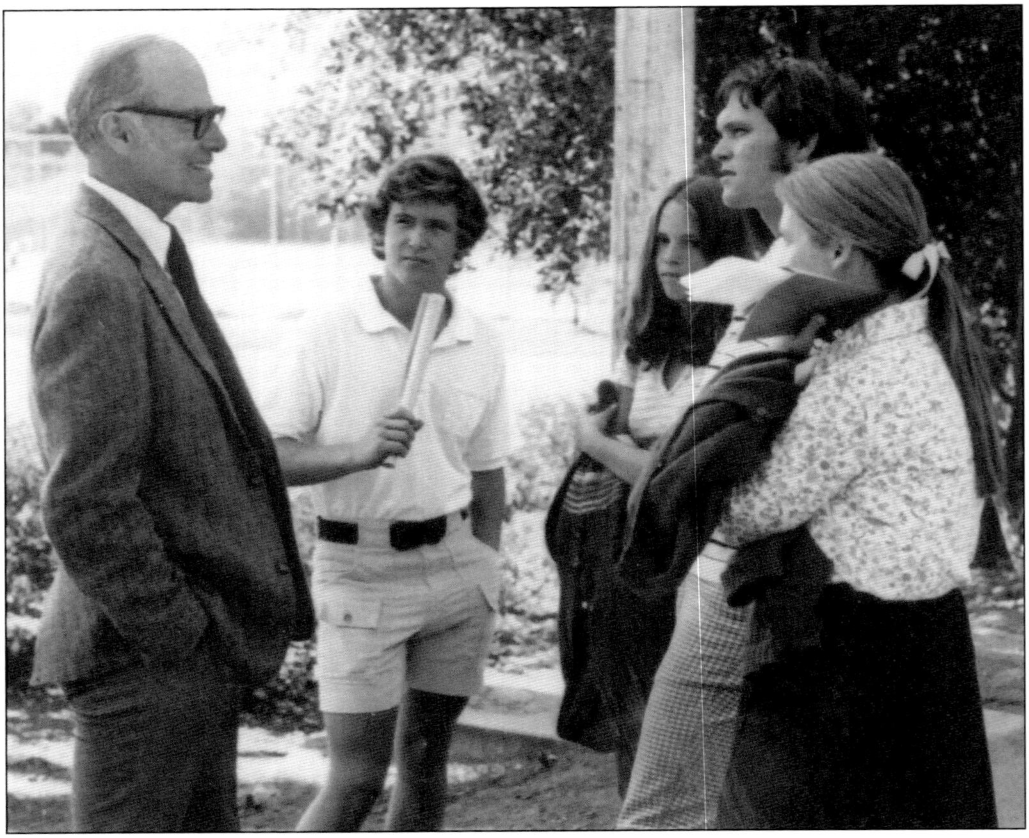

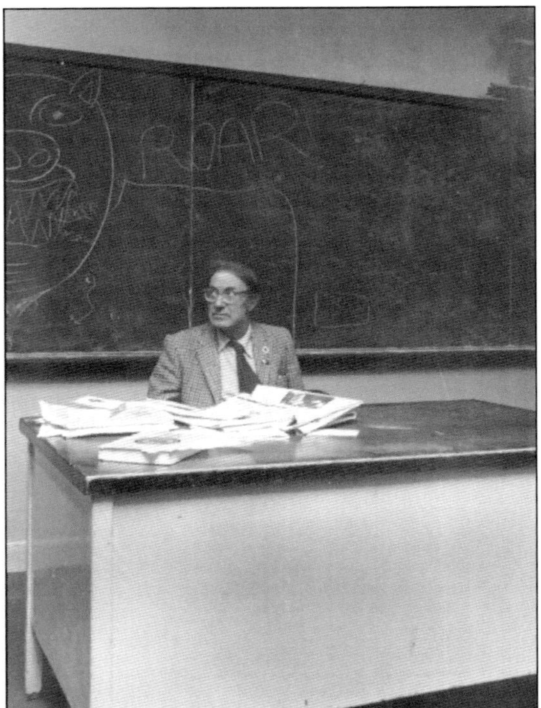

Why should history be studied? Napoleon famously maintained that "history is a set of lies agreed upon." Thomas Jefferson said, "I like dreams of the future better than the history of the past." On the other side of the ledger, Marcus Garvey, the Jamaican black nationalist leader, said, "A people without the knowledge of their past history, origin, and culture is like a tree without roots," and Winston Churchill said, "Study history; study history. In history lie all the secrets of statecraft." Thacher's history teachers, such as Fred Lamb (above) and Marvin Shagam (at left), have guided their students through this challenging maze, instilling in them not only a sense of what has gone before but also of the relevance of those events to their lives today and tomorrow.

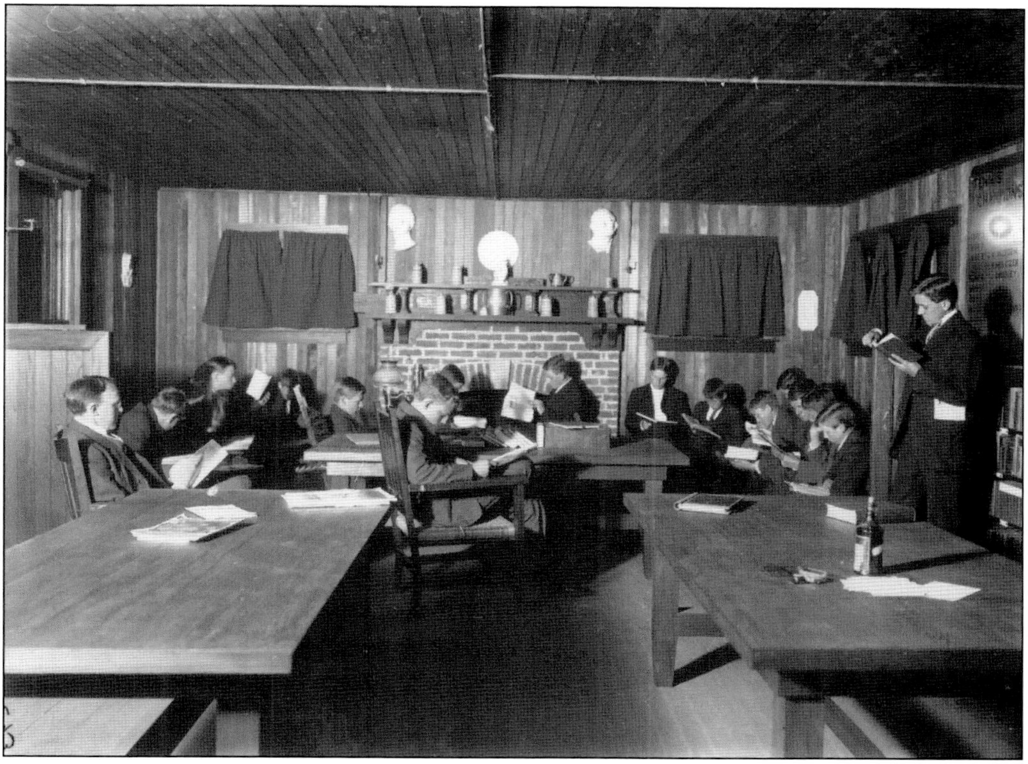

The library is one of the centers of academic life at Thacher. The first library (above) consisted of a set of books housed in a campus room. The books were donated by William Kent, a parent and friend of The Thacher School. In 1928, a dedicated facility was constructed adjacent to the Upper School. This building and its collection of material were added to over the years. In 1991, the library underwent a complete renovation and was renamed the James G. Boswell Library. It now houses books, periodicals, and over 10,000 classical records (most of them donated by Fred Lamb). The library also provides students with access to an ever-growing array of digital resources, including several million volumes via the interlibrary loan program.

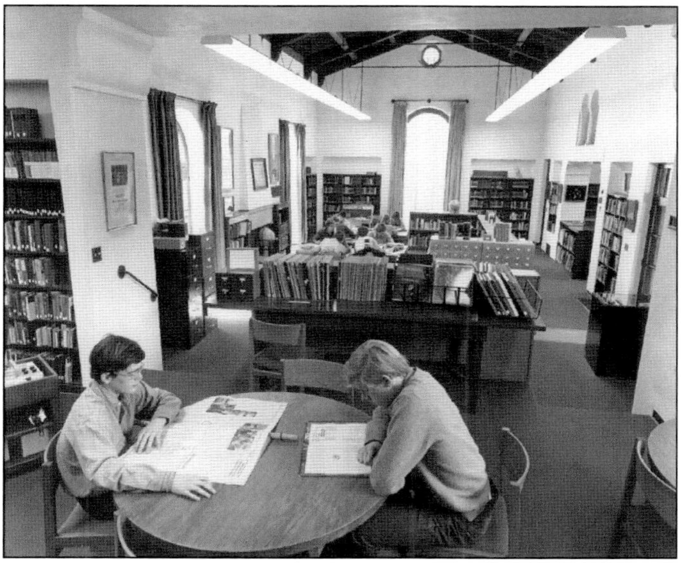

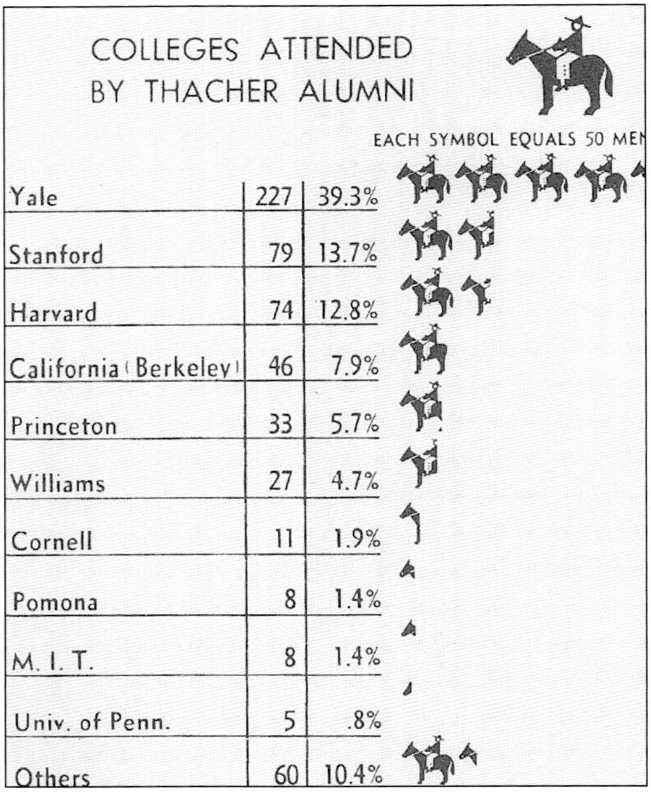

COLLEGES ATTENDED BY THACHER ALUMNI

EACH SYMBOL EQUALS 50 ME

Yale	227	39.3%
Stanford	79	13.7%
Harvard	74	12.8%
California (Berkeley)	46	7.9%
Princeton	33	5.7%
Williams	27	4.7%
Cornell	11	1.9%
Pomona	8	1.4%
M. I. T.	8	1.4%
Univ. of Penn.	5	.8%
Others	60	10.4%

For much of its existence, Thacher (like many boarding schools) served as a feeder school for such institutions as Yale, Harvard, Stanford, and Princeton. Shown at left is a graphic from the 50th anniversary that indicates the success that The Thacher School had in that regard. Since the 1960s, however, there has been an increasing focus on matching a student's capabilities and interests with an appropriate college or university. Longtime faculty members Jack Huyler and Bob Miller took on the task of college counseling as a collateral duty, and with the addition of full-time college counselor John Friborg in 1987, this program concentrated on helping students find the best fit at the best colleges and universities in the nation.

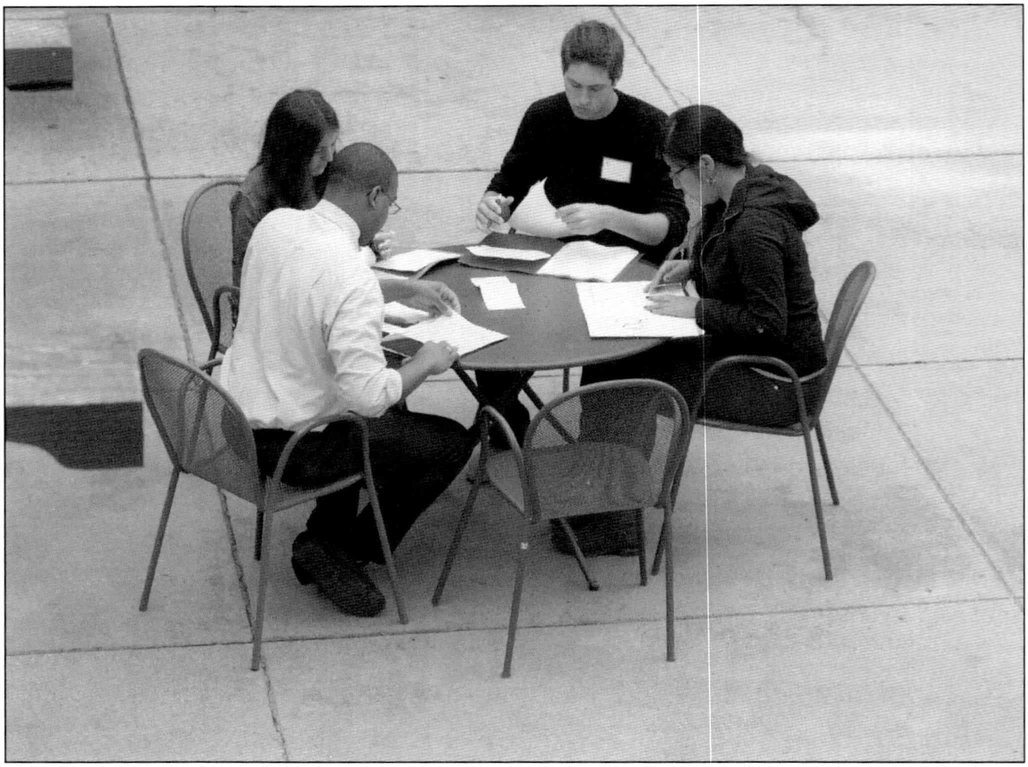

Six

Equis Armis Delectamur

There is probably nothing more iconic about The Thacher School than its horse program. Other private schools have excellent academic and athletic programs, and some may even offer equestrian activities, but none has Thacher's intimate connection with the equine world. In fact, with its 130-head remuda, The Thacher School may be the largest noncommercial owner of working horses in the country.

Thacher's horse program was born of necessity, not recreation. However, as Thacher grew and as cars became more common, Sherman Thacher recognized the value of horses as a core part of his unique curriculum. He famously said, "There's something about the outside of a horse that's good for the inside of a boy." This part of the Thacher curriculum teaches responsibility as well as horsemanship. Caring for a 1,000-pound animal that is totally dependent on the student-owner for food, water, exercise, and health care is a significant task, and becoming comfortable with such a task teaches a student as much about himself or herself as about the horse. Some have called this the "relentless responsibility."

Gradually, three categories of horse-based activities—camping, gymkhana, and trail riding—became integral to the overall program Sherman Thacher offered his students. Eventually, the broad scope of the horse program would be an aspect of the institution that set it apart from every other school, public or private, in the country.

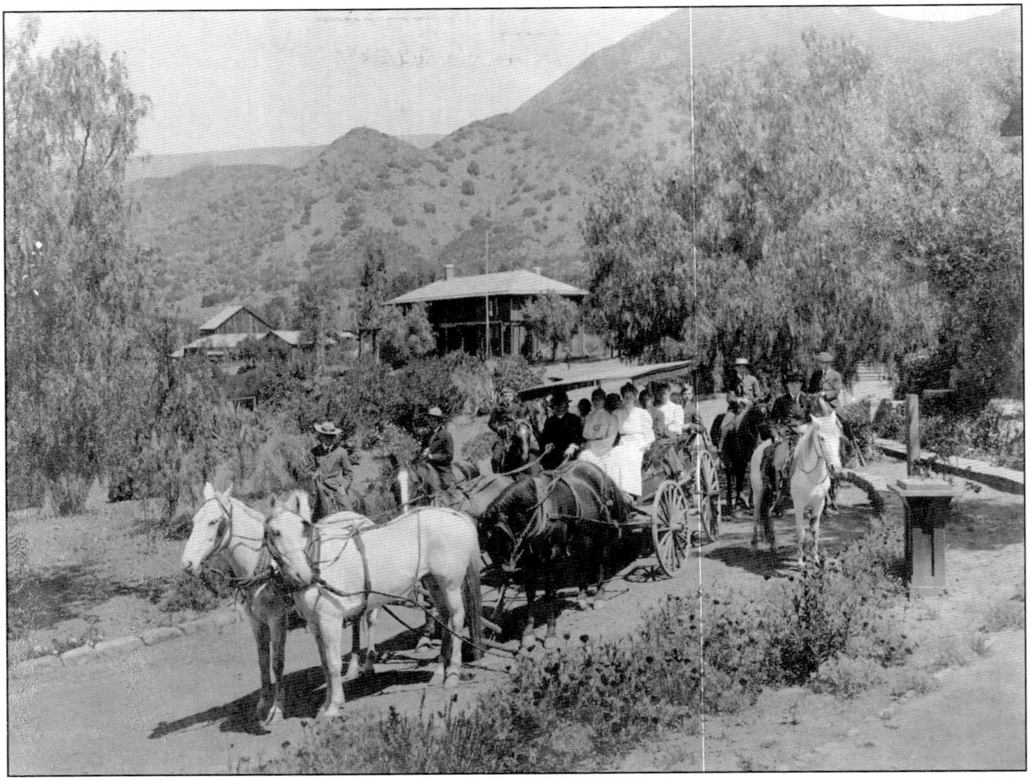

When Sherman Thacher purchased Casa de Piedra in 1888, horses were the only available means of motive power for agriculture and transportation. Since the ranch was nearly five miles from Nordhoff, horses and carriages were a necessity, not a luxury. Here is a group of horseman and a family, probably the Thachers themselves, going for an outing in the 1890s. In the image below, a large number of students and probably some faculty head out from Thacher, perhaps to go to Nordhoff for a lecture. In the days before public transportation, athletic teams would actually ride horses to Cate (then known as the Santa Barbara School) for a weekend of gymkhana and athletic events and then ride home. This might have been the departure for such a trip.

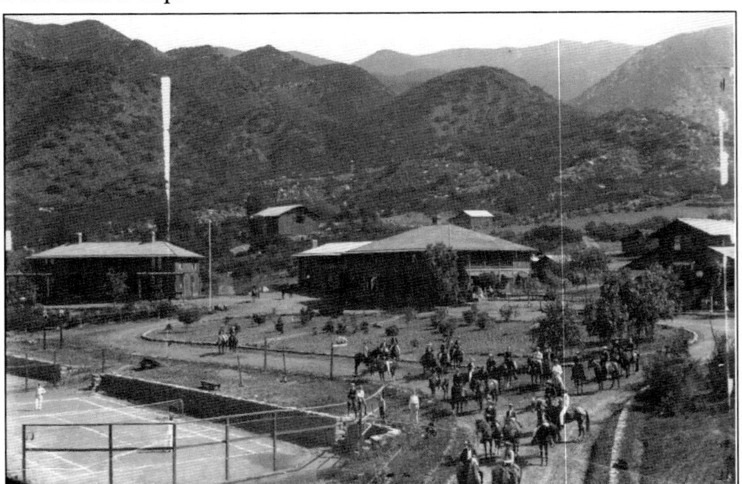

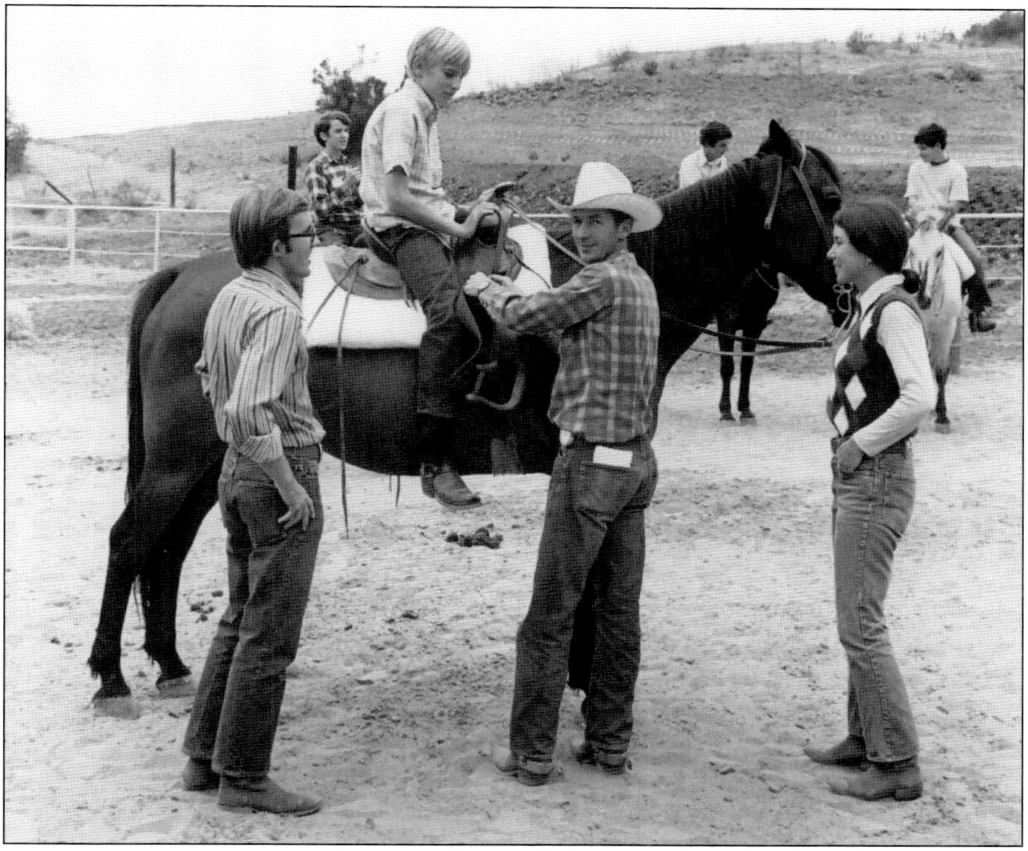

Few students, either then or now, have had much experience with horses prior to coming to Thacher. Under the watchful eye of the director of the horse program, older and more experienced horsemen take these tenderfeet under their wings, imparting to them the basics of horsemanship (such as which end of the horse eats and which end kicks), teaching them how to care for their new 1,000-pound best friend, and introducing them to the mysteries of tack. Within a matter of just a few weeks, boys and girls who had previously never seen the world from the back of a horse are riding on their own and planning their first gymkhana event or camping trip.

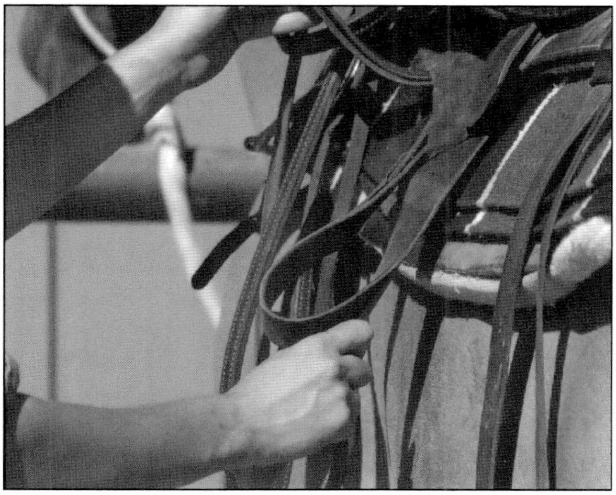

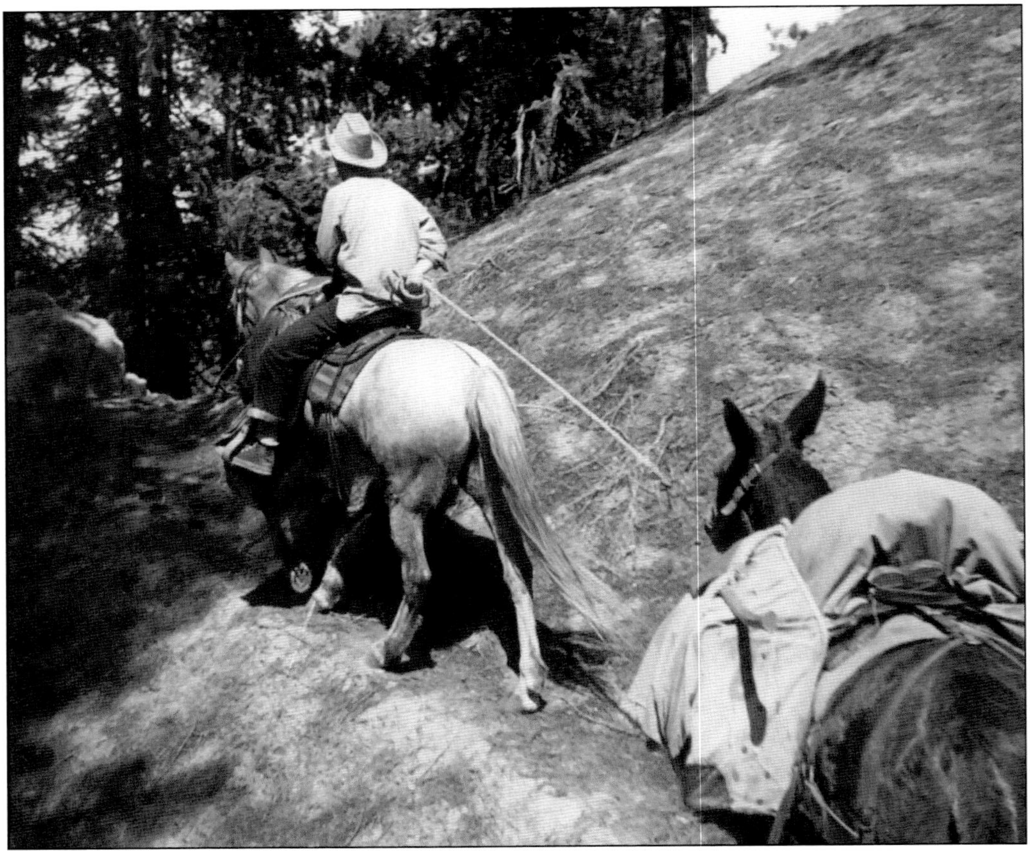

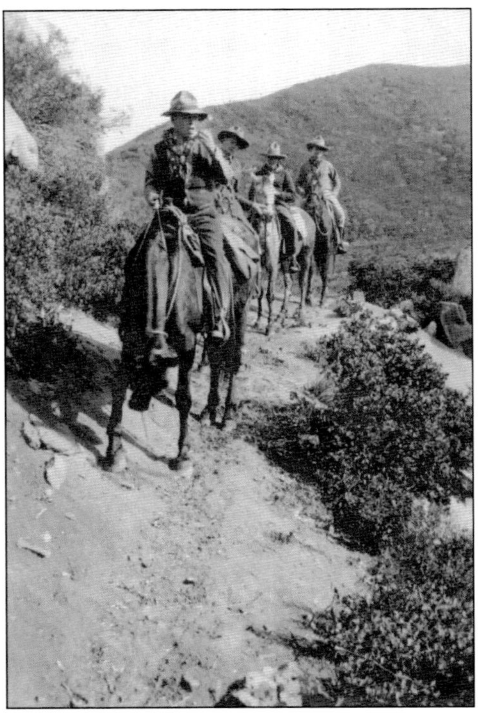

In the spring of 1891, two Thacher students—Ernest Hill and Horatio Newcomb—accompanied by Yale graduate student Samuel Knight, borrowed horses and pack mules from Thacher's herd and made an overnight trip to the Sespe. They crossed the ridge by way of Senior Canyon and camped overnight at a ranch along the Sespe. As far as is known, this was the first camping trip undertaken by Thacher students. Since that time, hardly a weekend has passed that campers on horseback or with packs on their own backs do not leave Thacher for a sojourn somewhere in California's backcountry.

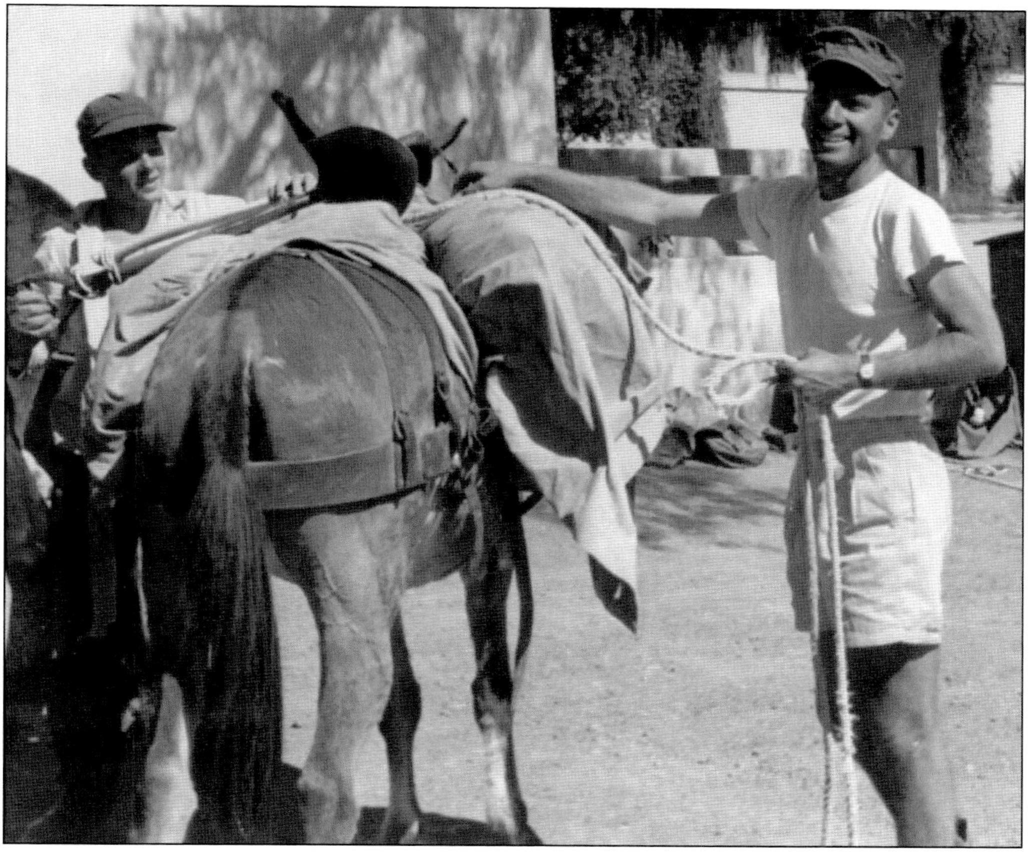

From 1891 to the present, camping has been a crucial aspect of a Thacher education. For the first 70 years, virtually all camping was by horse and was mostly confined to the Los Padres National Forest area that abuts The Thacher School. Campers left on Thursday afternoon and returned by Sunday dinner, often covering 40 or 50 miles in the Sespe and beyond. Once a year, an 8- to 10-day "extra-day trip" (now two five-day trips per year) was scheduled, which allowed campers to go even farther into the wilderness. Since that time, backpacking (either carrying one's own packs or using pack animals), kayaking, and island trips have been added, and destinations such as Golden Trout Camp in the High Sierra and others more remote are now available to students.

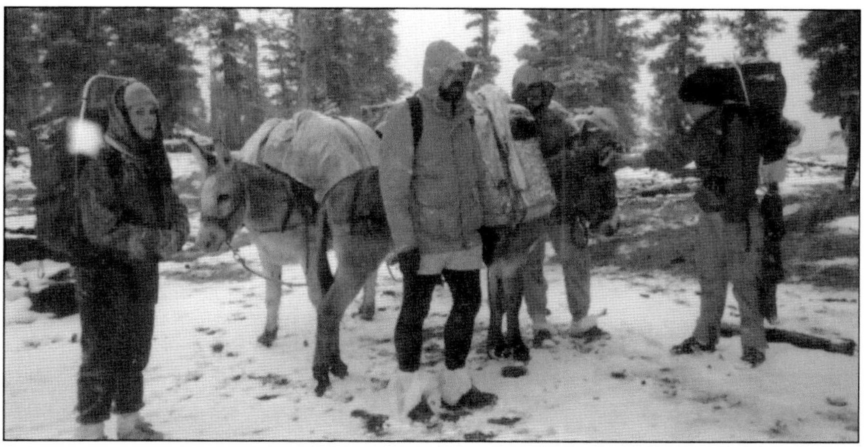

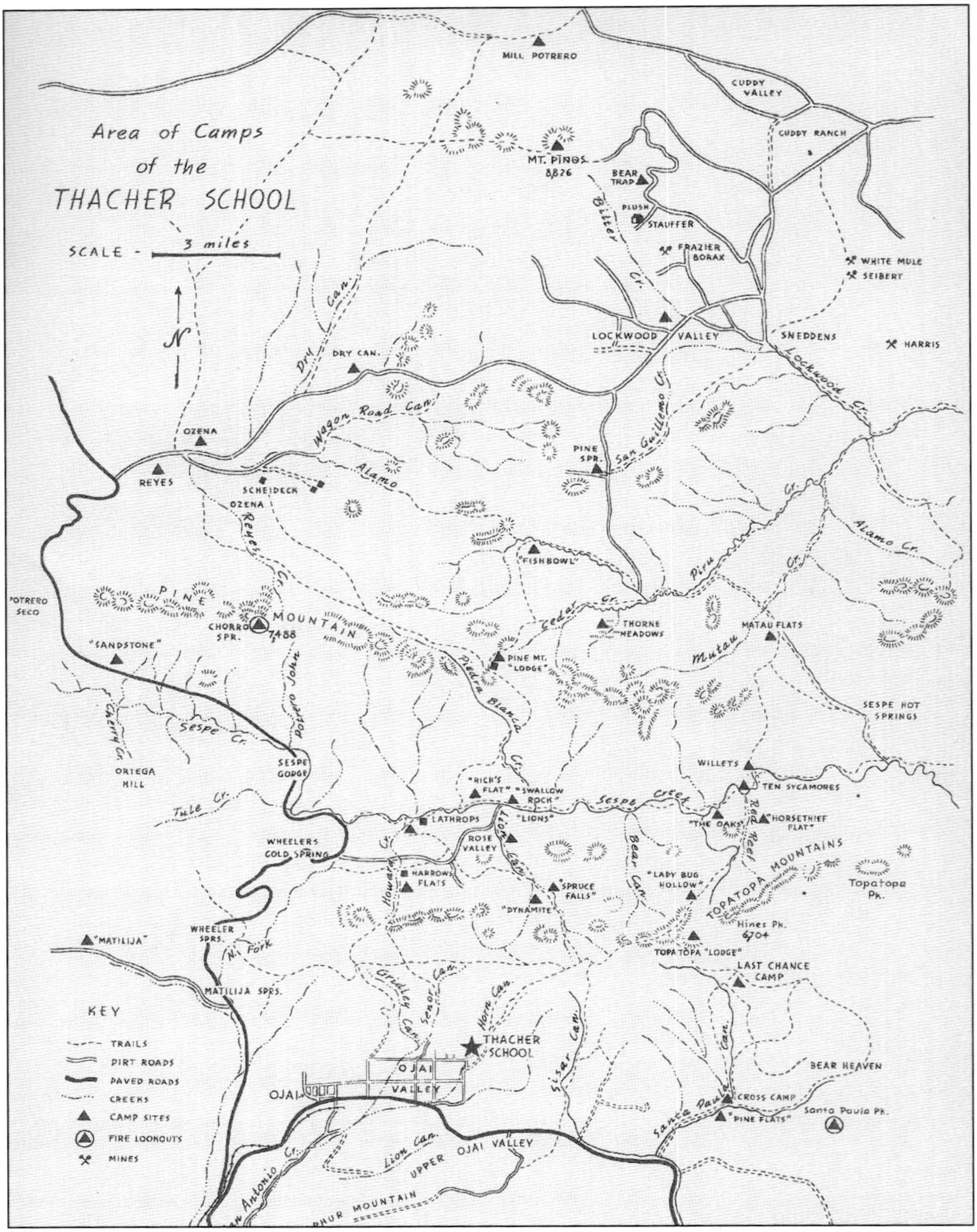

"Our camps are our laboratories. We have to use our hands and our heads and our hearts, and we learn that work and hardship are joy, and that the hard earth is friendly, and that the dark night is not to be feared. And I would almost say that the star-lit camps are our sanctuaries." These words from Forrest Cooke, a member of the Thacher faculty from 1912 to 1946, underscore the value of camping in Thacher's experiential curriculum. This map from the 1930s shows the major locations used by Thacher campers in the Los Padres National Forest. Within this nearly 200-square-mile area are such familiar locations as Ladybug, Patton's Cabin, Pine Mountain Lodge, Timber Canyon, and Mutau Flats. With the acquisition of the famous Green Machine (a bus converted to carry both people and horses) in 1963 and the purchase of Golden Trout Camp in 1966, there is almost nowhere that a Thacher camping trip cannot go.

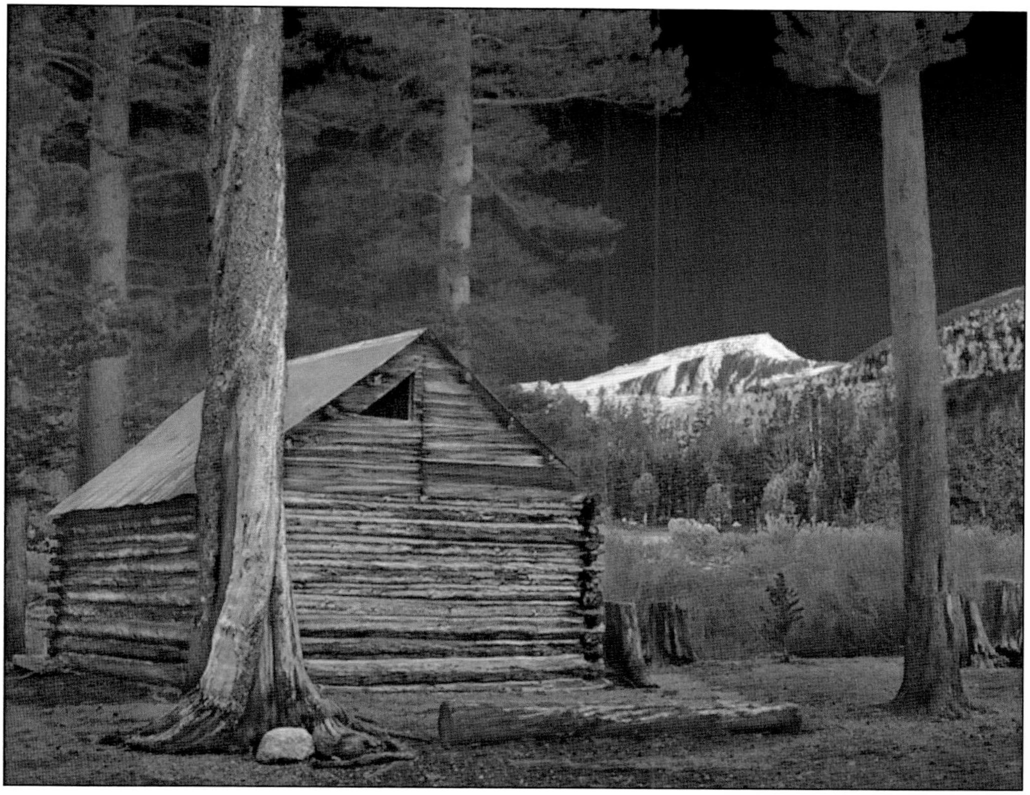

The idea of a wilderness camp was first proposed to Sherman Thacher by Ike Livermore in 1929, but for a variety of reasons, the concept did not gain traction until the 1960s. In 1966, Thacher acquired an 80-acre campground in the Golden Trout Wilderness above Lone Pine, California. The camp (shown above just as the sun catches the top of Mount Langley in the early evening) is situated at the southern border of the John Muir Wilderness in California's Sierra Nevada range and serves as a staging area for camping trips into this special wilderness area. This added a new dimension to the camping program. Horse trips were still popular outings, but backpacking in the High Sierra provided a new opportunity for Thacher's camping program.

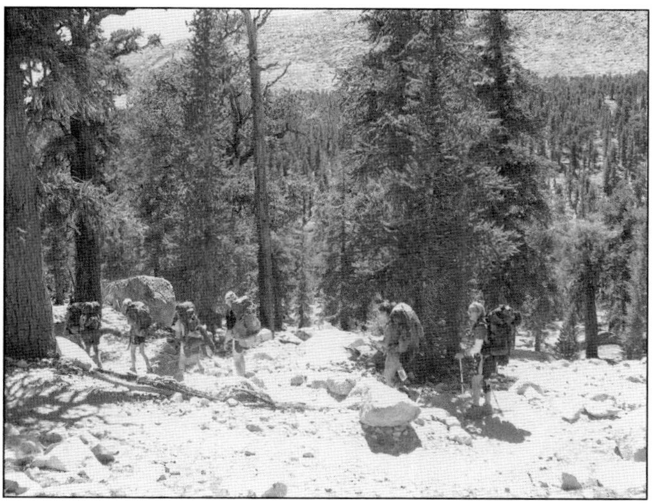

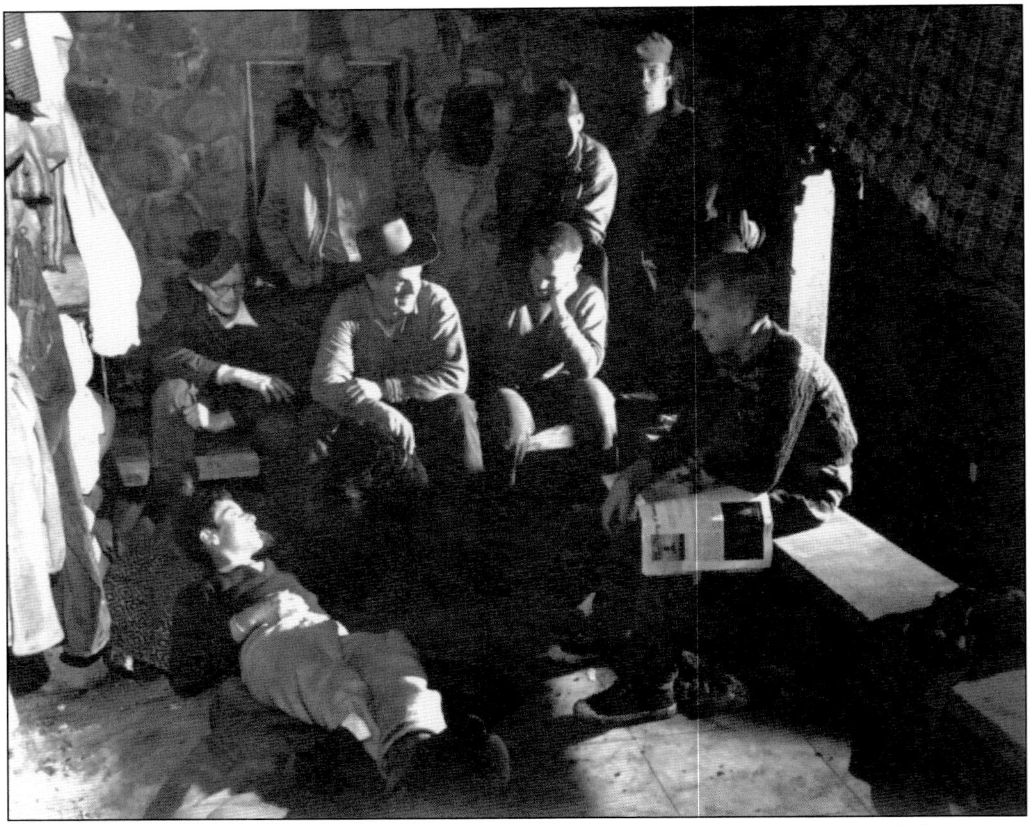

Patton's Cabin is one of the most popular destinations for Thacher campers and also serves as a staging point for trips farther into the backcountry. It is a welcome sight on days when the weather is less than perfect, and it is always great to sit around a roaring fire and plan for the next day's outing. The location saw lots of use over the years but also suffered the indignities of nature and some less considerate visitors. In 2006, a group of Thacher students elected to repair the site. New windows were installed, the roof was repaired, and rotten wood was replaced. Below, some of the participants in that renovation are seen carrying supplies across Sespe Creek.

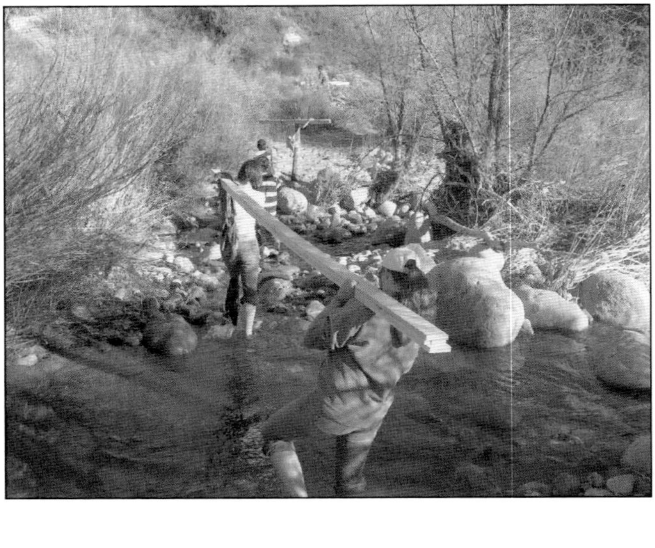

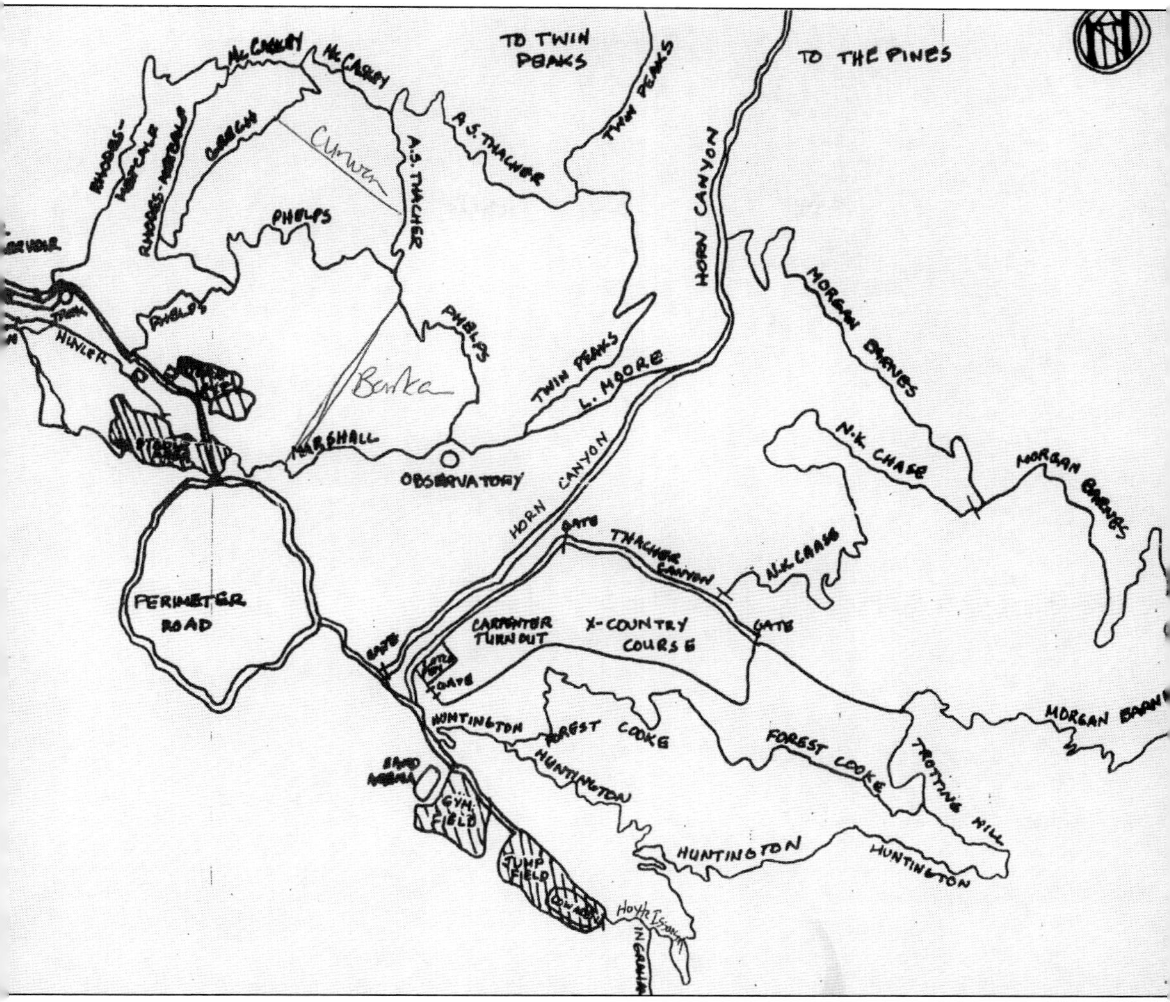

Early on, horses were as much a mode of transportation as they were an aspect of recreation. However, the urge to explore is a strong one, so students began to blaze trails into the foothills around Thacher as well as into the backcountry of the adjacent national forest. Soon, there was a network of interconnected trails, each cut and maintained by hand, leading to diverse locations from Senior Canyon to Twin Peaks. A map showing some of the nearby trails is shown above. Some trails are named for their destination, but many are named for the individuals that first rode them, including the Morgan Barnes, Anson Thacher, and Phelps (probably named for Austin Phelps CdeP 1924). It was mentioned earlier that trail maintenance was used as a punishment, but now it is viewed as community service. The Thacher trails are exemplars of challenging rides that are well marked and maintained.

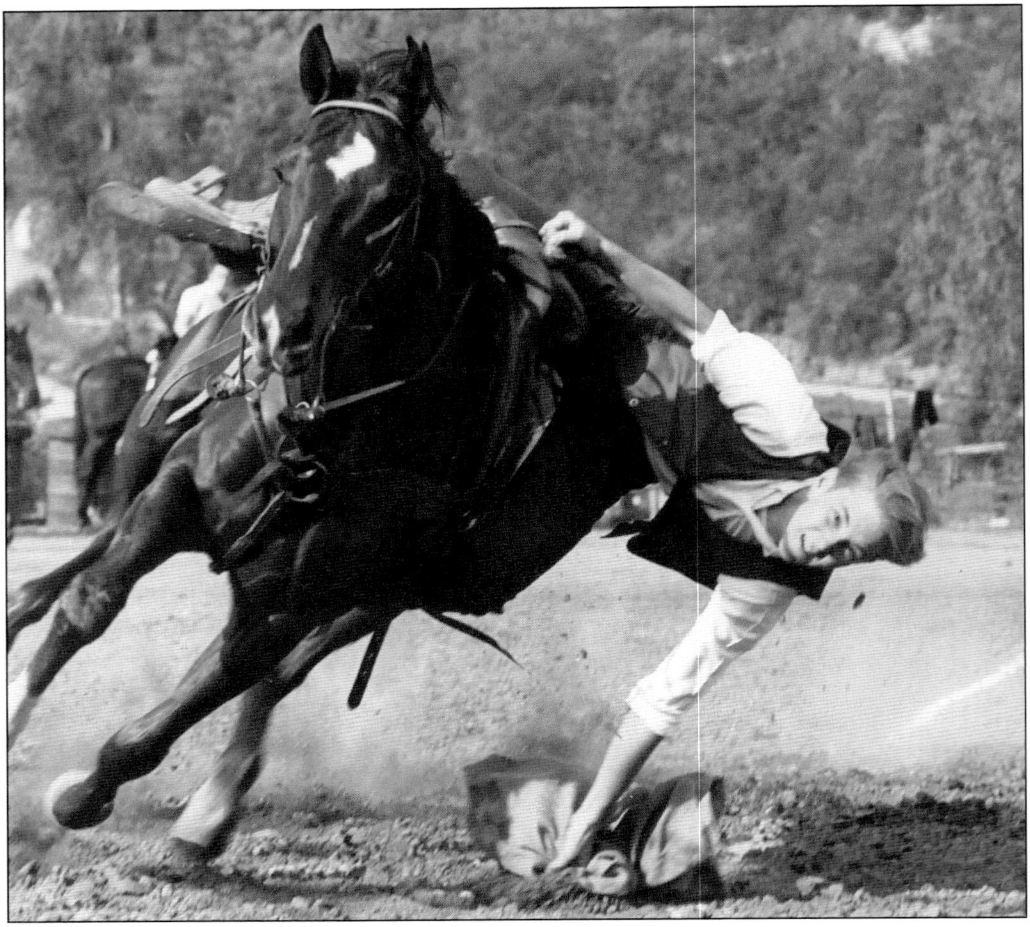

Gymkhana is defined as "speed pattern racing and timed games for riders on horses." Although organizations such as the California State Horsemen's Association and the National Saddle Clubs Association have a set of specific pattern races that are used in gymkhanas, Thacher has added several events, such as the sack race (demonstrated above by Fred Endsley CdeP 1967) that are unique to its competitions. It also includes several non-gymkhana events, such as equitation, trail horse, cattle penning, and English riding and jumping classes. The first Thacher horse show was in December 1897, and gymkhana formally began in 1904 (pictured below) and continues to be one of Thacher's truly unique activities.

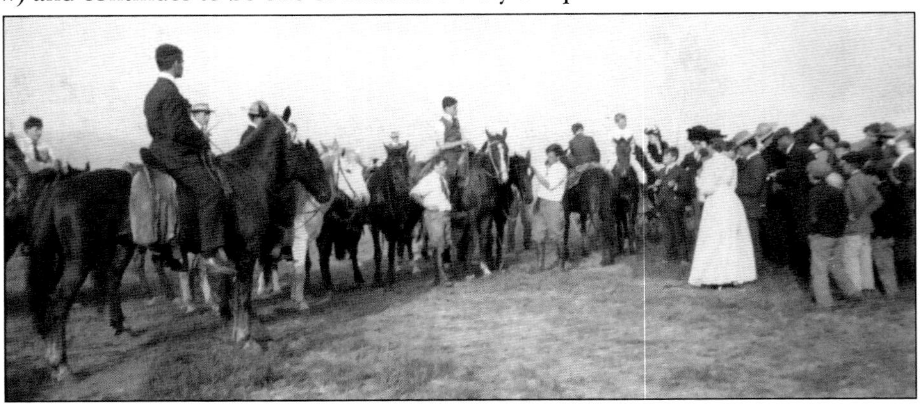

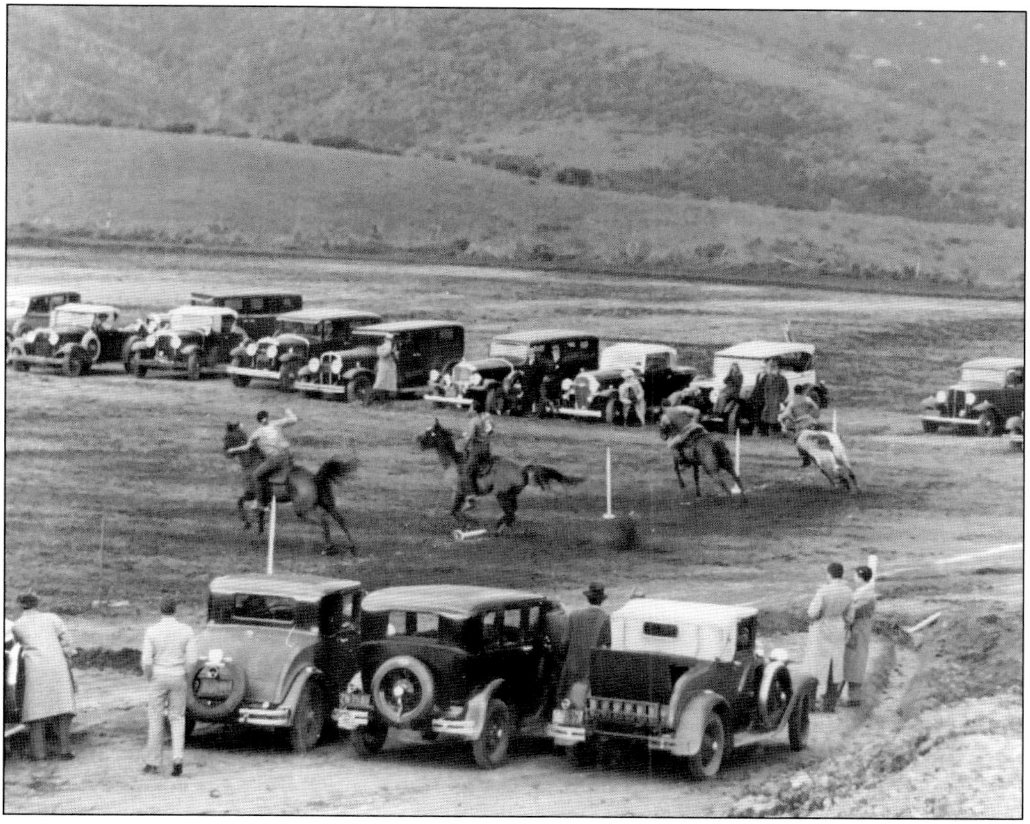

A number of classic gymkhana events involve maneuvering horses around poles or barrels, or into and out of confined spaces, all at high speed. These include pole bending, figure-eight races, quadrangle stake races, barrel races, and keyhole races. These were originally run in heats of four to six riders, as shown in this image of a 1934 gymkhana at the Santa Barbara School (now Cate). These races are now run individually as timed events.

The rescue race involves two individuals, one on a horse and one (initially) on the ground. In this event, one rider gallops toward his partner, who is waiting on the ground 100 yards away. As the horse makes the turn, the person on the ground must jump aboard (and must remain on until they cross the finish line).

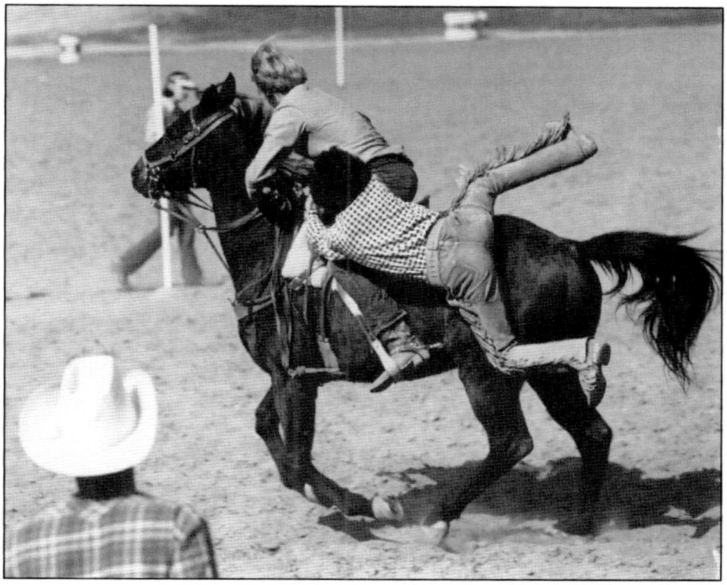

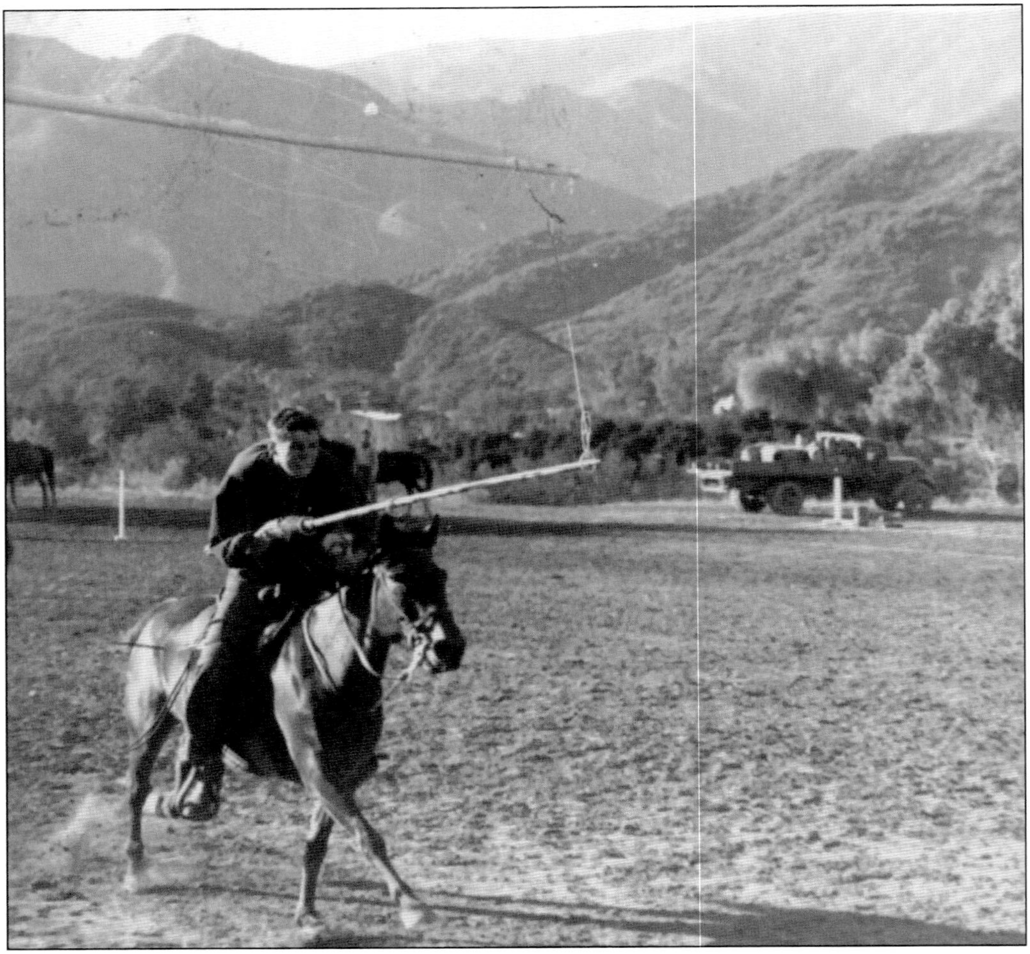

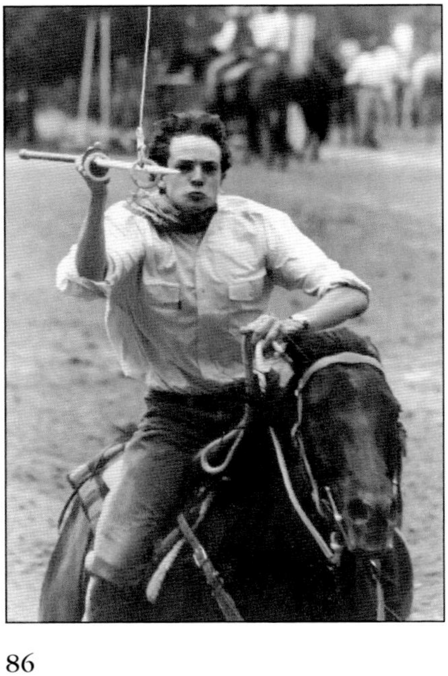

Tilting, or ring spearing, is a much less dangerous form of medieval jousting. The rider with a spear rounds a tree at the west end of the gymkhana field and gallops over a 100-yard course where three rings are hung an equal distance apart. The rider must spear the rings, and for each one he or she misses, a five-second time penalty is assessed. The rider makes three passes, and the times are totaled. For many years, Thacher had its own take on the event, with long spears and big rings (above), but those disappeared in the late 1960s in favor of the standardized short spears and small rings (below).

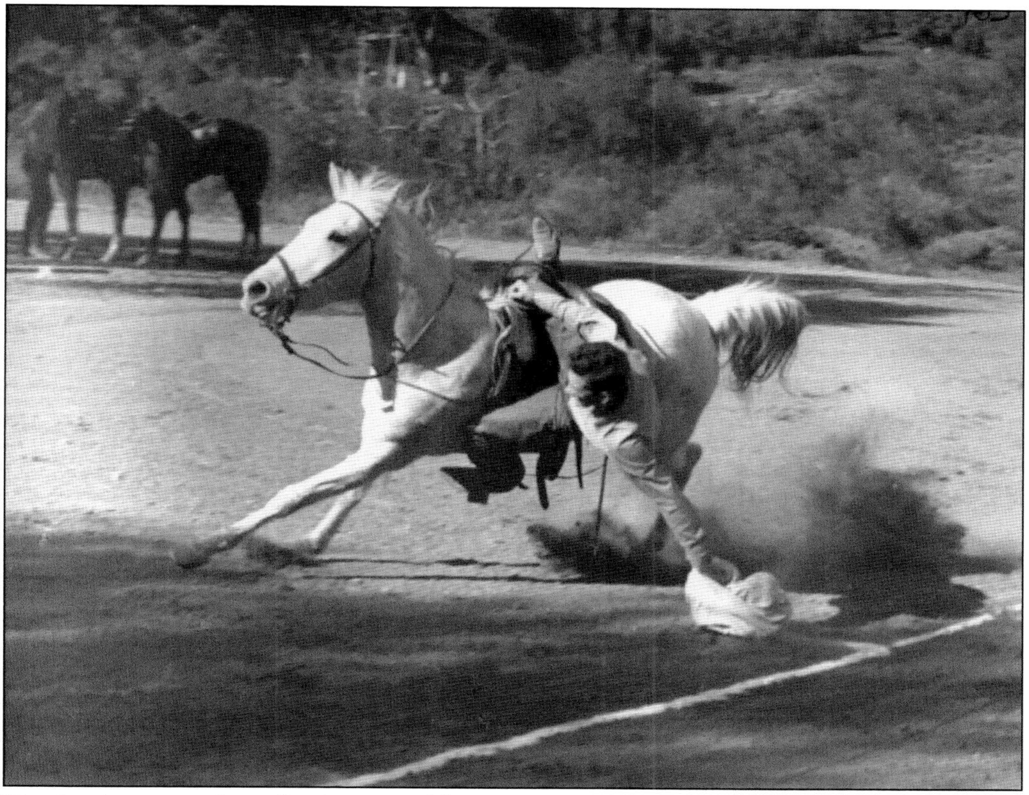

Thacher has a number of unique gymkhana events. Perhaps the most iconic of these is the sack race (above). The rider (after carefully checking the girth) gallops 100 yards toward a burlap sack sitting on the ground. Rounding the sack at a gallop, he or she leans down from the saddle, picks up the sack, and gallops back to the finish line. A slower but still challenging version of the sack race is the orange race. In this event, the rider must pick up five oranges from the ground, one at a time, and drop them behind the start line. The most challenging of the retrieval events involves picking up a silver dollar from the ground at a gallop, as demonstrated below. Success grants a coveted membership in the Silver Dollar Club.

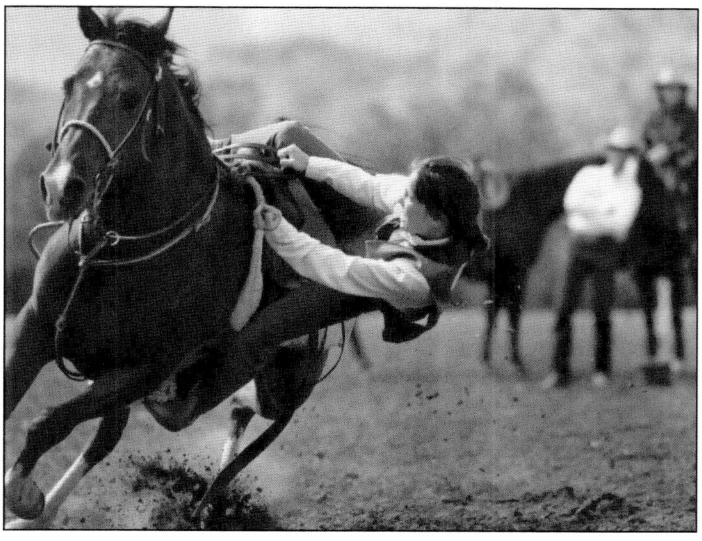

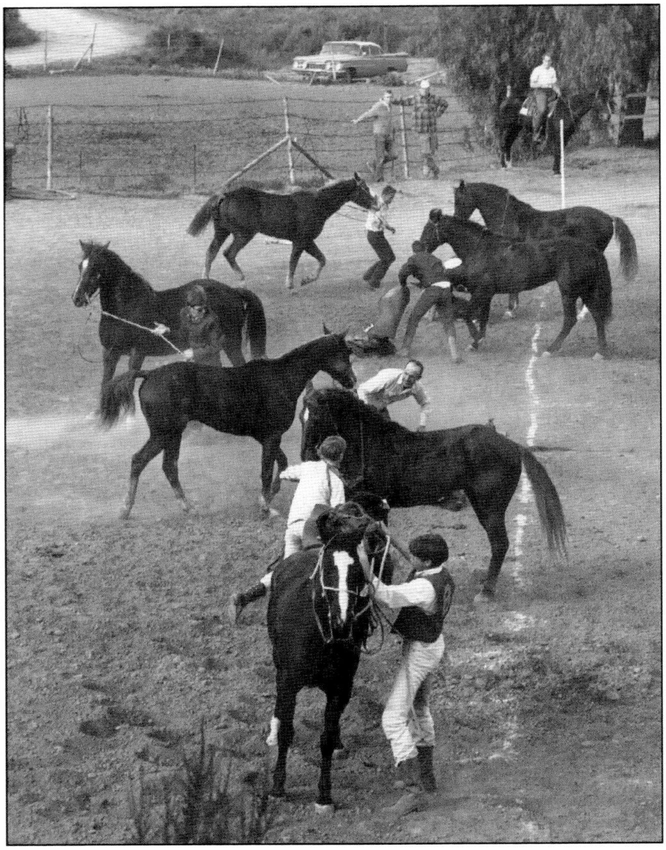

Two other unique Thacher events are the saddling and packing races. In the saddling race (at left), the rider is bareback and the object at the end of the 100-yard run is a saddle. The galloping horse is reined to a halt (hopefully in the vicinity of the grounded saddle), and the rider saddles at breakneck speed and jumps aboard, hoping against hope that the saddle does not slip during the race to the finish line. In the packing race (below), a horse or mule wearing a pack saddle is led to a location between two panniers, a grain bag, a tarp, and a rope. The two packers put the panniers, grain bag, and tarp onto the pack saddle and throw a diamond hitch. Then the team heads to the finish line, frequently with ropes dragging and the pack animal bucking.

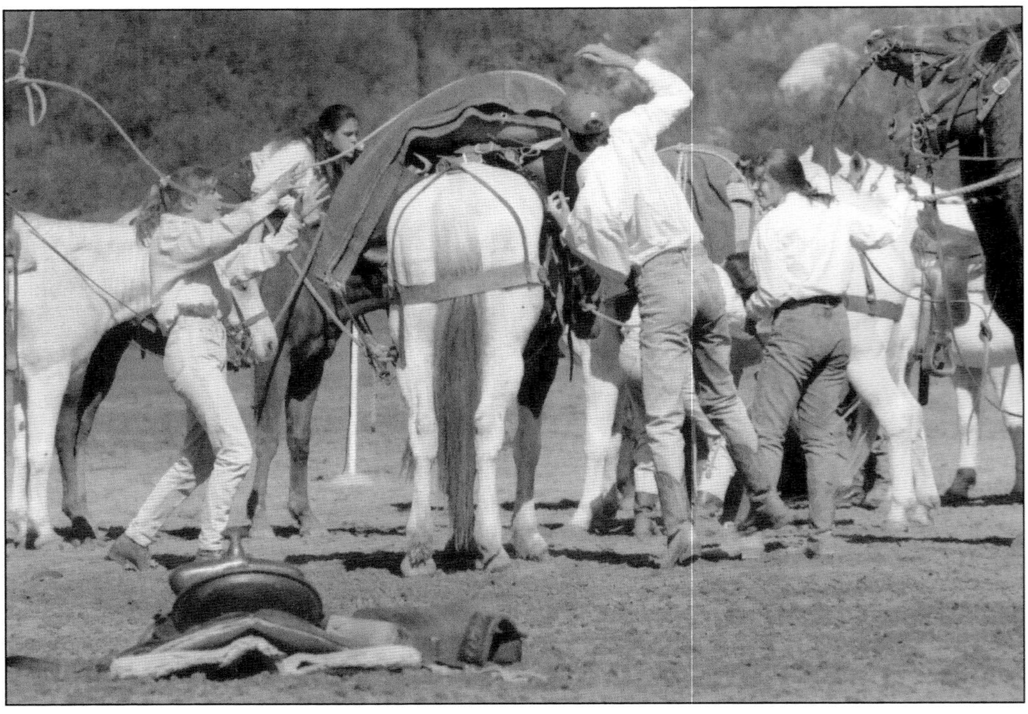

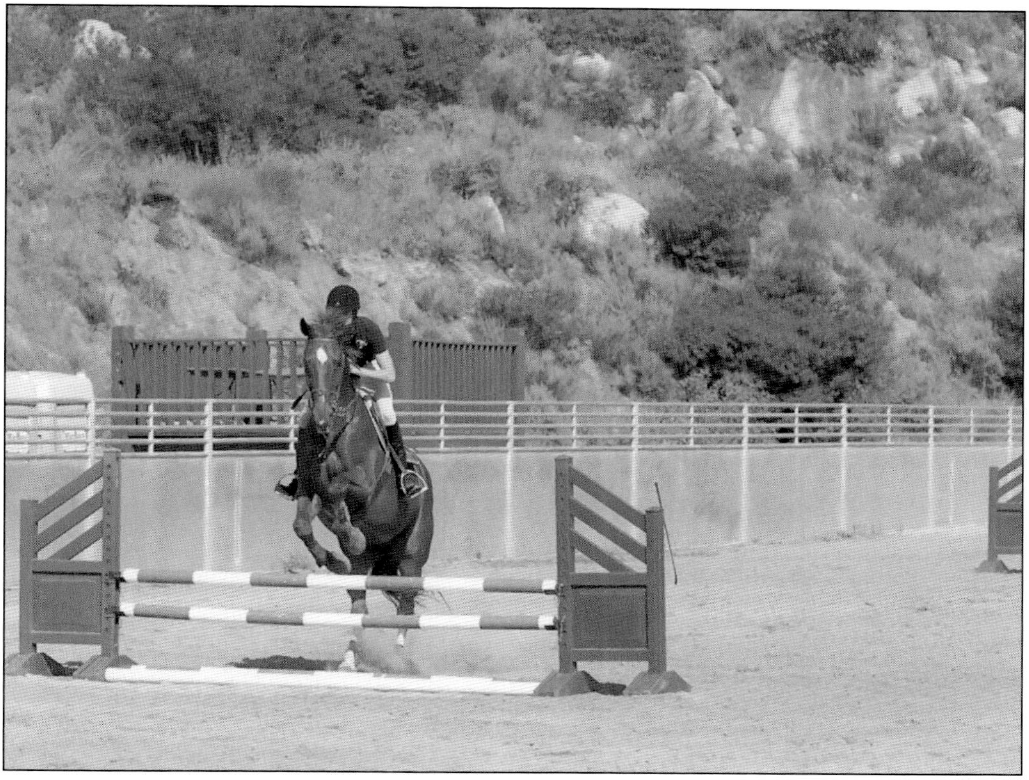

English classes—equitation, dressage, and show jumping—were added to the gymkhana menu in the late 1970s. These events, which are very challenging for both horse and rider, provided a new dimension to the traditional Thacher equestrian programs and allowed riders to participate in a wider range of activities and outside events.

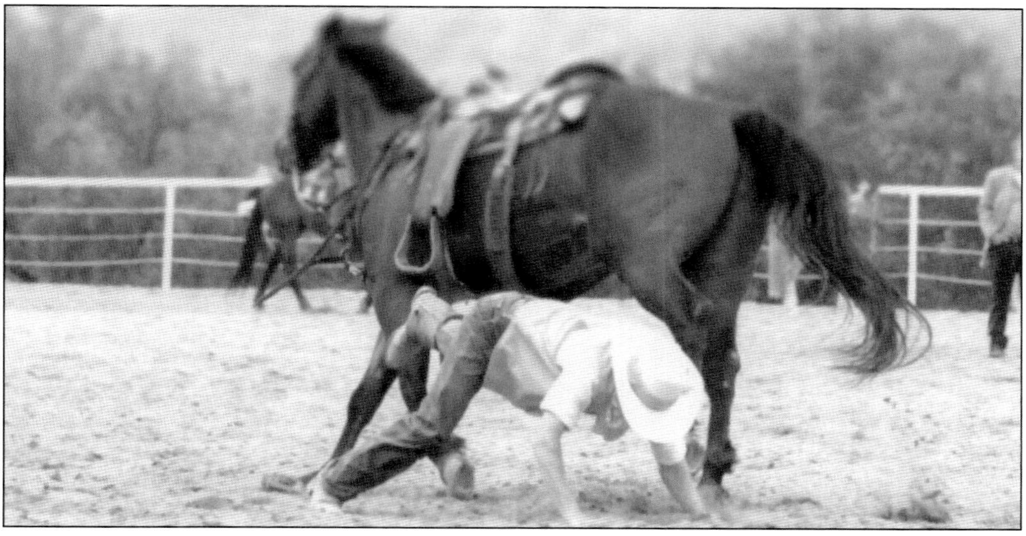

One of the inevitable consequences of learning to retrieve a sack, crest a jump, or round a stake at a gallop is finding oneself face down on the dirt of the gymkhana field as the horse trots (or gallops) off on its own. When this happens, there is nothing to do but stand up, dust off, catch the horse, and try again, knowing that one is in good company.

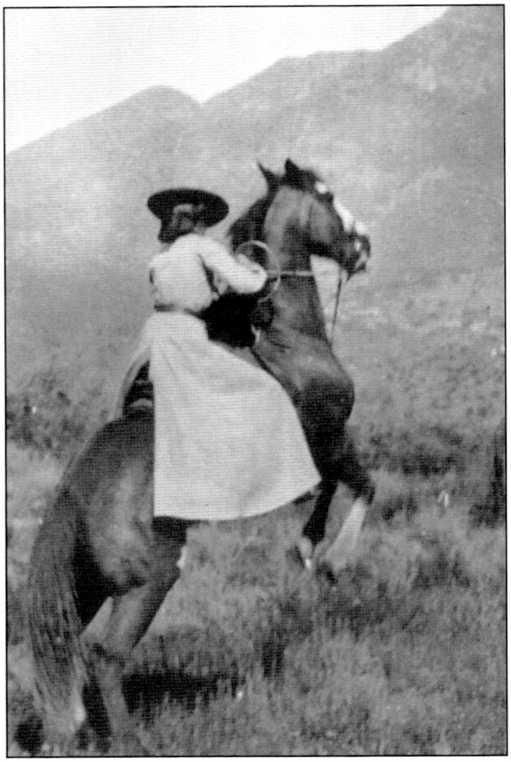

Given the importance of the horse program to Thacher, the director of the horse program has always been a key faculty position. Thacher has been blessed with several exceptional directors, including the current director, Cam Schryver, who has led the program since 1992. Three of Schryver's predecessors deserve special mention for their tenure and their devotion to the program. The first of these was Margaret Clark Hunt. Hunt came to The Thacher School in 1908 and remained as the director until her retirement in 1943—a remarkable 35-year tenure. The first horse she bought for Thacher was Noheli, a dark bay, "popular as a camper and good at gymkhana."

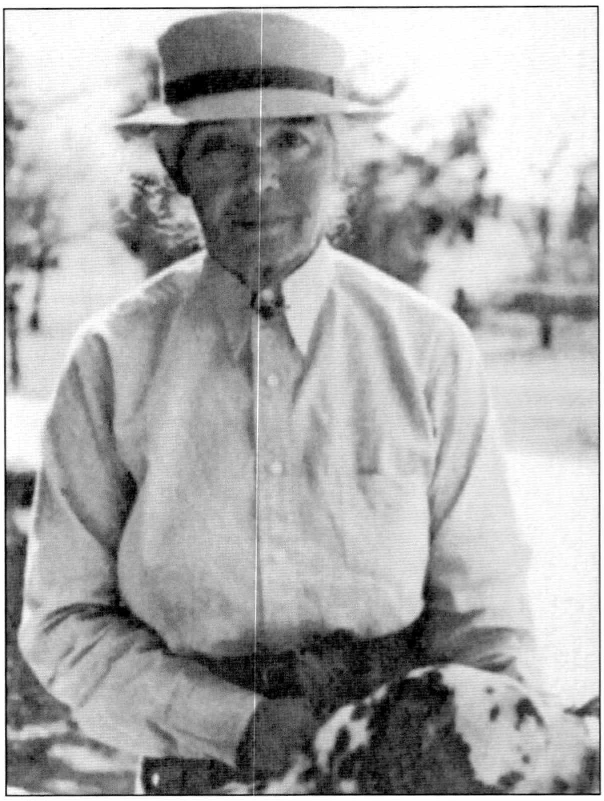

Jesse Kahle and his wife, Clarice, came to Thacher in 1948, and although he formally retired in 1972, he remained an active member of the Thacher community until his death in 2005, an outstanding 57 years of service. Jesse's wiry six-foot, three-inch frame, classic country sense of humor, soft-spoken nature, and uncanny ability to match horse and rider and to train even the most tender of tenderfeet to be a confident and capable horseman made him one of Thacher's most iconic faculty members. His renditions of "Tales of Uncle Josh" were legendary at assemblies. In addition, he was an accomplished gymkhana rider and horse exhibitor in his own right, taking a number of his own horses to the California state championships.

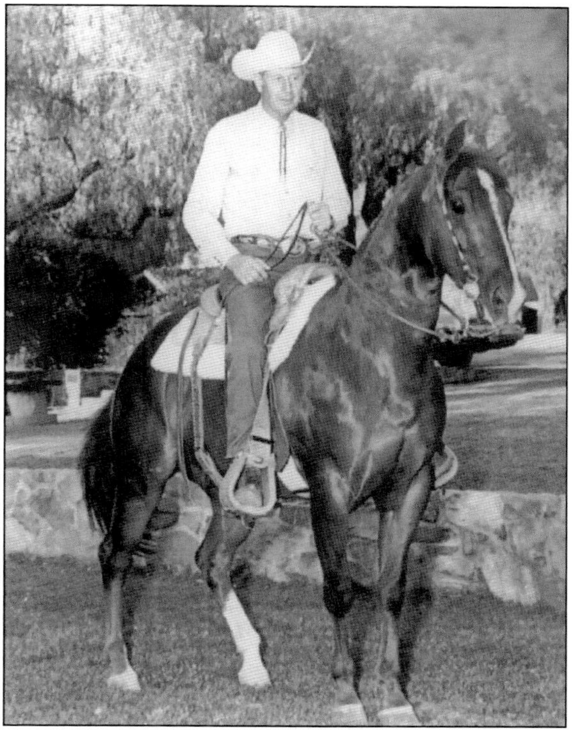

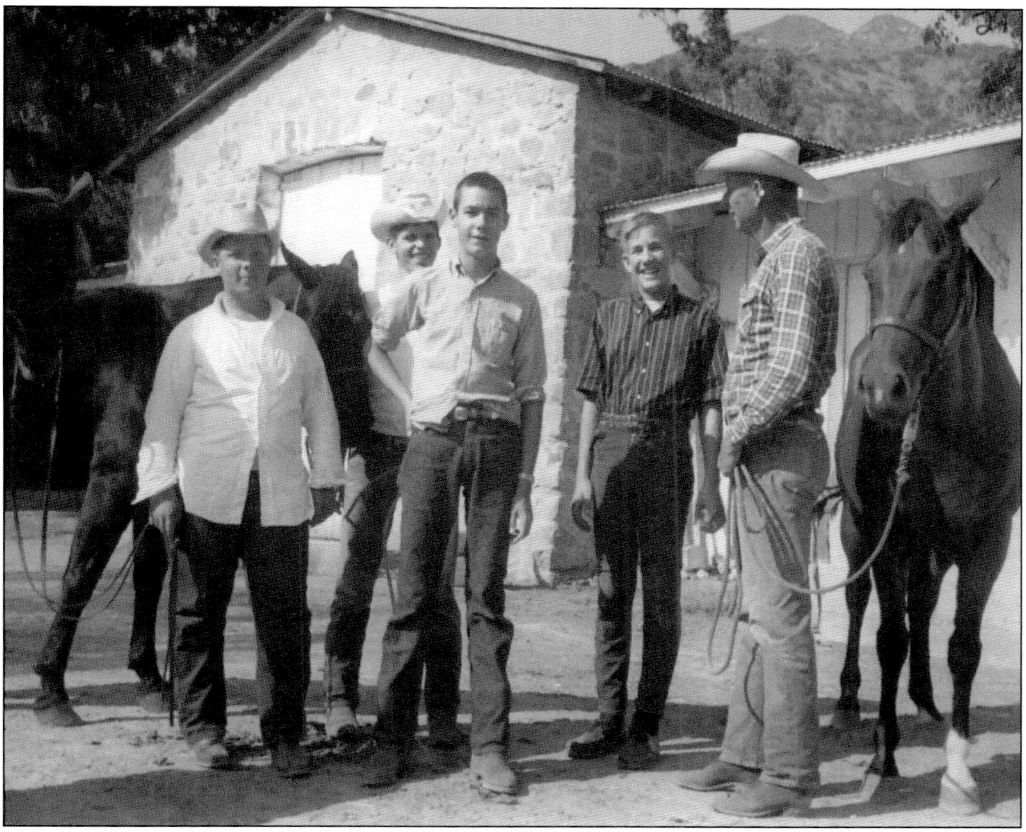

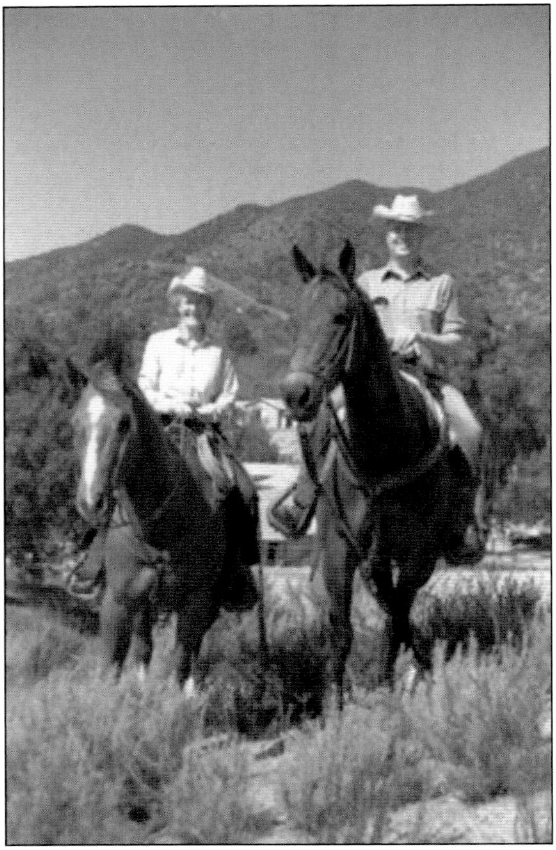

Jack Huyler, known variously as "Black Jack" and the "Shakespearean Cowboy," arrived at Thacher in 1949 with his wife, Margaret (at left), two small children, and two horses. During his more than 50 years at Thacher, he served as assistant director of the horse program, interim director of the horse program, assistant headmaster, interim headmaster, head of the English department, and college counselor. He and Jesse Kahle (below, right) worked together for several decades, keeping Thacher's horse activities a vibrant and meaningful part of the unique Thacher experience. Jack, too, was an accomplished horseman in his own right, holding several California state records in gymkhana events. In addition, he authored one of the classic histories of Thacher, *The Stamp of the School.*

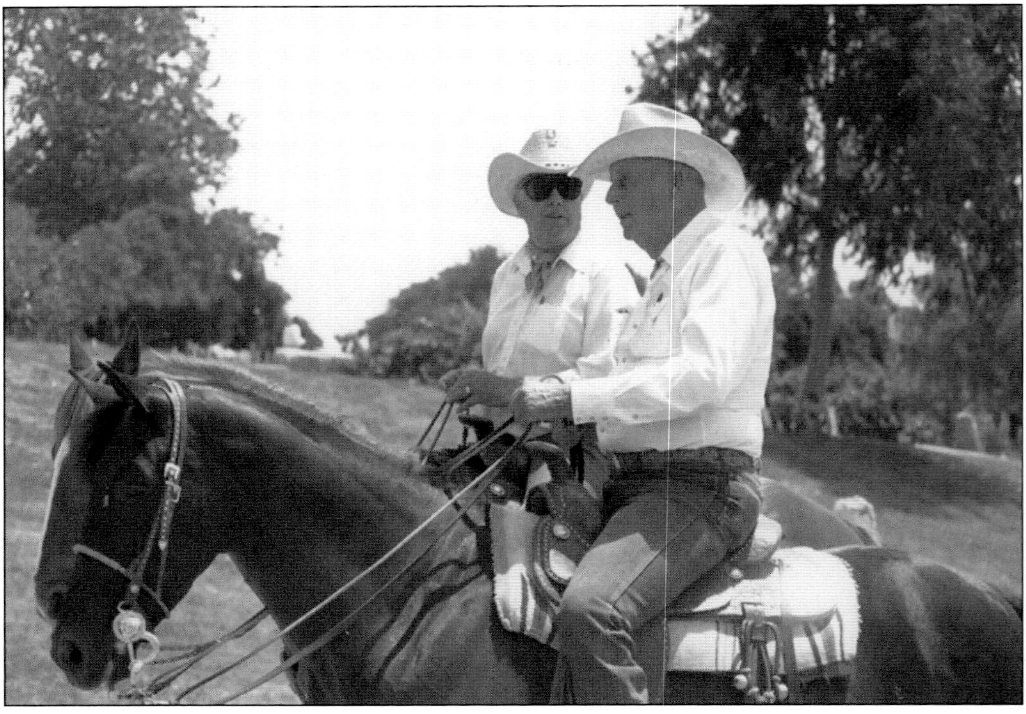

Seven

THE ARTS

In one of his earliest advertisements for The Thacher School, Sherman Thacher noted music as a key aspect of the comprehensive college-preparatory education that he was providing. Many boys brought their own instruments from home. Singing, however, became one of the most popular activities. Over the years, the *Thacher Songbook* has undergone a number of revisions. Many of the revisions incorporated new songs or new verses that had become popular. Other revisions removed songs, verses, or words that had become outdated or politically incorrect. Still others kept up with major changes, such as the advent of coeducation in the 1970s.

F. Barreda Sherman, a member of the class of 1911 and one of Thacher's first trustees, recalled:

> Singing at Thacher was one of the things that meant most to me. We had the little songbook developed by Mr. Barnes. It contained the words of about 100 songs without music; but Mr. Barnes, who had a perfectly extraordinary memory for tunes and words, would lead us in singing them. We had a lot of fun singing school and college songs and songs of many kinds from Spain, France, Germany, and England such as 'The Roast Beef of Old England' and 'Men of Harlech.' These are the good ones.

For almost 50 years, Jack Huyler carried on this Morgan Barnes tradition.

In the early days, Thacher was an isolated place for much of the year. There were few automobiles, and Ojai, a small village even today, did not have a lot of entertainment to offer young men. As a result, Thacher was relatively self-sufficient when it came to entertainment. As noted, music was popular, and drama—initially skits and small plays but later major theatrical productions—became commonplace. This trend has continued to the present.

Visual arts—painting, photography, ceramics, woodworking, and sculpture—have also become important aspects of student life. With the addition of the Humanities Building, the Royal Barney Hogan Woodshop, and a fully equipped wet darkroom, students have the opportunity to indulge their artistic sides in virtually any medium.

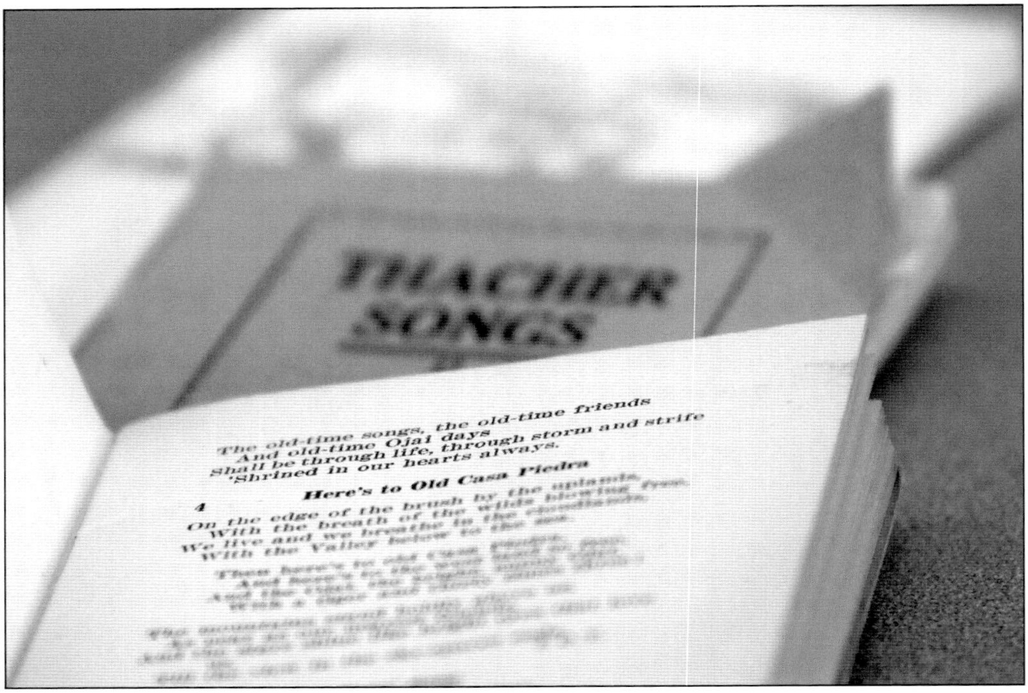

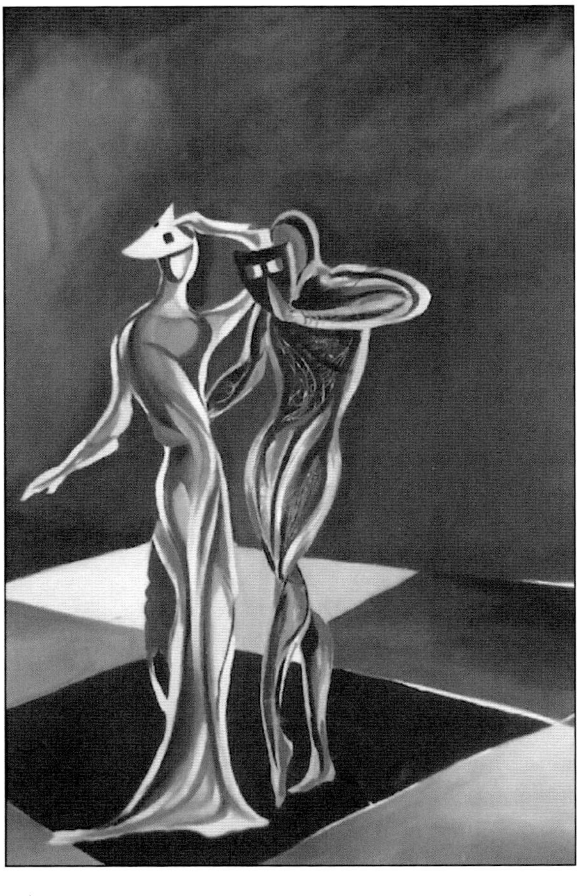

Throughout The Thacher School's history, art in all forms has been a key part of the Thacher experience. The contents of the *Thacher Songbook* reflect the history of The Thacher School and the nation. Classic patriotic songs, college songs from across the country, unique Thacher songs, and old favorite sing-alongs were staples of the after-dinner sings.

Visual arts, including those by former Thacher art director Gui Ignon (his painting *Dancing Masquers* is shown at left) are seen all over campus. A student summed it up very well, "If you have any desire to be an artist, you can be one at Thacher. Whether within the curriculum or outside of it, no specific genre dominates."

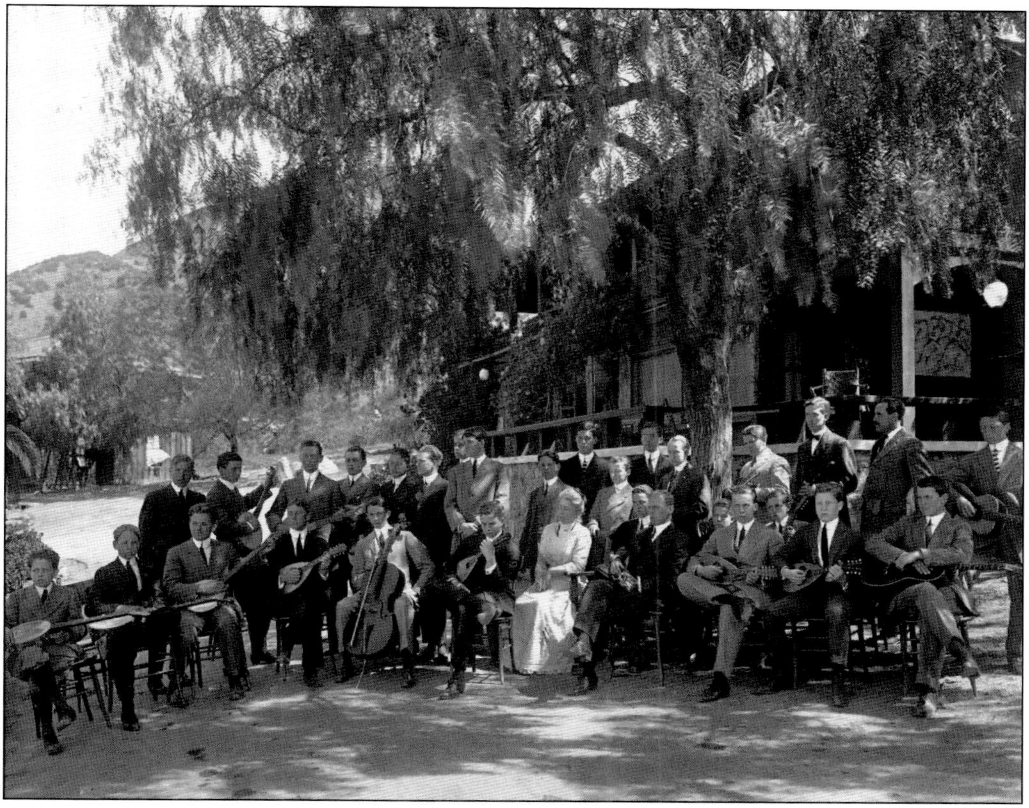

Music has always been a significant part of the Thacher experience. There were frequent school-wide musical activities such as concerts, musical theater, or Tuesday and Thursday after-dinner singing. In many of these instances, individuals from around the valley were invited to watch or even participate. Other students formed small groups or played individual instruments—everyone was involved in music to one degree or another. The 1912 image above shows a gathering of musicians with a number of stringed instruments below the Pergola. The 26 individuals (students and faculty) represent a majority of Thacher's population. The image below shows a student practicing violin in her dorm room.

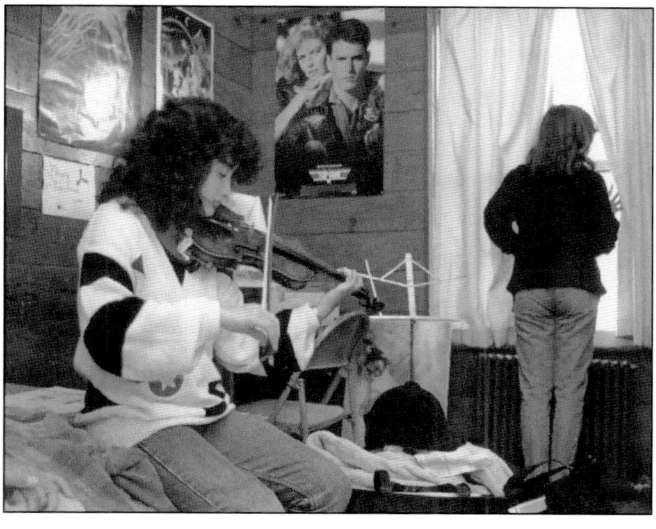

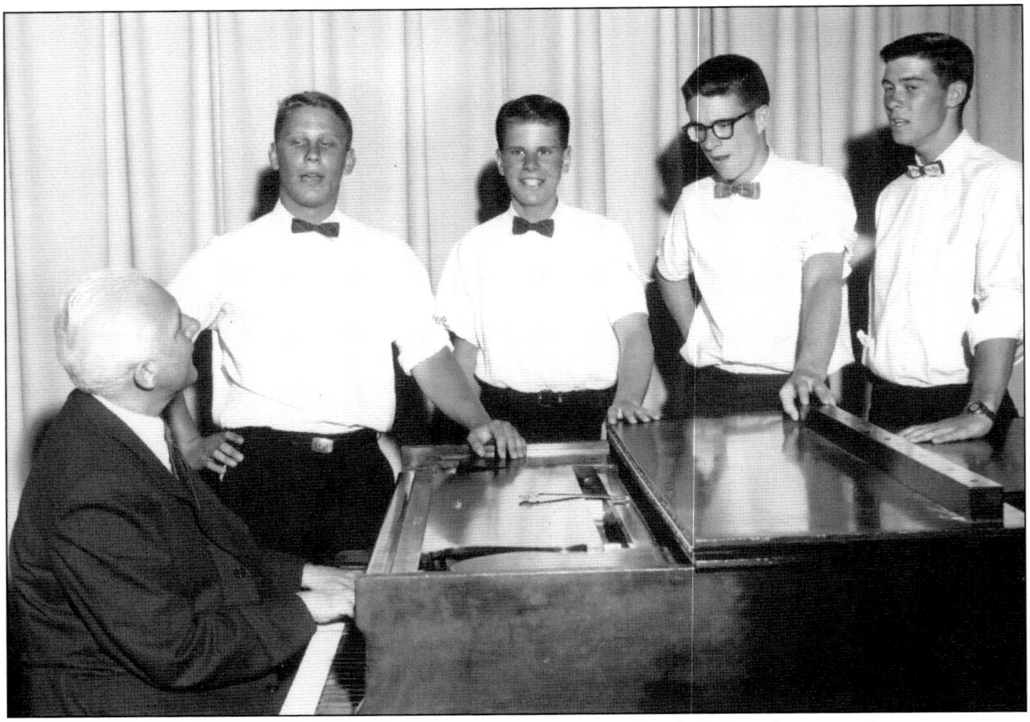

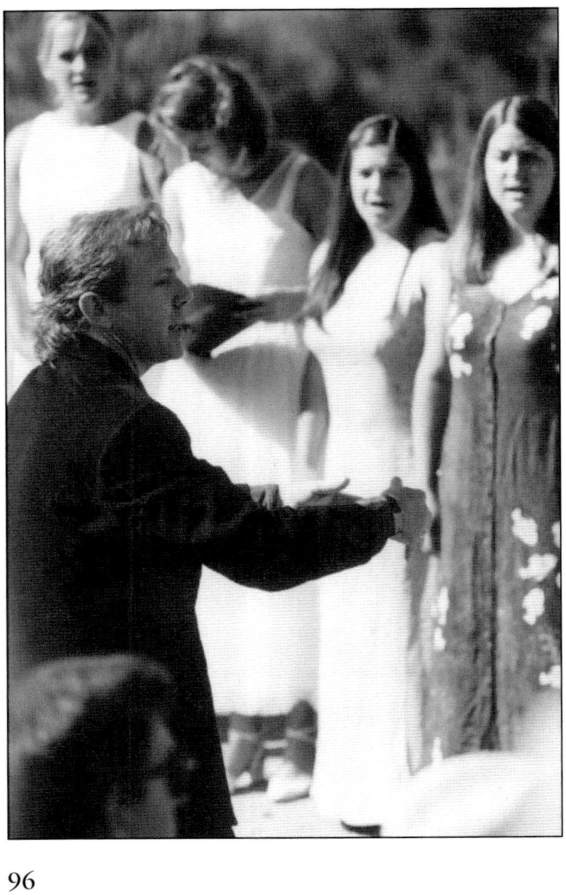

Michael Ehrhardt, seen above with a 1960s quartet known as the Honeytones, was the music teacher at Thacher from 1946 to 1977. He held court in a small square building on the road to the stables that was logically called the "Music Box." All students passed through the Music Box at one time or another during one of the required music appreciation classes, and many returned for private lessons.

Today, much of the musical activity (under the direction of Greg Haggard) takes place in the Milligan Center, which includes a 450-seat performance venue as well as practice rooms. Additional practice rooms are nearby in the Thacher Commons. Popular classes include digital music and music theory.

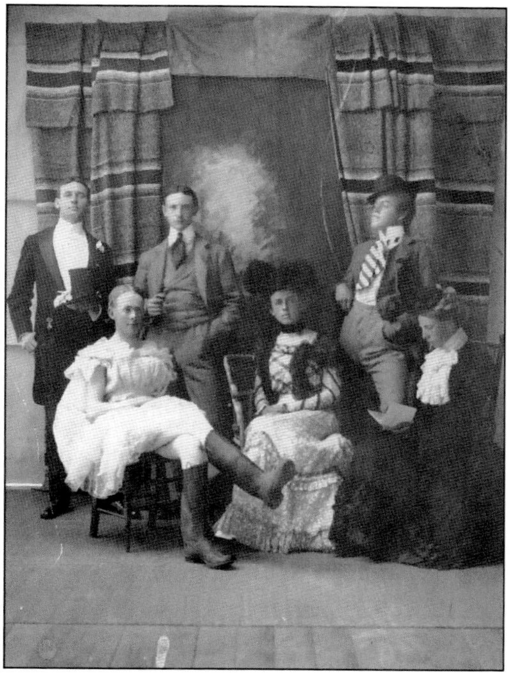
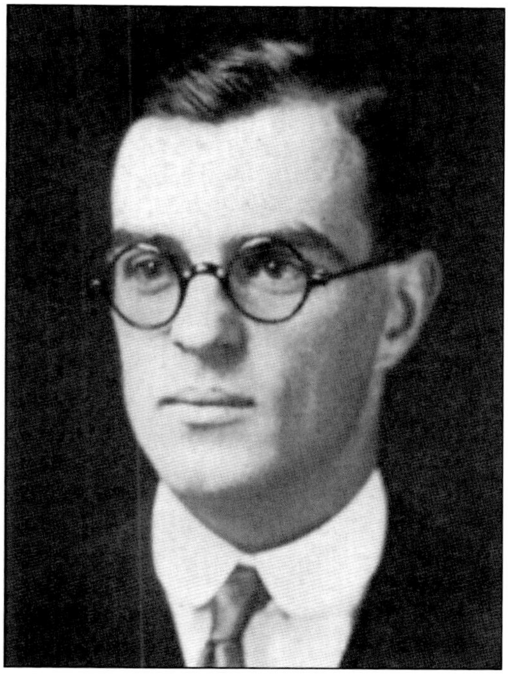

The Casa de Piedra Dramatics Club, a great-grandfather of the present-day Masquers, was formed in 1898. One of its first productions was *My Awful Chum* (above left), put on in conjunction with the Nordhoff Tennis Tournament. Attendees remarked that "the acting was remarkably good." A drama participant of some note in Thacher's early years was future Pulitzer Prize–winning playwright Thornton Wilder (above right) of the class of 1913. Note that until girls were admitted in 1977, Thacher's dramatic offerings embraced the Shakespearean tradition of men playing women's roles. Shown below is Don MacDougall, a teacher of biology, French, history, Latin, English, public speaking, and drama from 1947 to 1975, transforming a Thacher boy into a femme fatale for one of the biannual Shakespearian productions in the Outdoor Theatre. (Above right, courtesy of Yale University; above left and below, courtesy of The Thacher School Archives.)

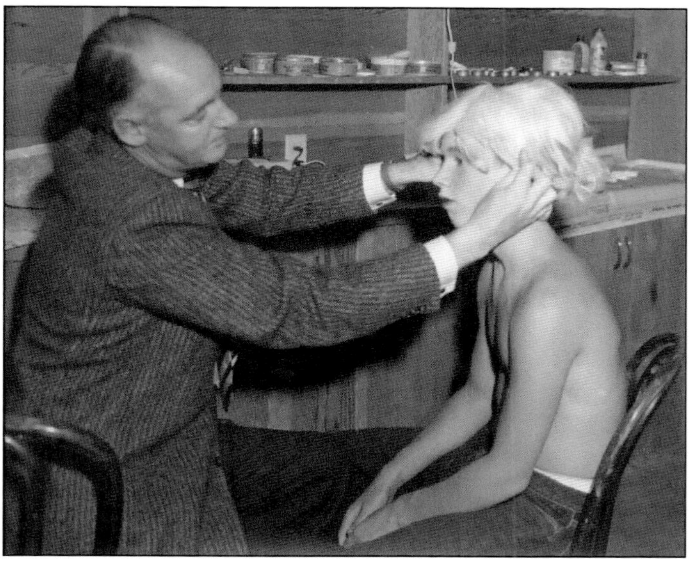

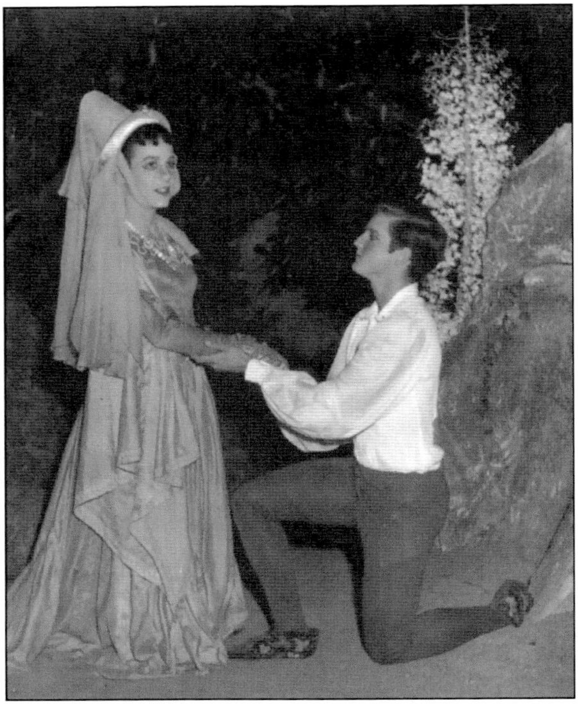

The Outdoor Theatre (originally called the Rustic Theatre) was constructed in 1908. The first real production in the theater was a Lower School performance of *Pyramus and Thisbe* directed by Morgan Barnes. It caused the audience "such mirth that . . . the house would certainly have been brought down if it had not been literally hewn out of the living rock." The image at left shows a Shakespearean production in the Outdoor Theatre in the 1950s. Pictured below is a 1965 production of *The Tempest* in the Outdoor Theatre. As before, note the authentic Shakespearean use of male actors as very convincing females.

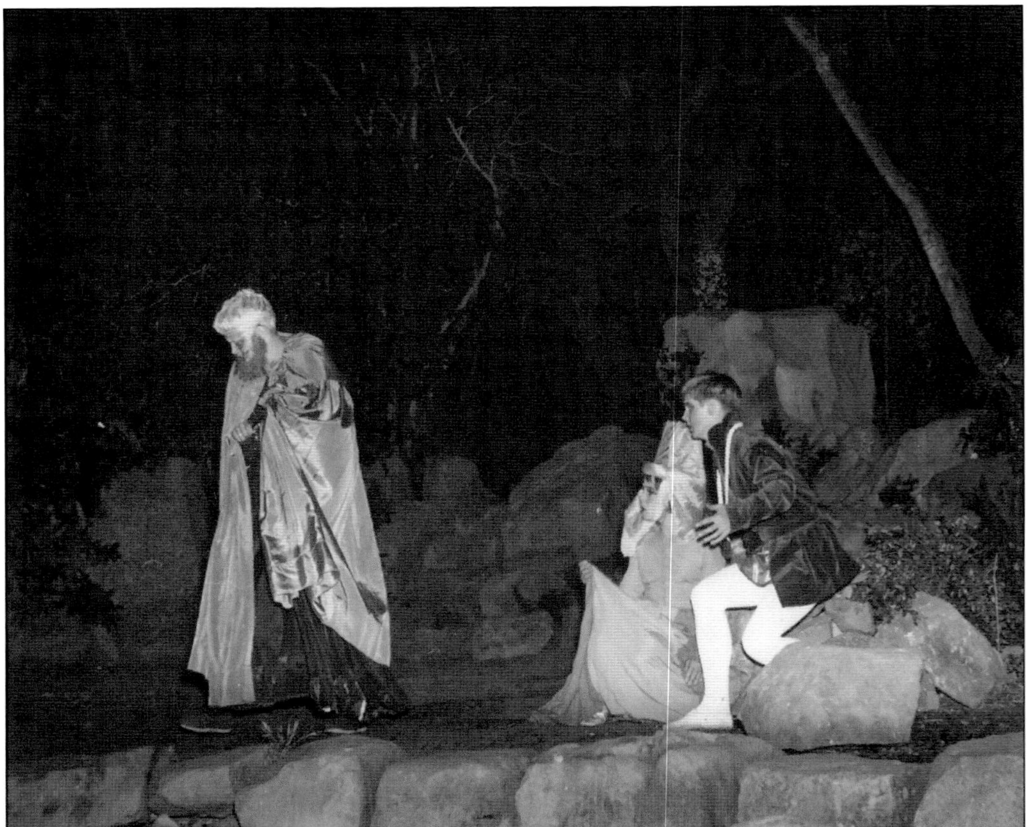

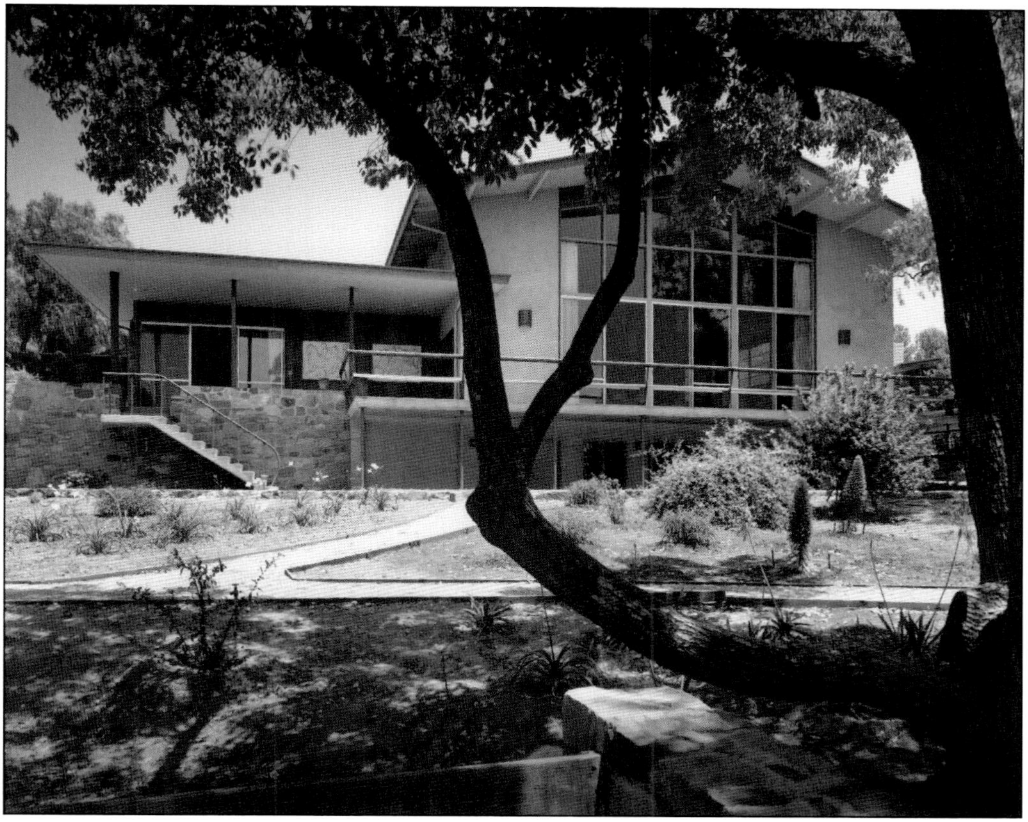

The Lamb Auditorium (above), named for longtime history teacher and tennis coach Fred Lamb, was completed in 1960 as an indoor venue for a wide variety of activities, from concerts and plays to lectures and dances, that had previously been presented in either the library or the west end of the dining hall ("the parlor"). By the early 21st century, however, Thacher had outgrown this facility, and in 2004, the Lamb Auditorium was taken down in favor of the new Milligan Performing Arts Center (below). This state-of-the-art facility has a 450-seat auditorium with full technical support for dramatic presentations, concerts, and lectures.

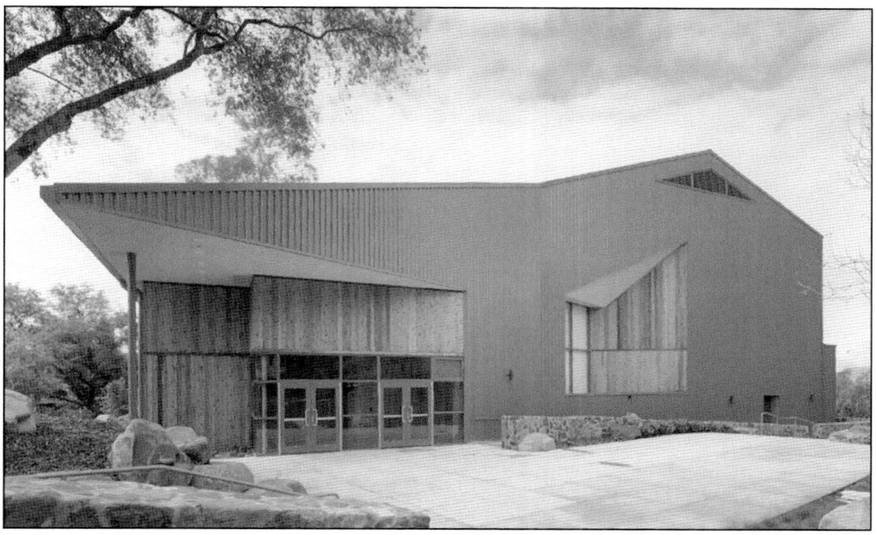

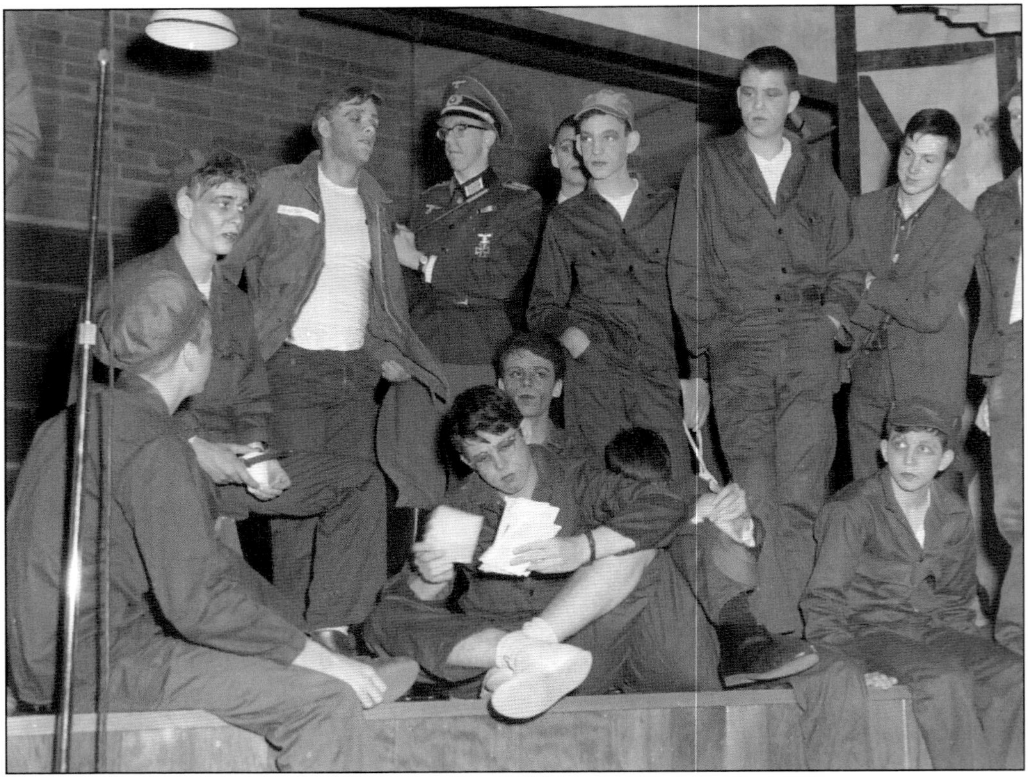

With the construction of the Lamb Auditorium in 1960 and the Milligan Center for the Performing Arts in 2006, more complex indoor theatrical productions, both dramatic and musical, became possible. Shown above is the 1962 production of *Stalag-17*, and below is the 2004 production of *The Music Man*. Although most products are directed by a faculty member, students, under faculty guidance, do all the rest of the work for each production—manning the lights, making the props and sets, managing the sound system, and, of course, doing the acting and singing. These productions have always attracted enthusiastic audiences from the student body and the surrounding area.

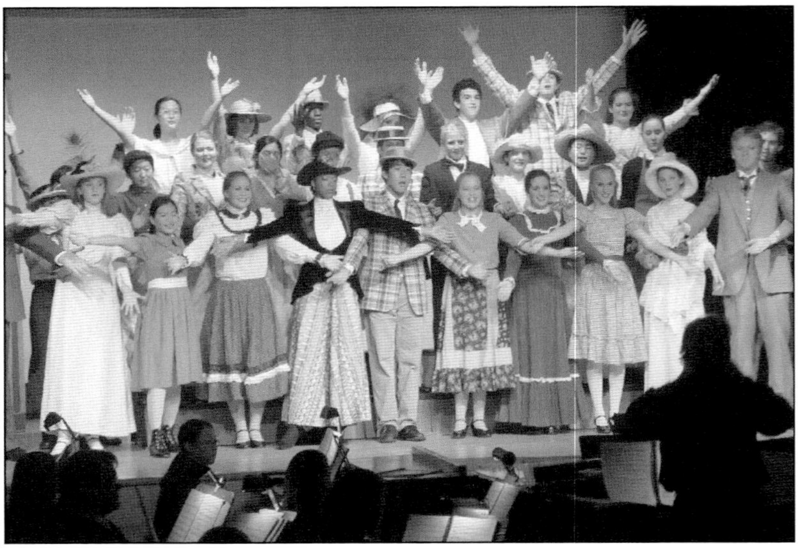

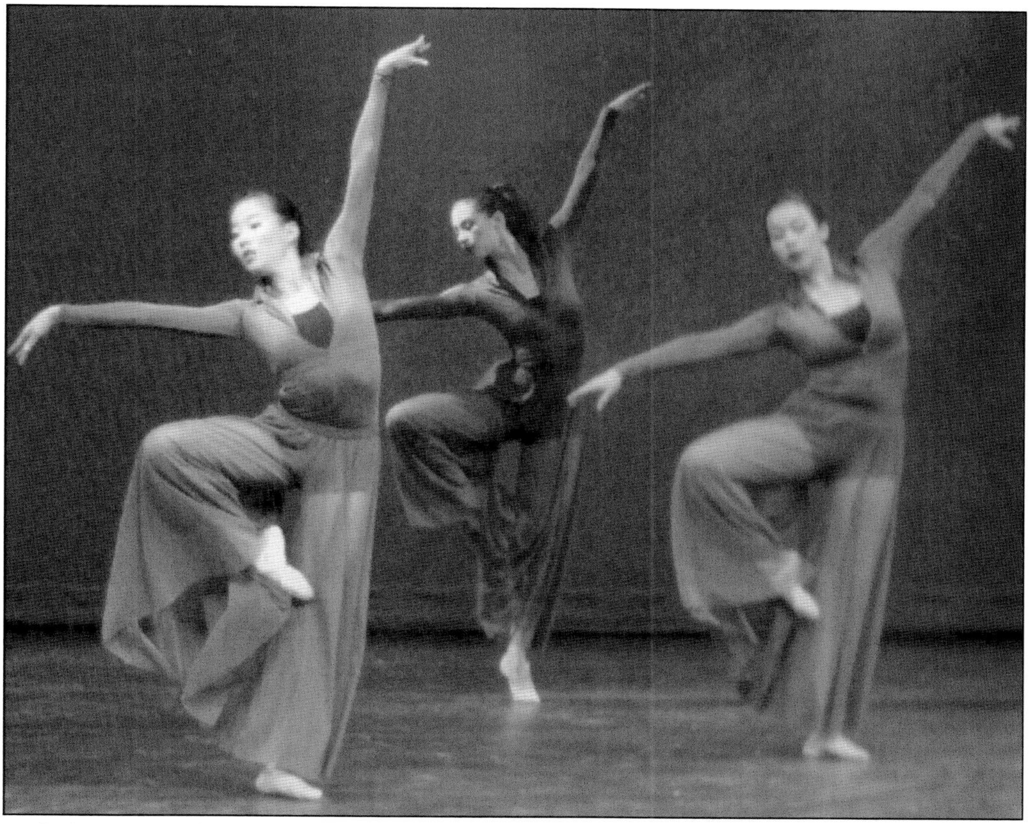

With the arrival of coeducation, creative dance became an art form of choice for many Thacher students. Both modern dance and classical ballet were/are performed, and the expertise of the dancers is used in the choreography of the musical productions that grace the stage of the performing arts center. Since Thacher attracts students from around the world, dances that reflect other cultures are performed as well. Both men and women participate in the dance program, and Thacher dancers have been featured in publications such as *Dance Magazine*. All of this is produced under the watchful eye of dance instructor (and math teacher) Gallia Vickery.

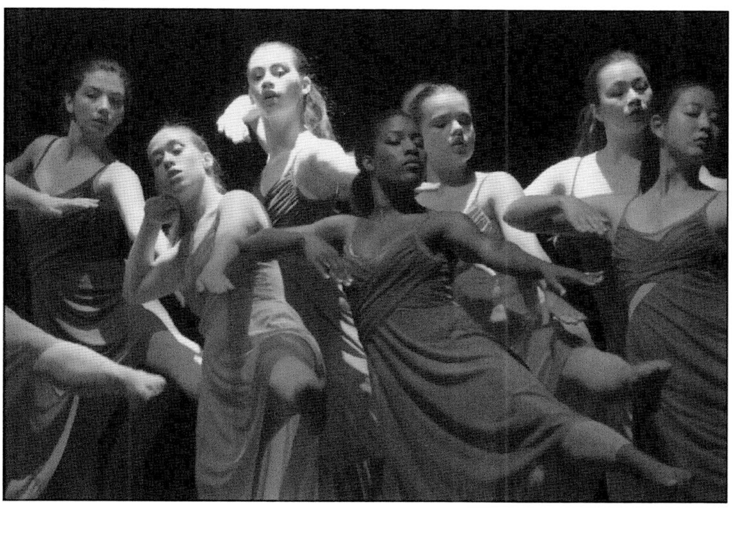

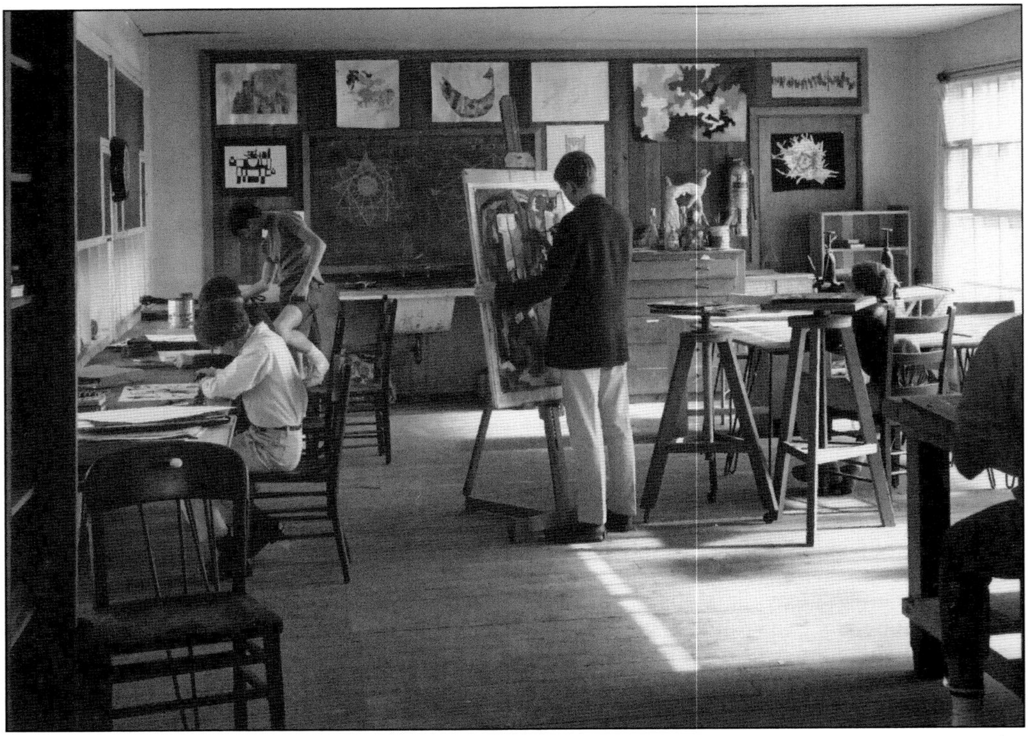

Visual arts offerings include painting, sculpture, ceramics, photography, and woodworking. The indoor handball court above the Upper School, originally constructed in 1930, was converted into a studio to accommodate the growing interest in art, especially painting. Gui Ignon, a renowned Postimpressionist artist, was hired to head the art program. Following Ignon's untimely death in 1963, Chilean artist Edgardo Catalan took over the program, emphasizing the creative process rather than just the final product. This approach complemented Thacher's overall academic philosophy of developing well-rounded, thoughtful, and creative graduates. The photograph above shows students working in the art studio in 1967. The students below are working with ceramics.

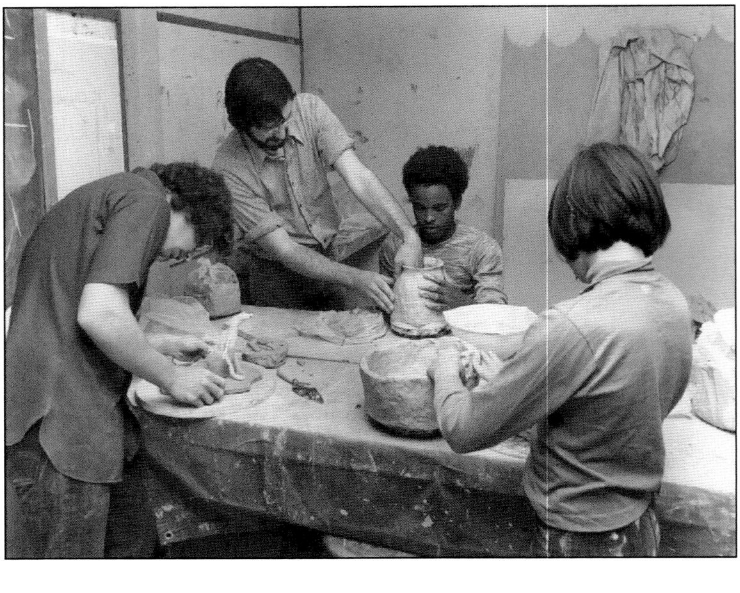

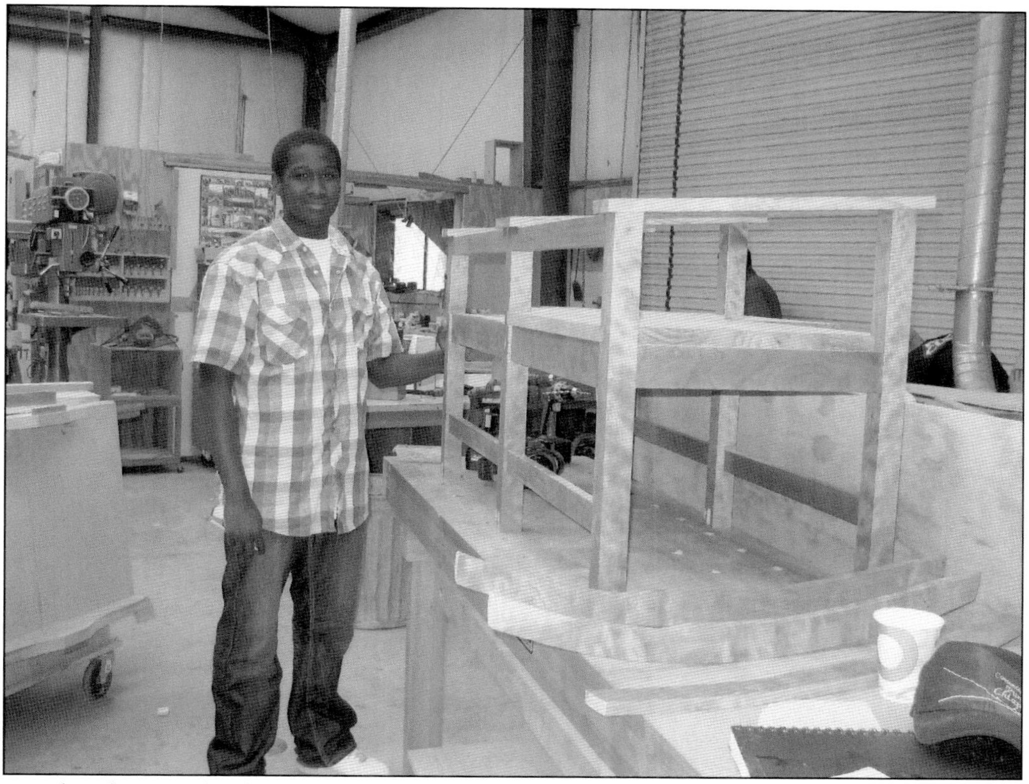

Woodworking, under the direction of John Bueti, has become a very popular artistic pursuit. The Royal Barney Hogan Woodshop, with tools that range from small chisels for detailed engraving to large planes and lathes for turning spindles or planing tabletops, was constructed near the maintenance facility in 1990 with a grant from the Bechtel family. Students can do anything from making intricate wood carvings to constructing furniture with fancy lathed spindles and intricate inlays. In fact, woodworking is so popular that a full-time craftsman was hired in 1997 to oversee activities in the woodshop. Classes in the shop fill quickly, so students who wish to pursue this artistic outlet must plan well in advance to secure a place.

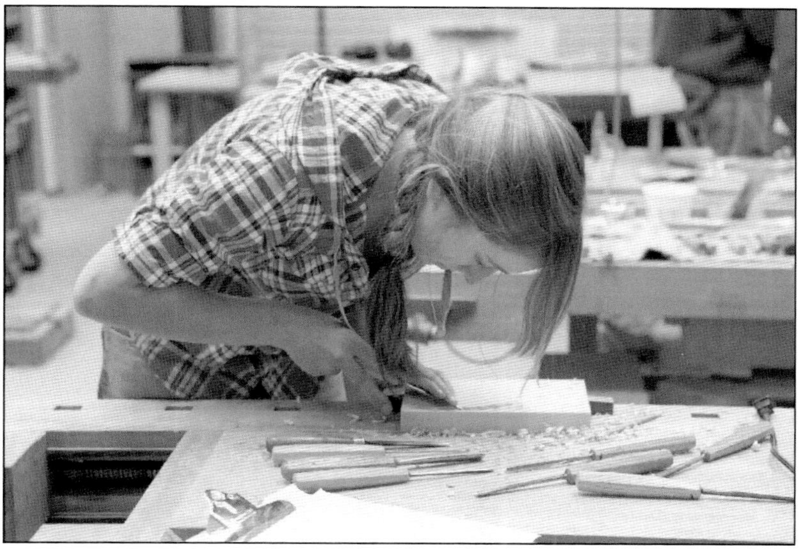

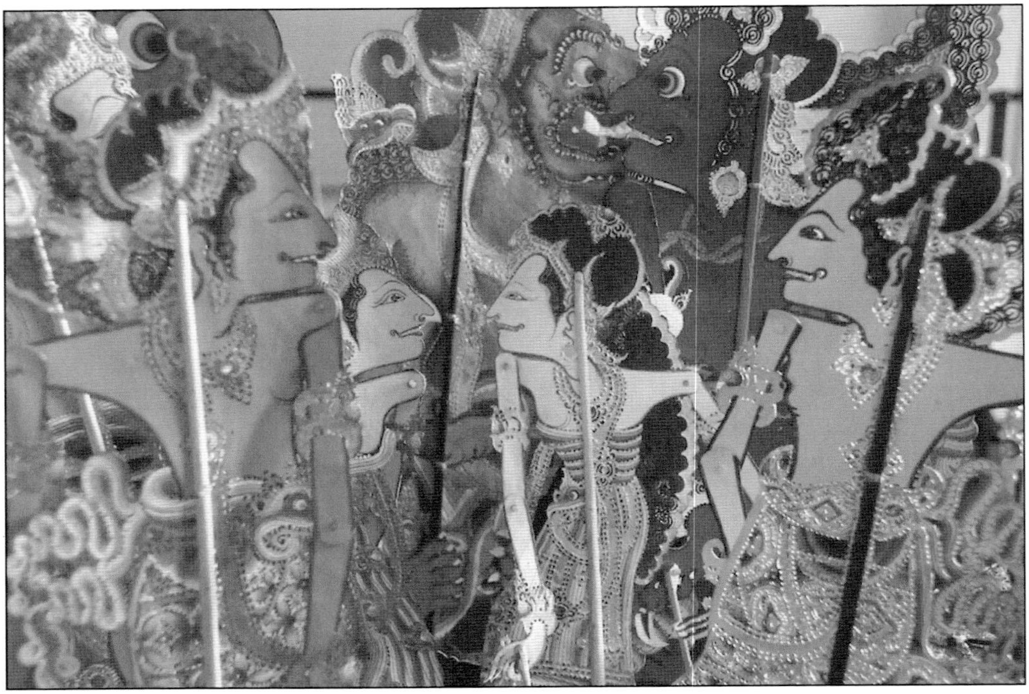

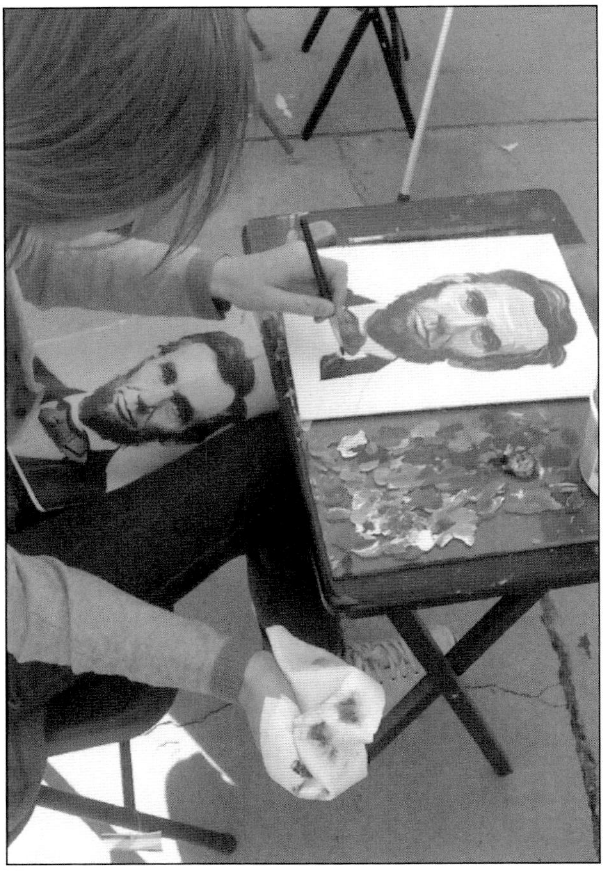

Every Thacher freshman is introduced to art. Those who wish to further pursue painting and/or drawing have numerous opportunities. Thacher offers programs in studio art, advanced studio art, and AP studio art within its fine arts department. Following the philosophy established by Edgardo Catalan and carried on by Bettie Saunders and (currently) Elizabeth "Liz" Mahoney CdeP 1988, students are given a solid foundation in technique and art theory and are then encouraged to follow their own creative impulses. In alternate years, Departmental Weekend, a winter weekend focused on in-depth exploration of particular subjects, is devoted to the visual arts. Examples of the art from the 2009 Department Weekend are shown here. Works by students, faculty, and artists in residence are displayed around the campus from the Brody Gallery (which also serves as a robotics laboratory) to the Thacher Commons.

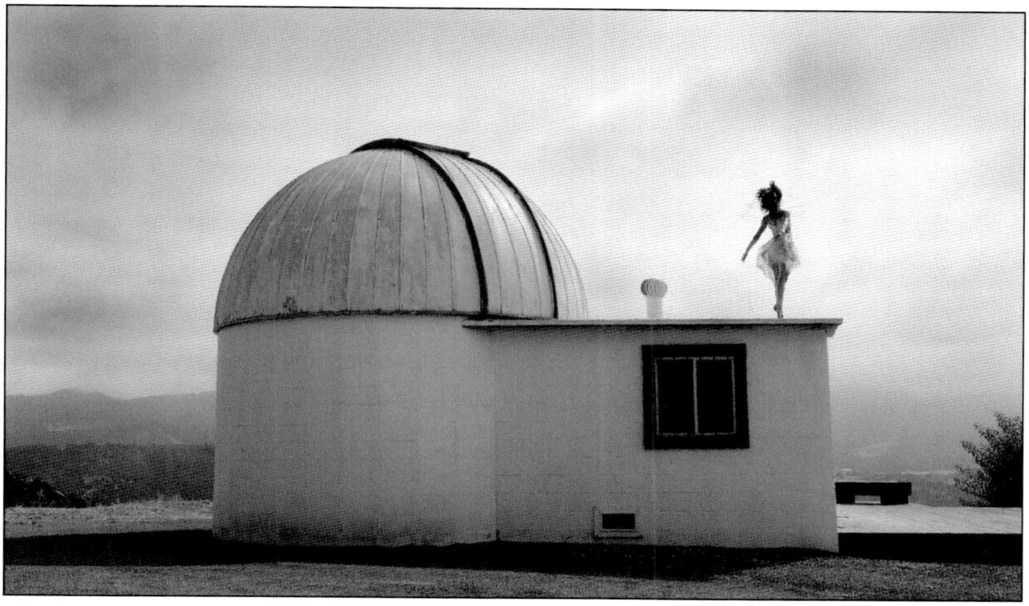

Thacher is something of a photographer's dream. There are endless opportunities to capture action shots, landscapes, animal studies, portraits, clouds, or whatever strikes one's fancy. Early interest in photography was fostered by longtime faculty member Marcus Dall, affectionately known as "Mr. D" during the 43 years he was associated with The Thacher School (1928–1971; head of the Art Department 1928–1949). Famous for his red Basque beret and enormous heart, his photographic archive captured hundreds of Thacher boys in their "natural surroundings." Today, both introductory and advanced photography classes are offered under the direction of Liz Mahoney, with an emphasis on technique, composition, wet darkroom skills (in a fully equipped darkroom in the Humanities Building), and digital photography.

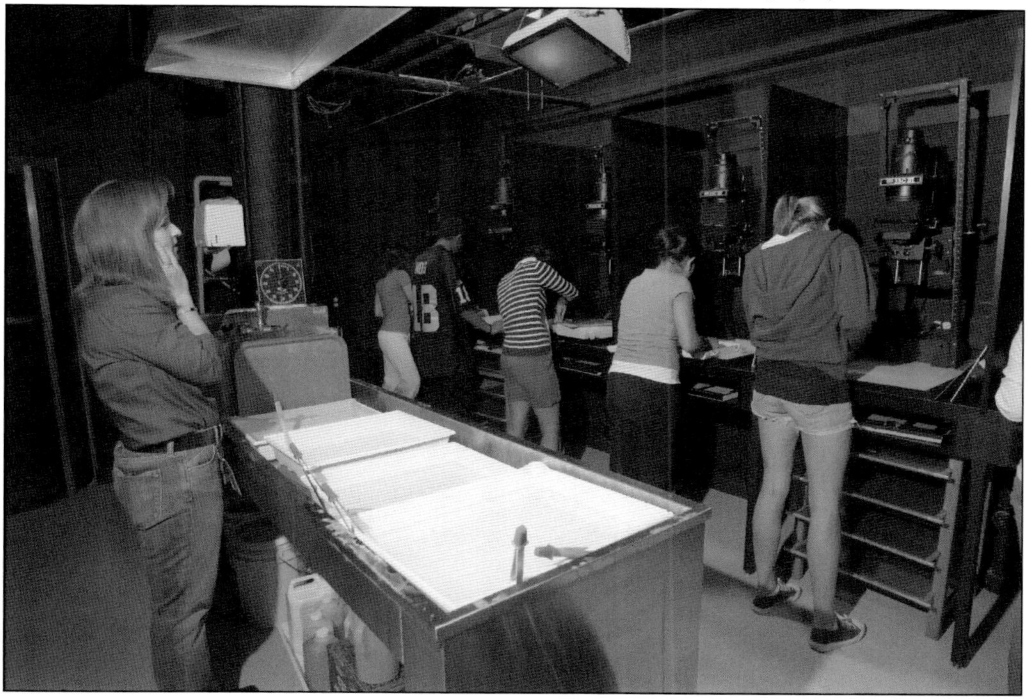

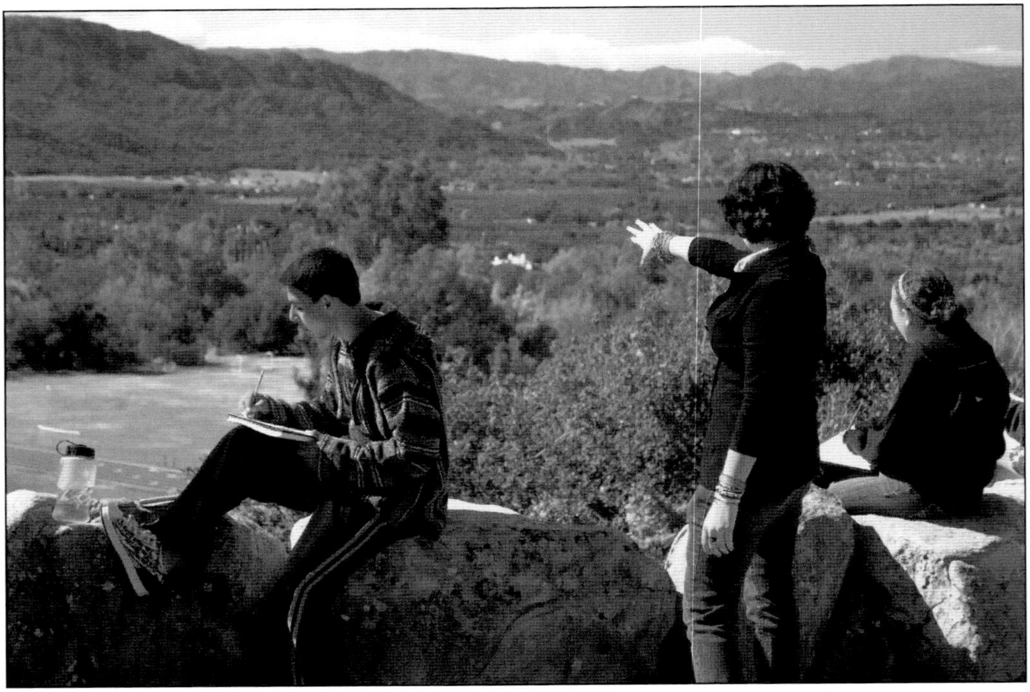

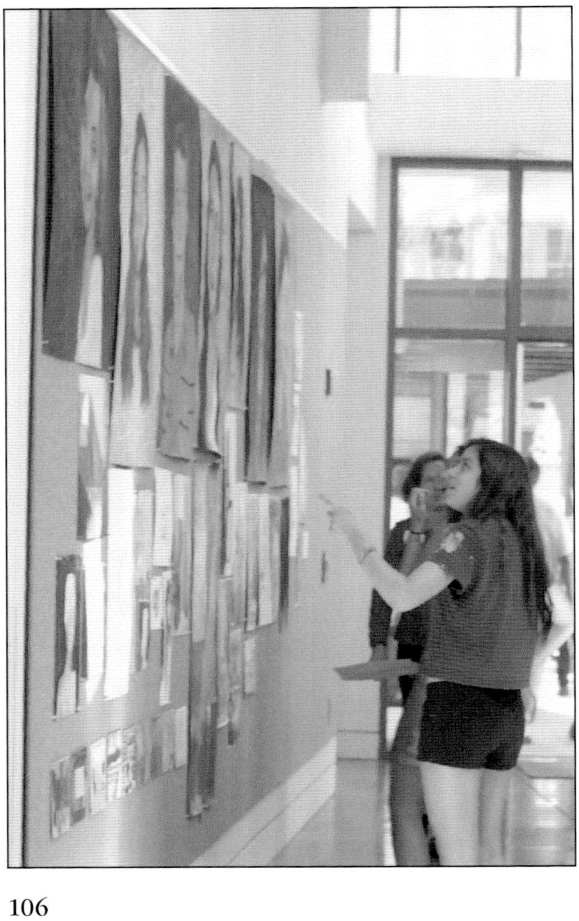

The Ojai Valley, with its stunning vistas and near-perfect weather, provides an ideal setting for budding artists. The combination of mountains, valleys, horses, and both vintage and modern architecture can inspire the photographer, the painter, the sculptor, the musician, and the writer—each in his or her own way. The strong tradition of drama fosters confidence and poise in the student performers. The richness of the venue itself, together with the emphasis on the creative process introduced by Edgardo Catalan in the 1960s, has made Thacher's programs in music, drama, and the visual arts an integral part of each student's educational experience.

Eight

ATHLETICS

The importance of athletics to a well-rounded secondary curriculum has long been recognized. Some have called sports "the outdoor classroom" because they teach life lessons that simply cannot be learned in a strictly academic setting. Thacher refers to this as the "second scoreboard"—a measure of sportsmanship, effort, and character rather than simply the final score.

In addition, athletics provides a critical outlet for young men and women to blow off steam in a relatively safe (yet challenging) environment. Although Thacher's horse program fills some of these niches, athletics also play an important role in the development of young people.

Sherman Thacher recognized this, and by the time Thacher had reached an enrollment of about 20, baseball was becoming one of the most popular sports in high schools across the country. According to Leroy McKim Makepeace, "The game was played [at Thacher] all year, interrupted only when the balls were sent to San Francisco to be re-covered or the bat [there was only one] was broken."

In the early days, especially after the arrival of Sherman's brother William, a tennis star from Yale, tennis was also played. Other sports included hunting and trapping. As Thacher expanded, so did the athletic program, with track-and-field events and soccer added in the 1920s, basketball in the late 1930s and early 1940s, cross-country in the 1960s, lacrosse in the mid-1960s, and eight-man football in 2002.

When Thacher became coeducational in 1977, women's programs in softball, volleyball, soccer, basketball, and lacrosse were also added.

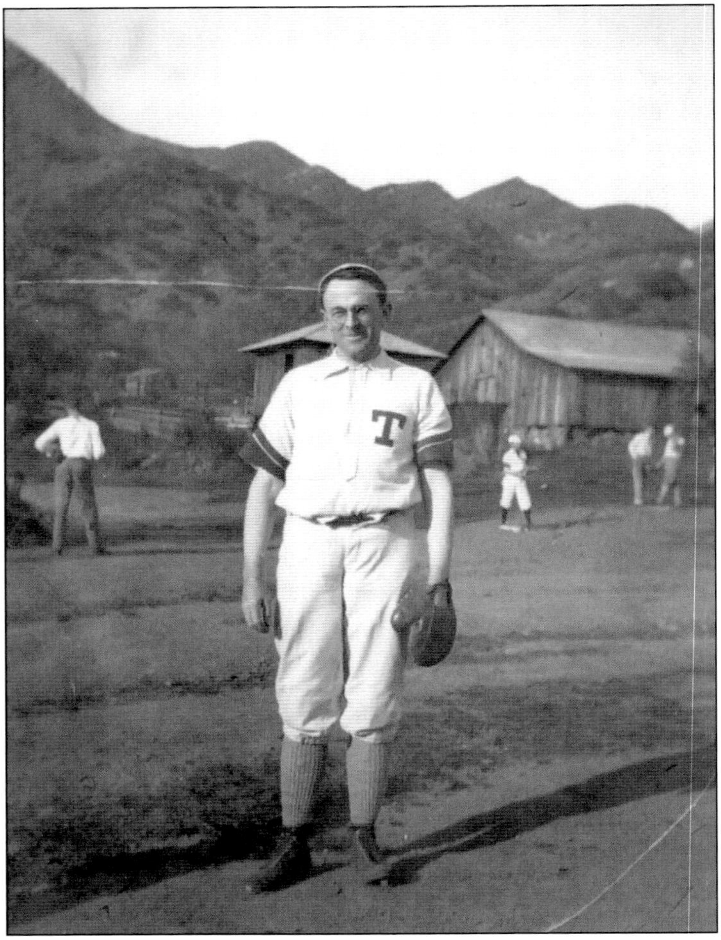

Sherman Thacher, shown at left in 1910 in the Thacher baseball uniform and below with one of his favorite horses, was an avid athlete himself. He noted, "Athletics, rightly conducted, are as important an element in the development of the human being as anything I know. But more important than the mere physical benefit is the chance they give to teach the essentials of honor, fairness, public spirit, and submission to authority . . . There is a vital relationship between wholesome physical skill and essential morality . . . Keeping a sound mind in a sound body is the basis for all successful service and all great adventure."

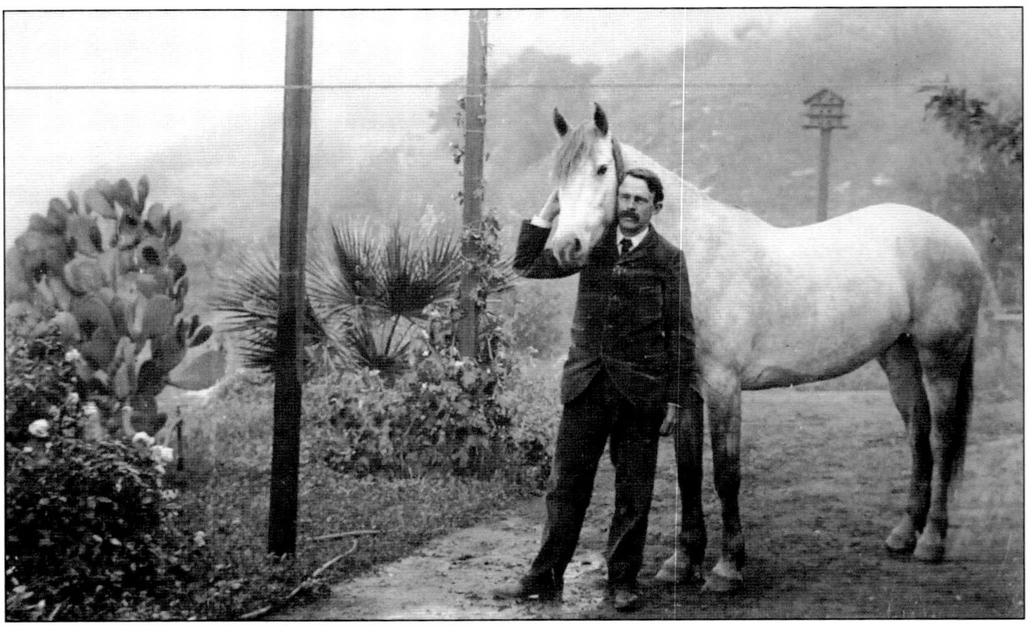

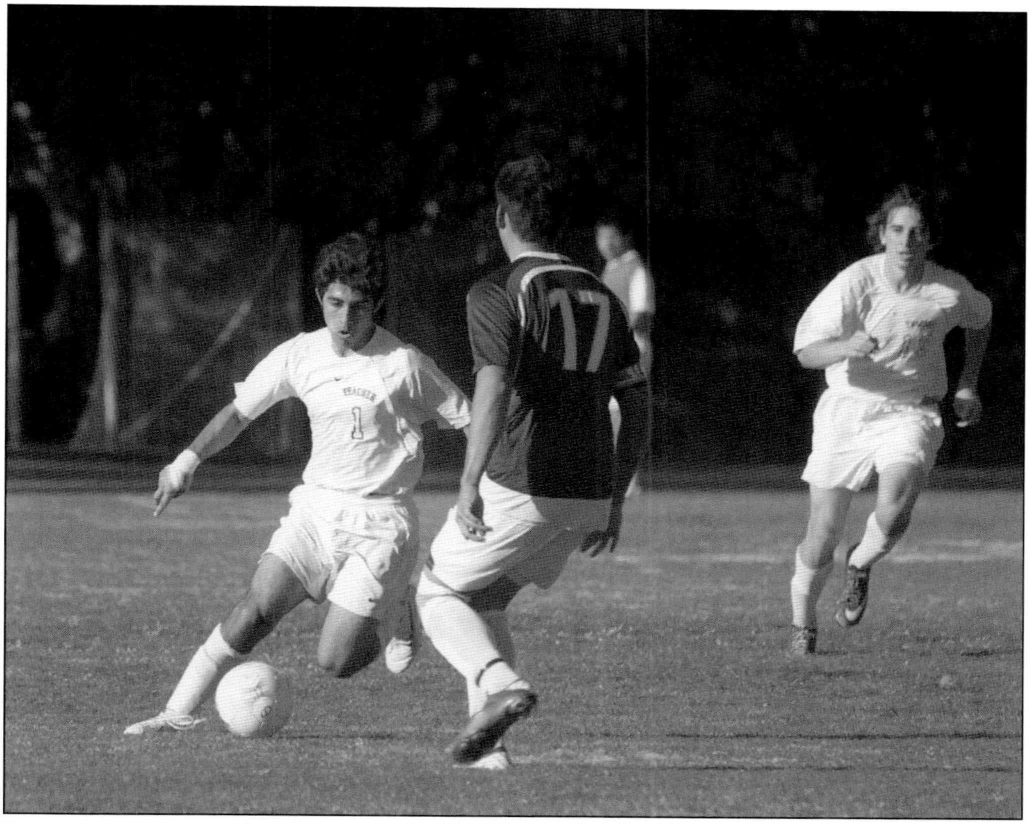

Soccer was first introduced to The Thacher School in 1920 and quickly became a popular fall sport. All students were required to participate, so as many as five teams (now only three) were fielded, playing on the dirt surface of the New Field and traveling to Midland (where the field was an even more primitive cow pasture), Cate (where the manicured grass was truly a luxury), and other schools in the area. For many years, competition between Thacher and Midland for the coveted Lowery Cup was one of the highlights of the athletic year. Soccer became a winter sport for both men and women in 2002 when football was introduced to the Condor League. Numerous Thacher soccer players have gone on to successful collegiate soccer careers.

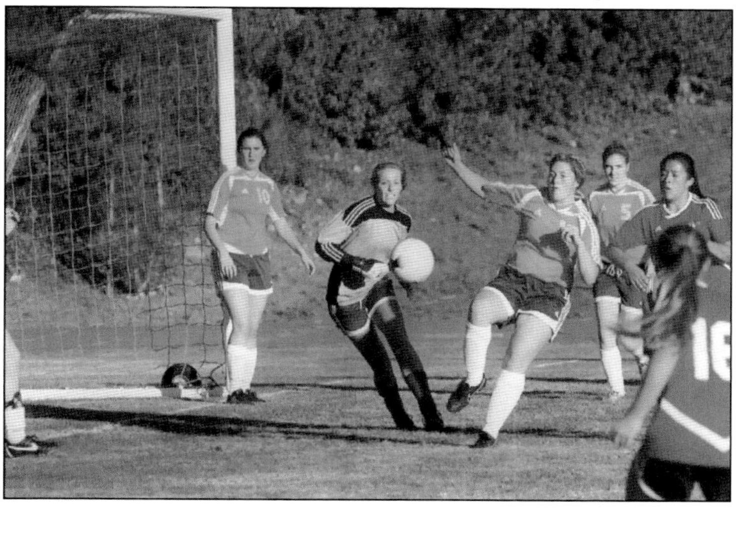

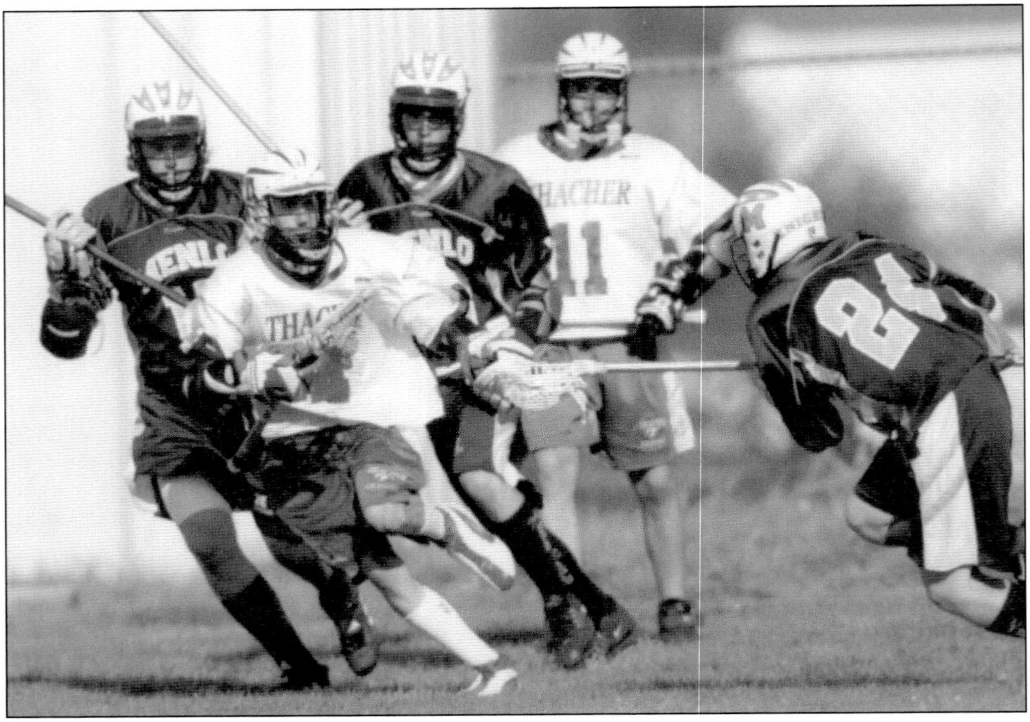

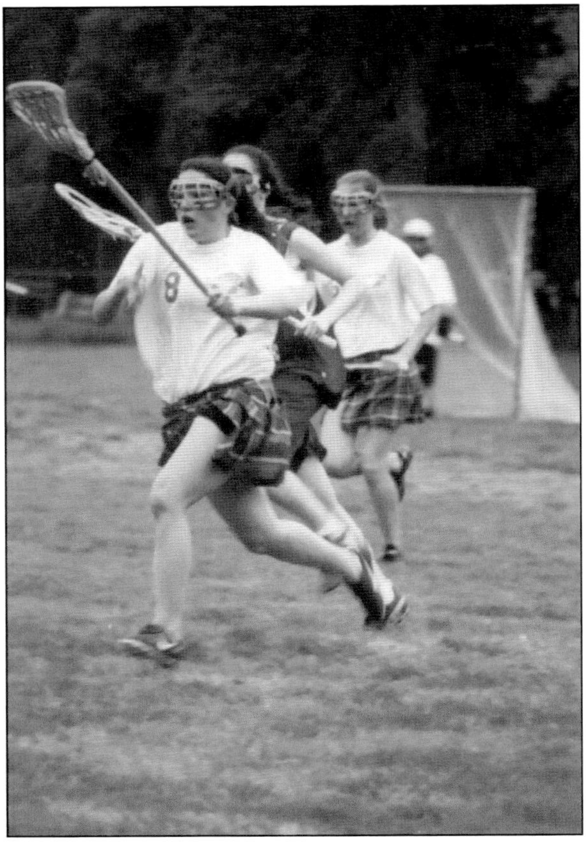

Lacrosse is a truly American sport, originating with eastern Native American tribes and some Plains Indians. Students who came to Thacher from the eastern United States frequently brought their lacrosse sticks and balls. However, it was the appearance of history teacher John Galloway in the fall of 1965 and the enthusiasm of Scott MacGregor CdeP 1967 that really kick-started lacrosse as a formal athletic activity. In fact, the first interscholastic lacrosse competition in California was held at Thacher in January 1966. Condor League competition began in 1967 for boys and in 1991 for girls.

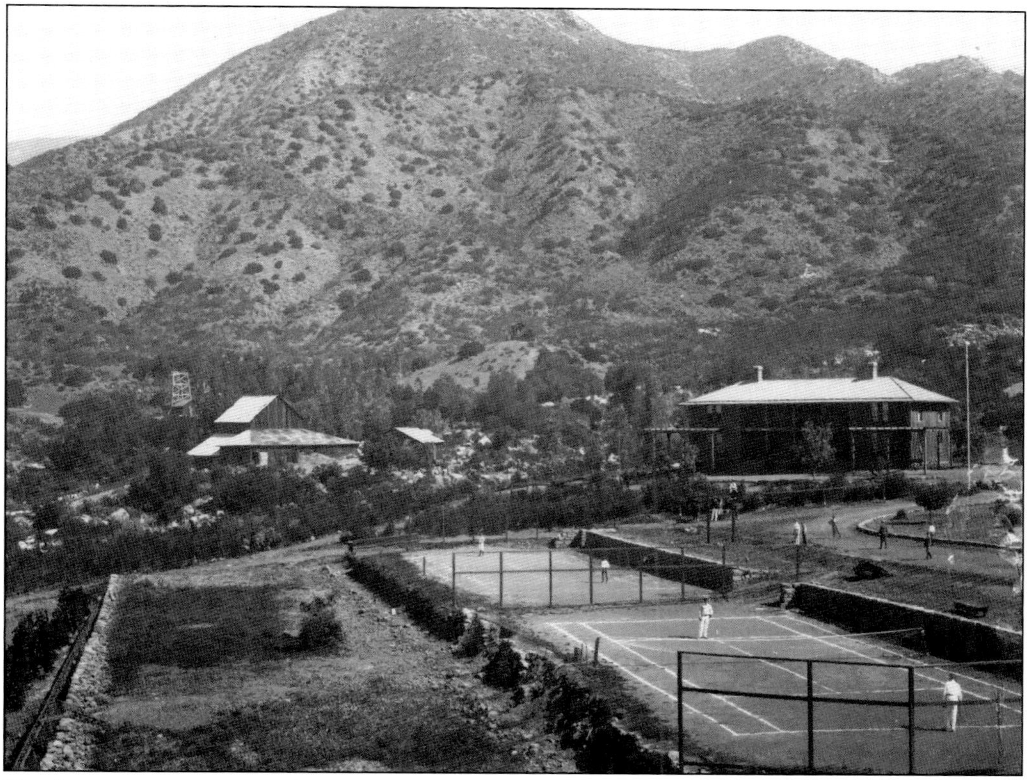

The first tennis courts in the Ojai Valley were built at Thacher in 1892 by Sherman Thacher's brother William Larned Thacher, a collegiate champion singles and doubles player at Yale. The image above shows dirt tennis courts at Thacher around the turn of the century. Pictured below is one of the early teams—note the long pants that were considered de rigueur for tennis competition early in the 20th century. Today, men's tennis is a spring sport, and women's tennis is a fall sport at Thacher. While uniforms have changed and the courts are no longer packed dirt marked with chalk, the popularity of the sport remains high, both as a formal team event and as a just-for-fun pastime. Thacher's involvement in the Ojai Tennis Tournament continues as an annual event, with participation by some students acting as ball boys and some adults assisting with overall tournament management.

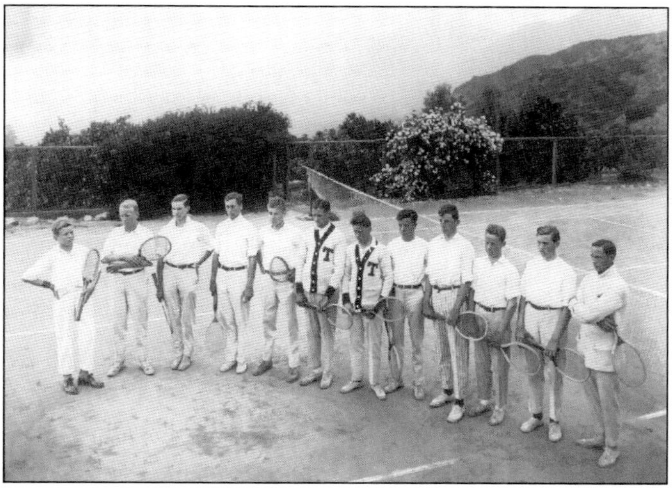

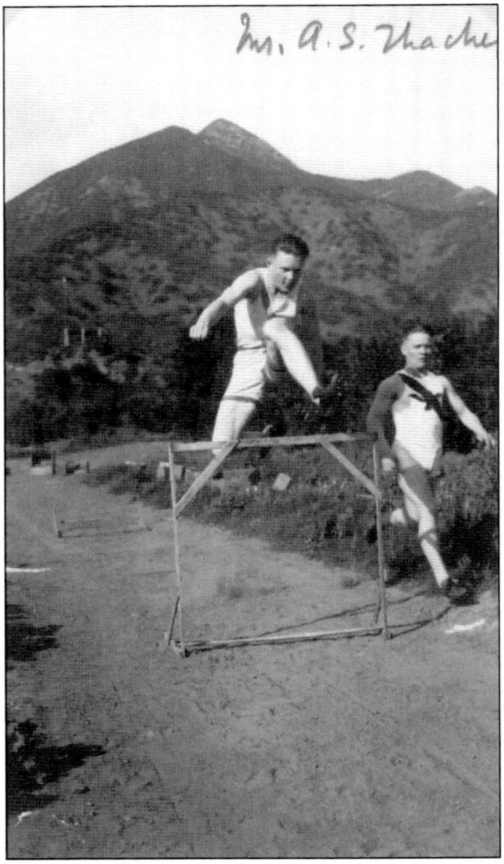

Running, jumping, and throwing have been celebrated since the ancient Olympic Games. In addition, they are the basis for most other sports. It is, therefore, not surprising that track and field has been a popular spring sport at Thacher since its earliest days. The image at left shows two members of the class of 1923—future headmaster Anson Thacher (the hurdler) and Bob "Cap" Bailard (the runner)—practicing at the New Field in the early 1920s. Thacher's foothill location and network of trails have always provided an ideal setting for training runners. Cross-country, first introduced in 1965, is a fall sport for both men and women.

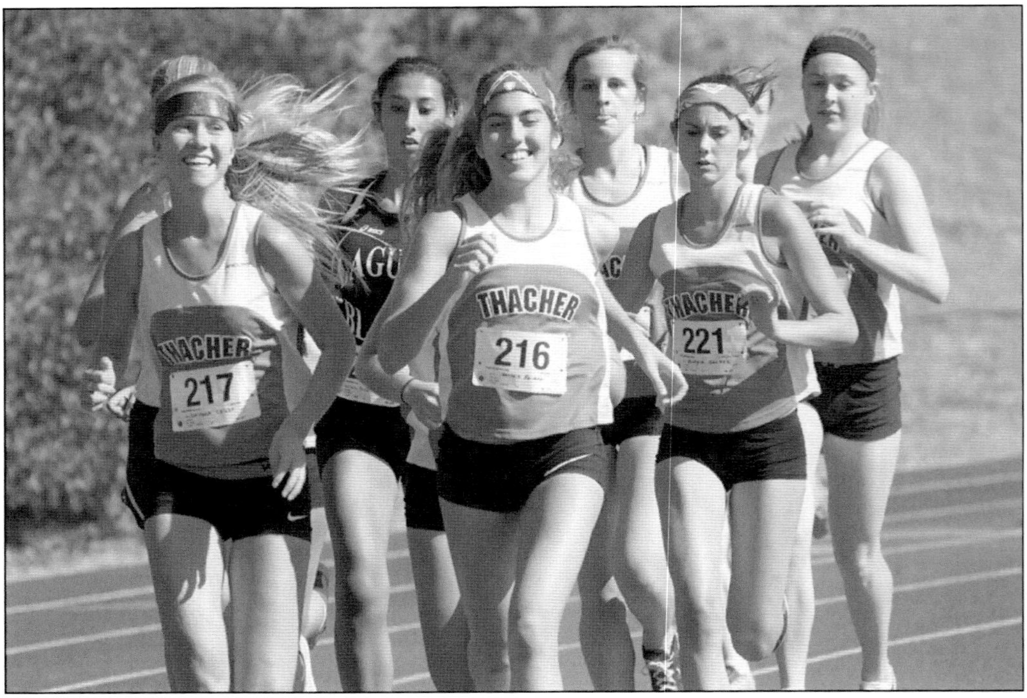

Basketball is first mentioned as a sport at Thacher in 1938, with official uniforms and organization in 1941. For almost half of the Thacher's subsequent history, basketball was played outdoors on the asphalt courts behind the Upper School, pictured at right, which also served as tennis courts. As a concession to teams from schools with indoor facilities, many of Thacher's home basketball games were played in downtown Ojai in the Nordhoff High School (now Matilija Junior High School) gymnasium. In the 1970s, as a part of Edgar Sanford's efforts to provide indoor venues for winter activities, the Voit Gymnasium was completed, and for the first time, Thacher's hoopsters could practice and compete indoors on their own real wooden court (below).

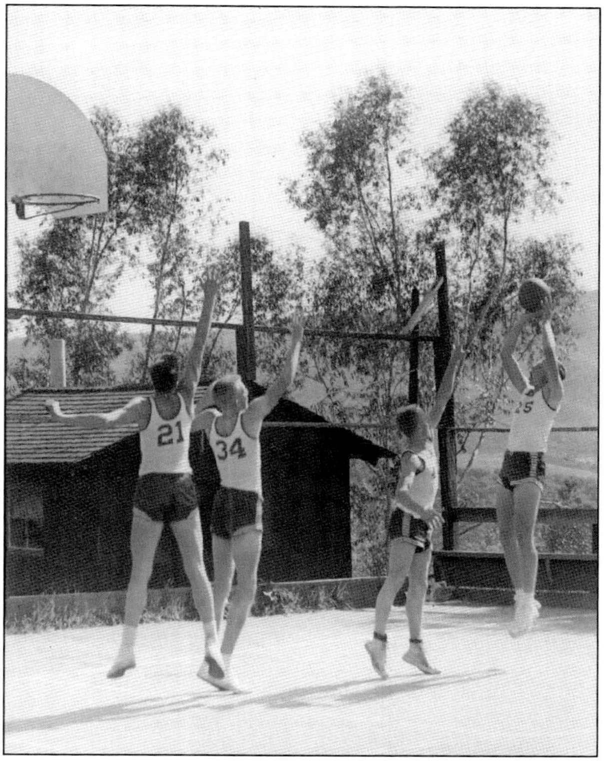

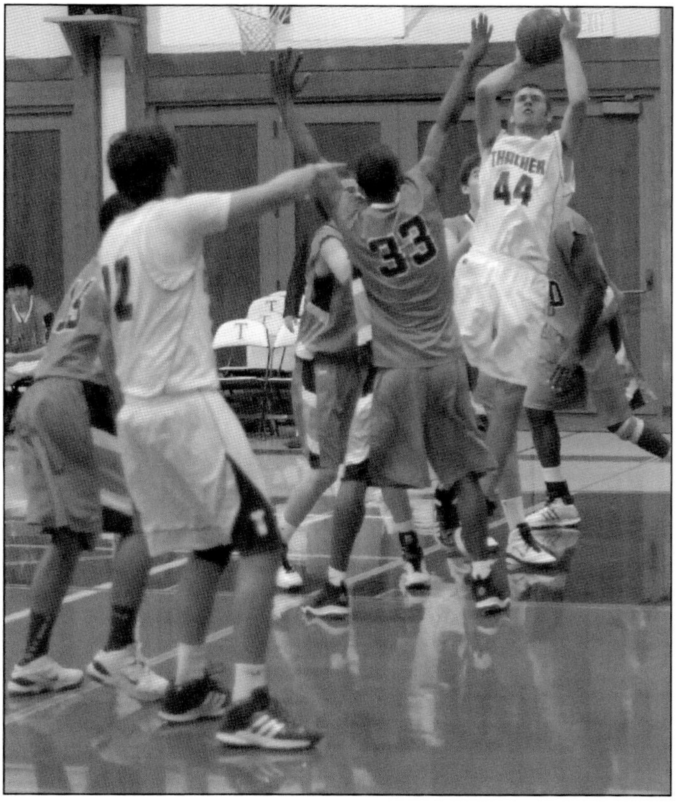

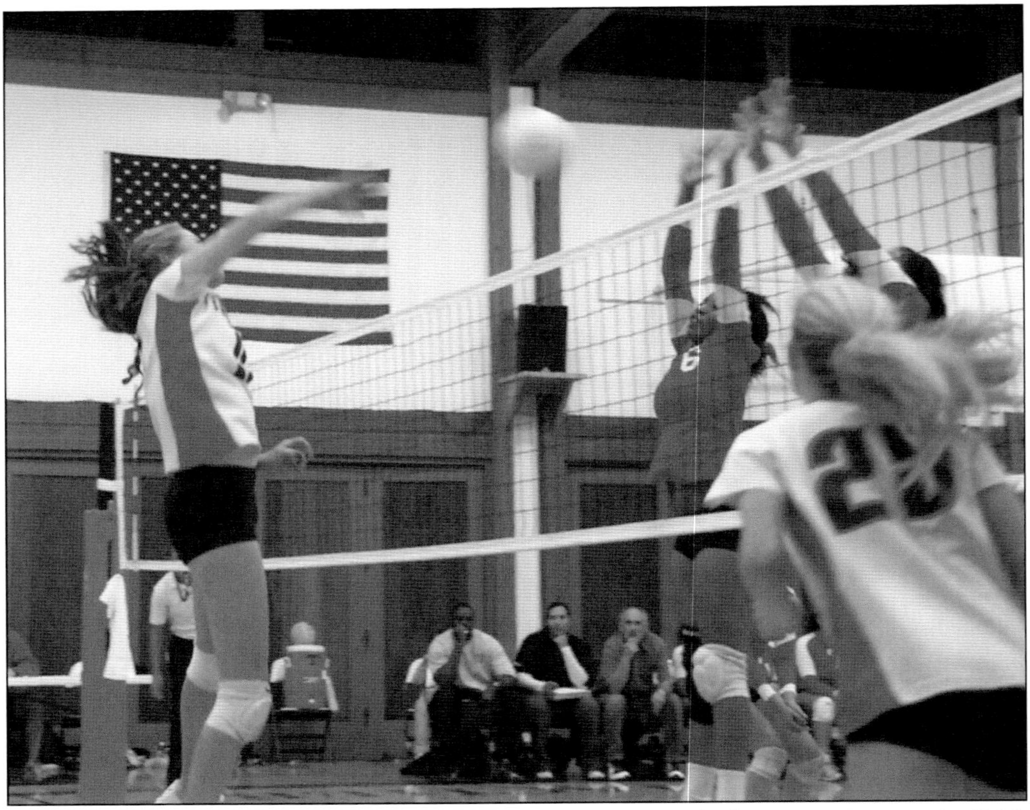

Volleyball, another authentic American sport, originated in Holyoke, Massachusetts, in 1895. This "gentle, recreational pastime" was introduced to Thacher as a fall athletic alternative for women shortly after coeducation in the late 1970s. As is obvious from the image above, this sport is no longer (and really never was) either gentle or recreational. It continues to be a popular fall sport, and Thacher teams have enjoyed considerable success both in the Condor League and against nonleague opponents. Several Thacher women have gone on to play collegiate volleyball. Basketball is also an extremely popular winter sport for women, with two women's teams competing with women's teams from nearby schools.

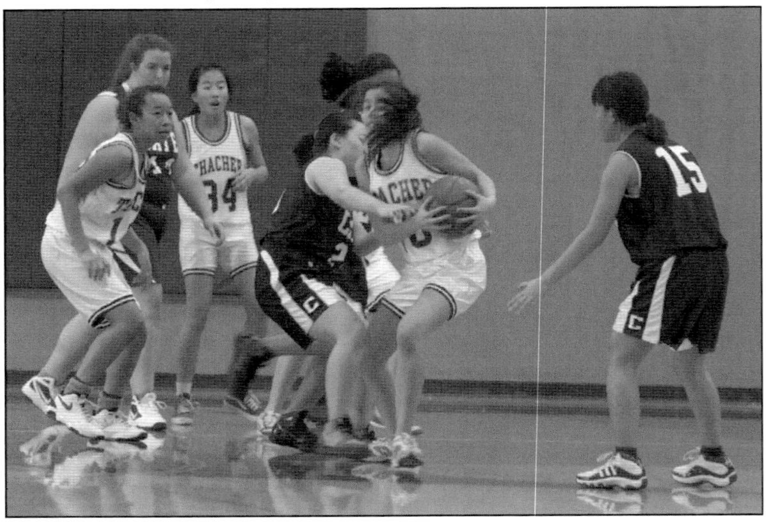

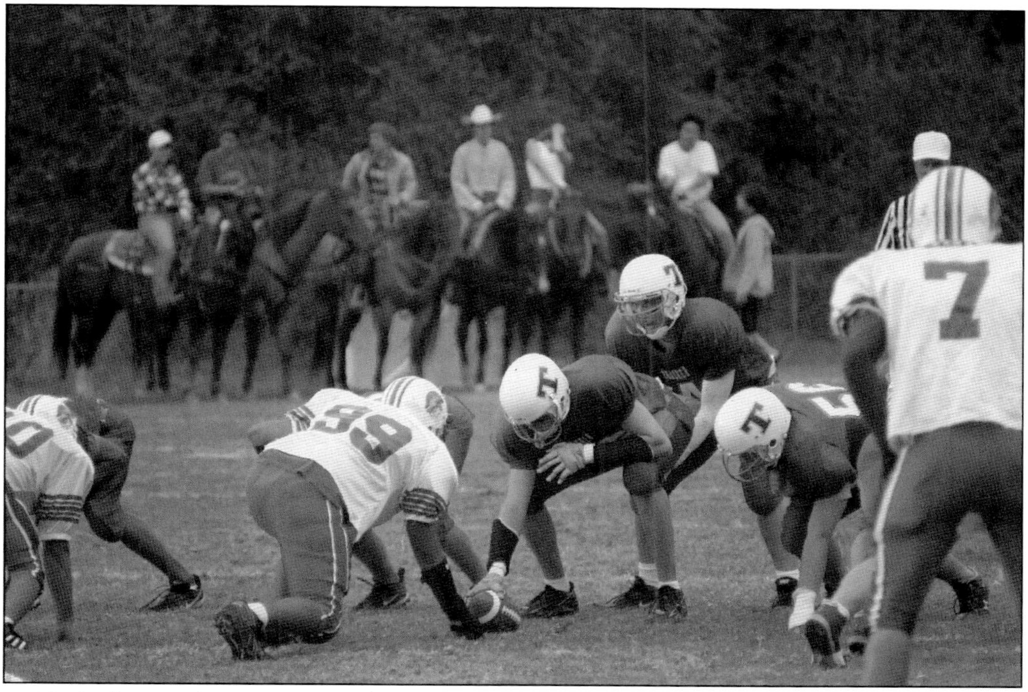

In 2002, the Condor League moved its soccer season from fall to winter. Because grass fields had been introduced at Thacher in the late 1960s, football became a viable activity, and after much debate, Thacher filled the void in fall sports by introducing eight-man football to its boys' athletic program. Since that time, football has become one of the favorite fall activities for both participants and spectators. Eight-man football is a faster version of its 11-man cousin and is frequently played by smaller schools like Thacher, which would struggle to field a full 11-man squad. The game involves more running than passing, and scores can be quite high. Note the unique Thacher phenomenon of spectators watching the game from the backs of their horses.

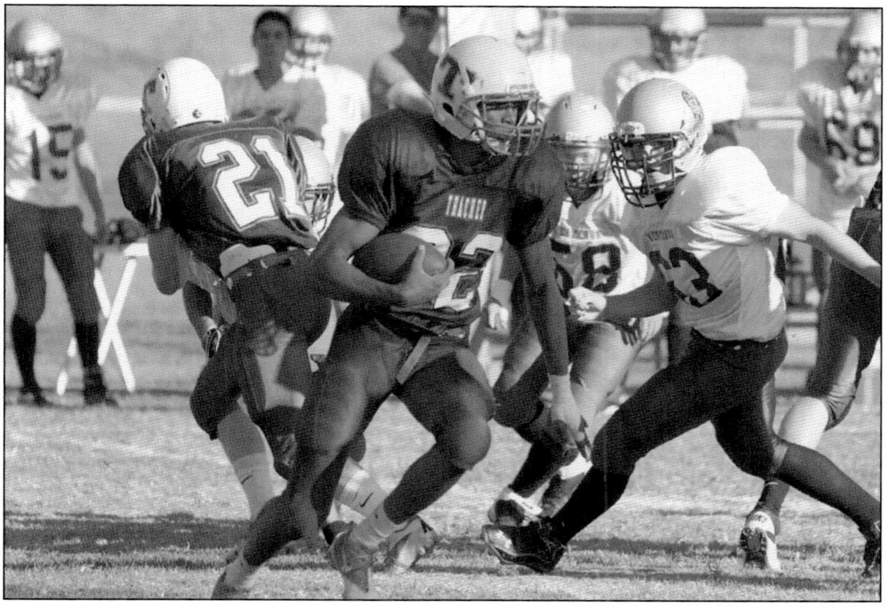

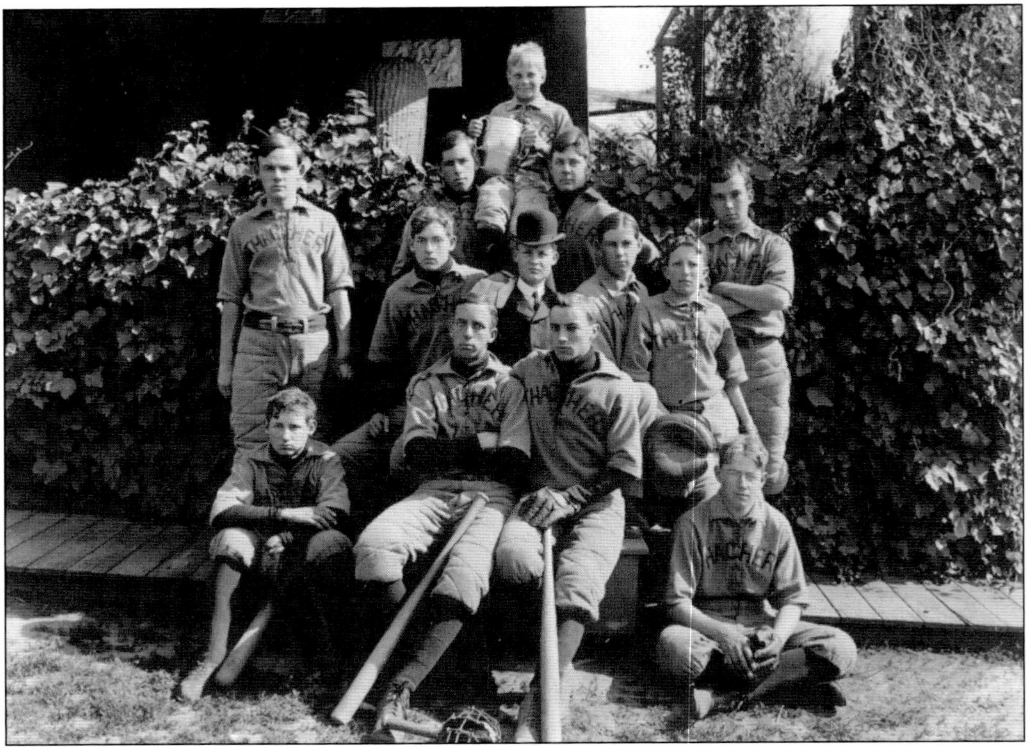

Thacher's very first interscholastic competition was a baseball game on March 1, 1893, against Santa Paula High School, which Thacher lost 17-14. The image above shows one of the early baseball teams posing in front of the "grandstand" at Jameson Field. Note the individual with the coat, tie, and bowler hat (perhaps the faculty coach or manager) in the center of the group. A favorite sport of Sherman Thacher, Anson Thacher, Newt Chase, and many others, baseball, now played on one of Thacher's grass athletic venues, has been a staple of The Thacher School's spring athletic program for nearly its entire history. For a time in the late 1970s and 1980s, girls' softball was also offered in the spring.

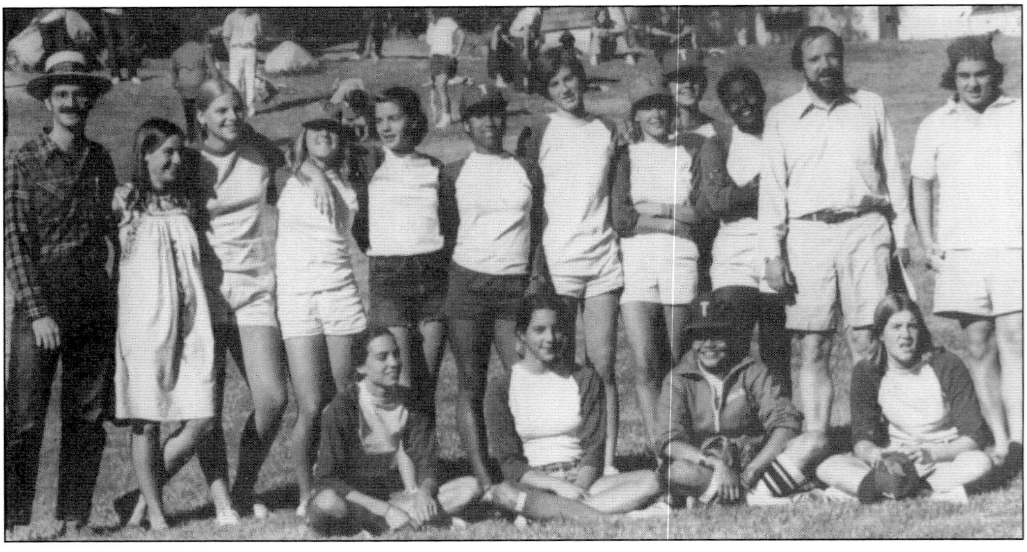

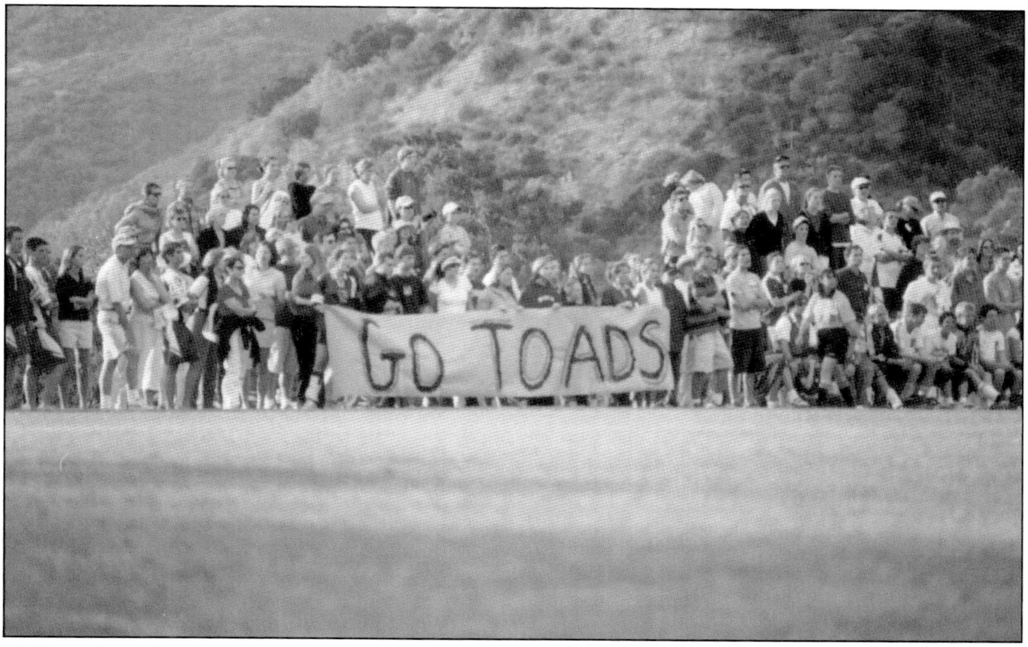

Although athletics have been an important part of The Thacher School almost from its inception, Thacher did not have a true mascot until the mid-1960s. Credit for naming the athletic teams the "Toads" has been variously attributed to Nick Thacher CdeP 1963, Stew Walton CdeP 1964, and Jock Hayward CdeP 1965, but regardless of the originator, the name stuck, and Mike Toad is now a fixture at Thacher athletic contests. The mascot, shown below with head of school Michael Mulligan, has even penetrated the administration—the faculty member who is on-call is known as the TOAD (teacher on administrative duty).

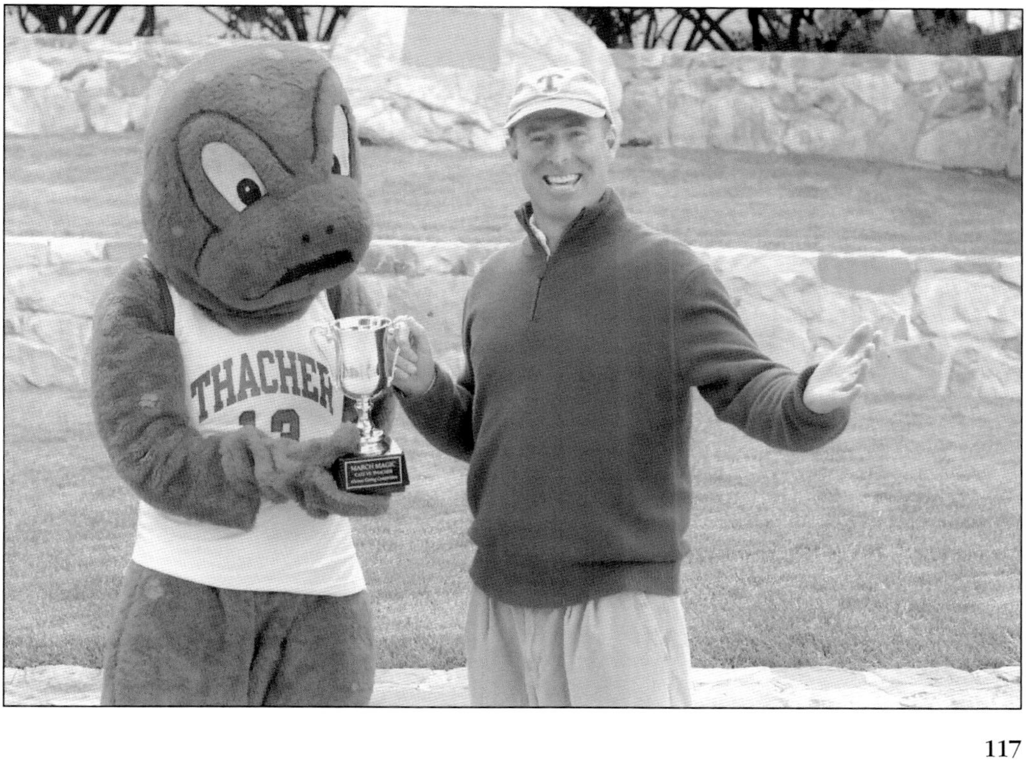

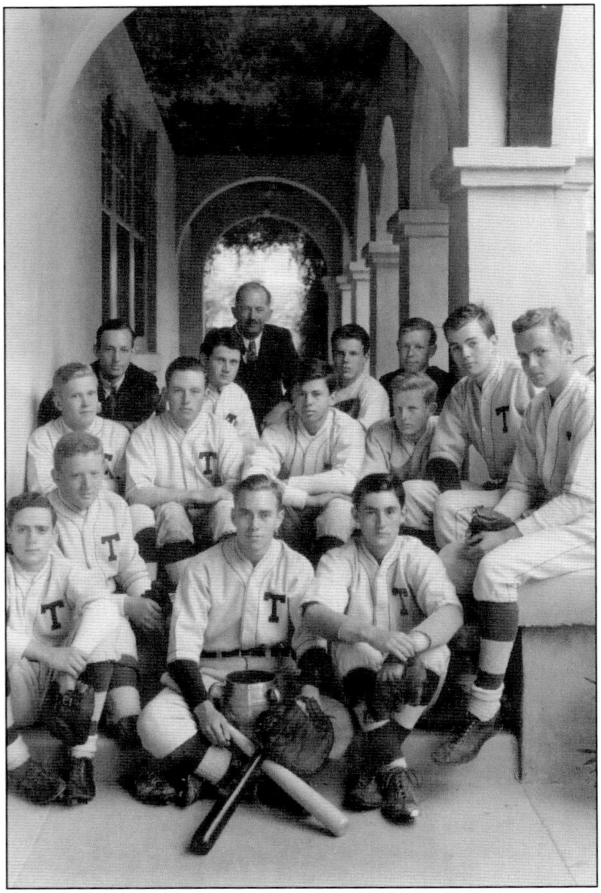

While winning is always a goal, it has never been the ultimate objective of Thacher athletics. From the early days of recess baseball to the modern days of football and lacrosse, participation has always preempted competition. This notwithstanding, Thacher has won its share of championships and trophies, both individual and team, and its athletes have gone on to compete successfully at colleges and universities across the country. However, every participant, from the fifth soccer team to the varsity lacrosse team, has learned lessons that have helped that individual be a better businessperson, lawyer, engineer, or artist. Lessons of success with humility and loss with dignity remain valuable all throughout life. The affirmation of Sherman Thacher's observation that "more important than the mere physical benefit is the chance [athletics] give to teach the essentials of honor, fairness, public spirit, and submission to authority" remains the highest goal.

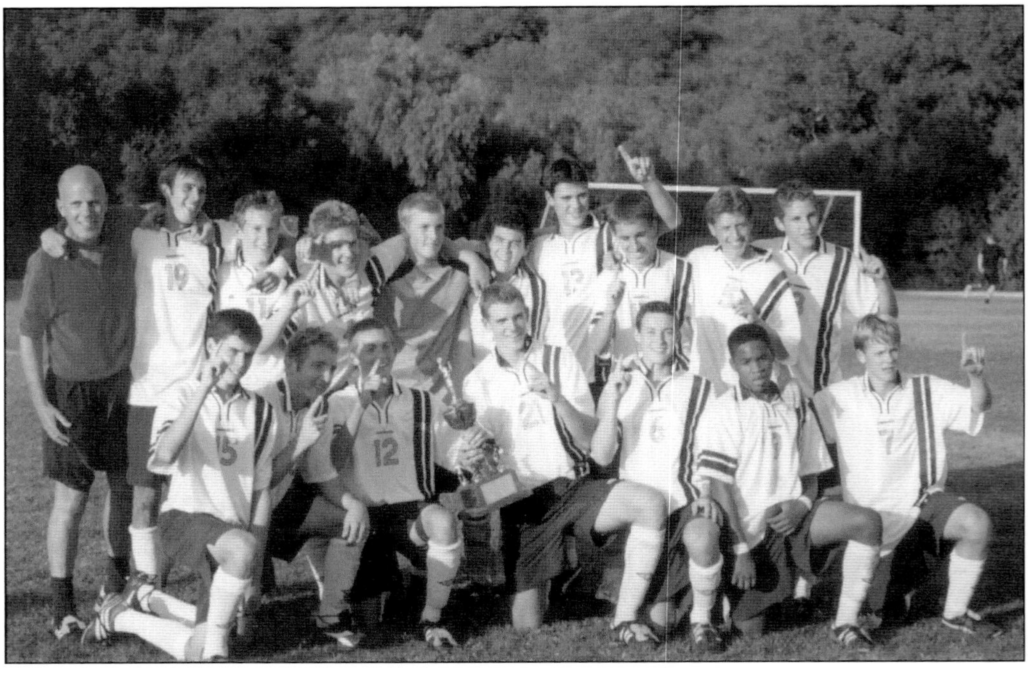

Nine

"May Old Casa Piedra Not Fade from My Heart"

Thacher's founding fathers—men like Sherman, William, and Anson Thacher; Morgan Barnes; and Forest Cooke—laid a foundation that persists to this day. Although The Thacher School has changed in many ways, from its facilities to its size and the introduction of coeducation, its basis remains as solid as the day when Sherman Thacher first built Casa de Piedra.

Each of The Thacher School's eight headmasters has left his mark on the institution and pushed it forward toward greater educational excellence. Sherman Thacher established the foundation. Morgan Barnes doubled the enrollment as he shepherded Thacher through the challenging days of the Great Depression. Anson Thacher continued in his father's footsteps, taking Thacher through World War II and keeping it on a sound financial footing without compromising its academic excellence. Newton Chase served twice and was a careful steward of Thacher's finances while, at the same time, starting to modernize many of the facilities.

David Twichell, a former student and son of a faculty member, brought some new and challenging ideas to the educational table that he integrated into the long-standing programs of outdoor activities. Edgar Sanford faced the challenges of the rebellious 1960s and saw Thacher through to calmer seas before he stepped down. Willard Wyman oversaw the biggest change in the history of Thacher when girls were admitted in 1977. Michael Mulligan, the second-longest-serving headmaster, has undertaken a number of strategic initiatives—upgrading faculty salaries and residences, renovating old structures, and building new facilities—and has brought the endowment to an astounding $120 million.

The conclusion of this volume recalls three compositions that remain in the heart of every Thacher graduate from 1890 to today: the Oath of the Young Men of Athens on the plaque at the Pergola; Forest Cooke's litany of Thacher; and the "Banquet Song," originally written by Sherman Thacher and appropriately modified when Thacher became coeducational in 1977.

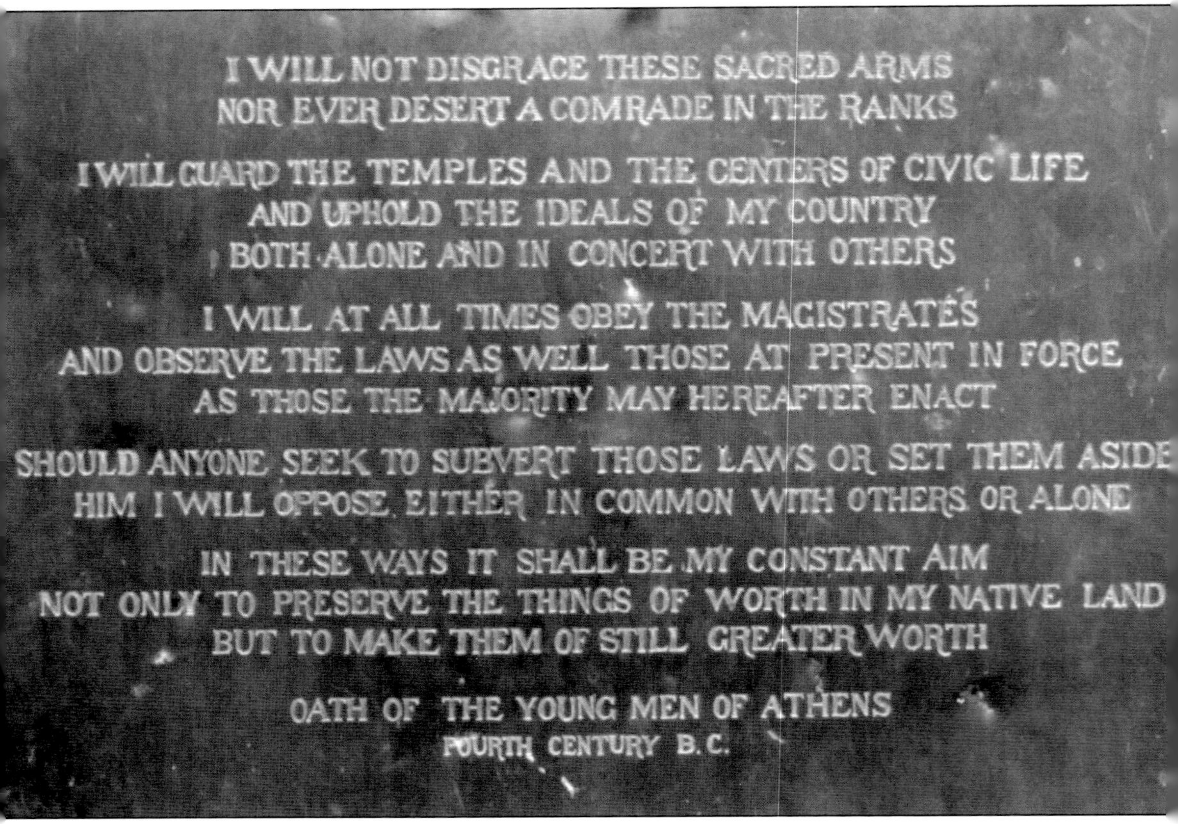

In ancient Athens, young men between the ages of 17 and 18 were required to swear an oath prior to being admitted to the Ephebate, the military training program that was required for citizenship in the Greek city-state. The oath was administered in the Temple of Aglaulus, one of the temples on the Athenian Acropolis. Although first noted by a Greek orator named Lycurgus in the fourth century BCE, the oath is thought to date to even more ancient times. Inscribed on a plaque at the Pergola, the Oath of the Young Men of Athens has been committed to memory by Thacher students for over 100 years. These words still speak volumes about the core values that underpin everything for which The Thacher School has come to stand. The astute observer will recognize the strong parallel between its last stanza and the last verse of the "Banquet Song," shown at the end of this chapter.

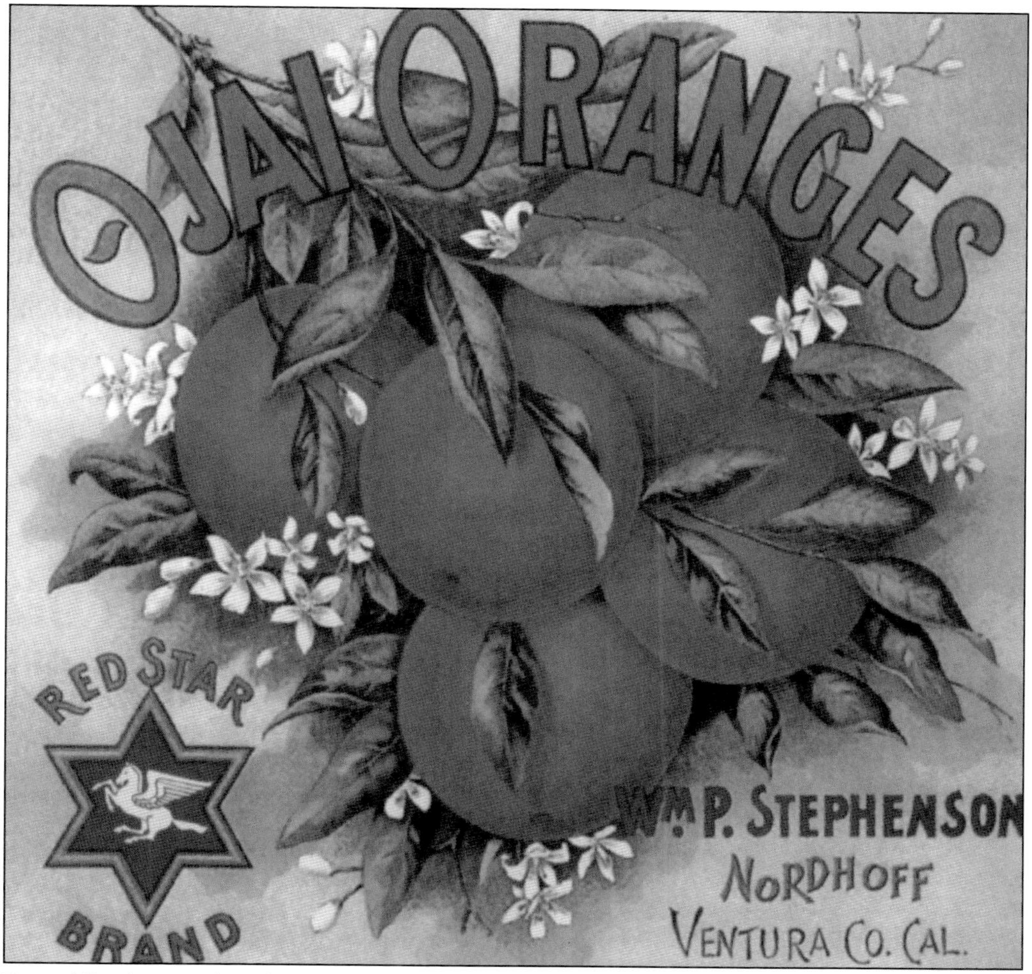

Every Thacher student becomes familiar, either directly or indirectly, with Forrest Cooke's litany of Thacher, which begins with the "The Ten Favorite Smells" and counts down to "The One Essential." They are as follows: "The Ten Favorite Smells—sage brush on a hot day; a well curried horse; orange blossoms in March; the top of Pine Mountain; bacon frying over a campfire; the wood fires in the sections; the fresh, earthy smell when you use a mattock on a trail; the clean paper smell when you open a new book; the dust smell when the first raindrops of the season fall; the Teachers' Club. The Nine Memorable Sights—Sunset from Memorial Hill; the view from Matilija Twin Peaks; Piedra Blanca by moonlight; horses swimming in the Sespe; a paper marked 100; a smiling face; clean finger nails; a team that pulls victory out of defeat; a letter from home in your mailbox."

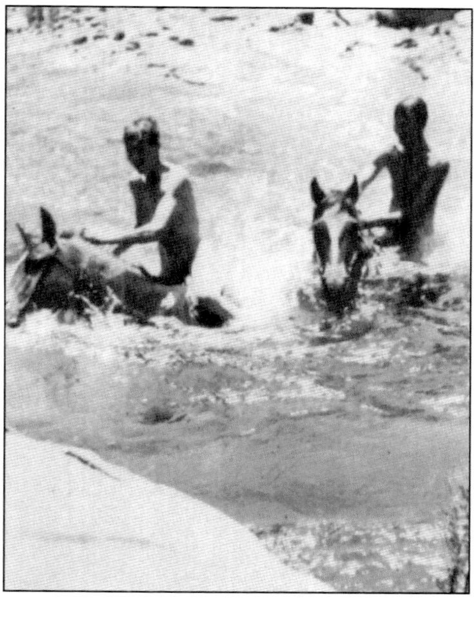

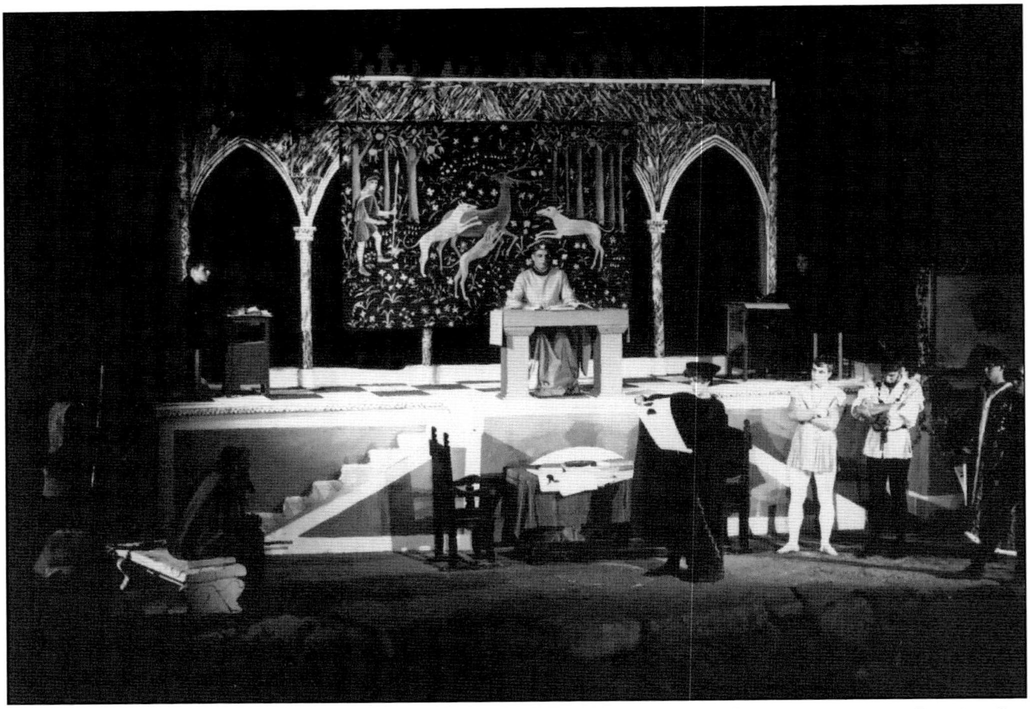

The litany continues with "The Eight Significant Sounds—Walker; music; orioles in the cottonwoods; a running brook heard from your sleeping bag under the stars; the starting pistol at the track; the whack of the ball against your bat when it soars out for a three-bagger; your horse nickering when you come to feed it; Shakespeare. The Seven Best Teachers—Your horse; the library; a lonely trail; a fair game; the friend you most admire; corrected mistakes; curiosity. The Six Things to Learn—To throw a good hitch; to cook a clean meal; to speak decent English; to look out for the other fellow; to do a thing right the first time; not to fool."

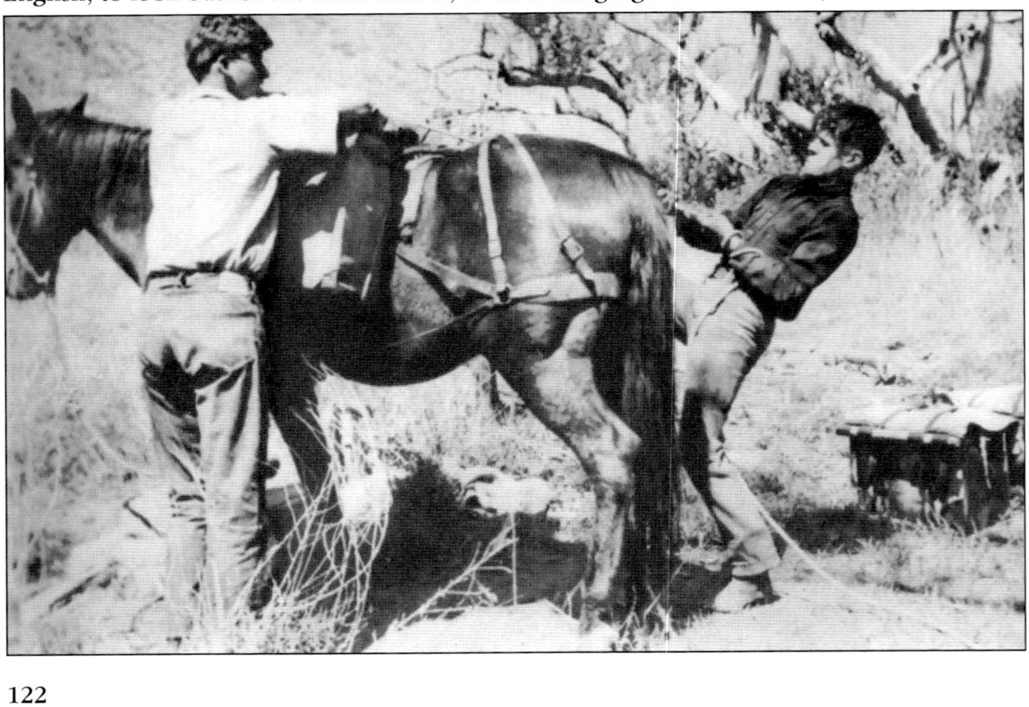

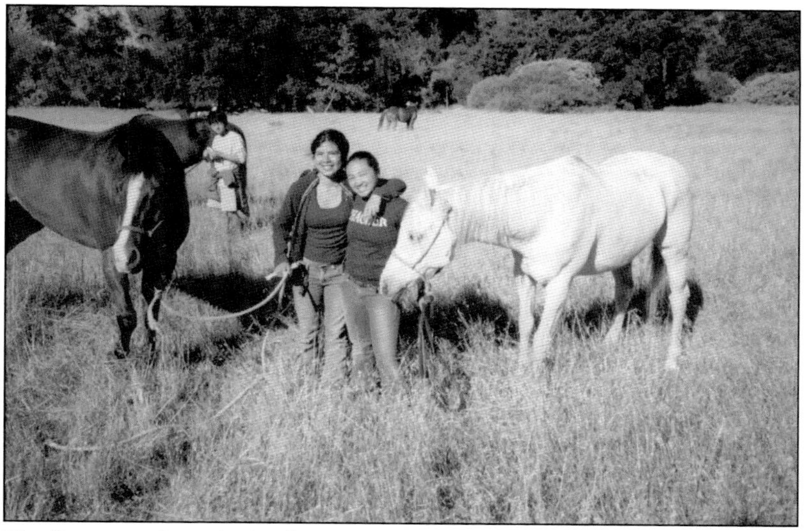

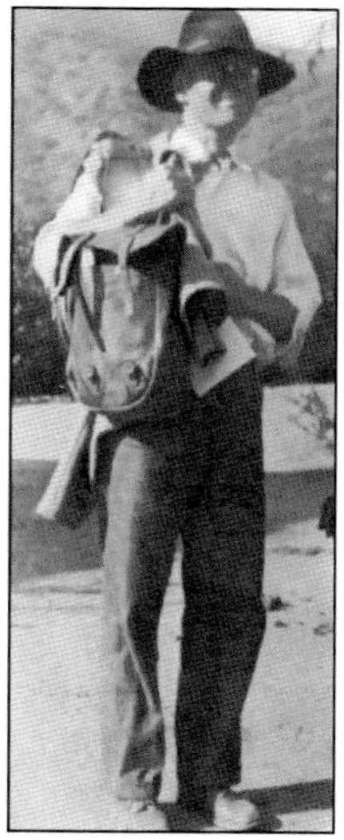

The litany ends with the following: "The Five Things to Avoid—A horse's hoof; misconduct marks; an easy life; the reputation of being lazy; borrowing other people's property. The Four Resorts in Times of Troubles—A teacher; the dictionary; your chum; yourself. The Three Great Letters: S.D.T. The Two Necessities: Courage and Understanding. The One Essential: Truth." The advice and principles in this litany of Thacher, penned by Forrest Cooke (shown above right and below) in the first part of the 20th century, are, indeed, timeless. Yes, the words may sound a bit arcane but the principles endure.

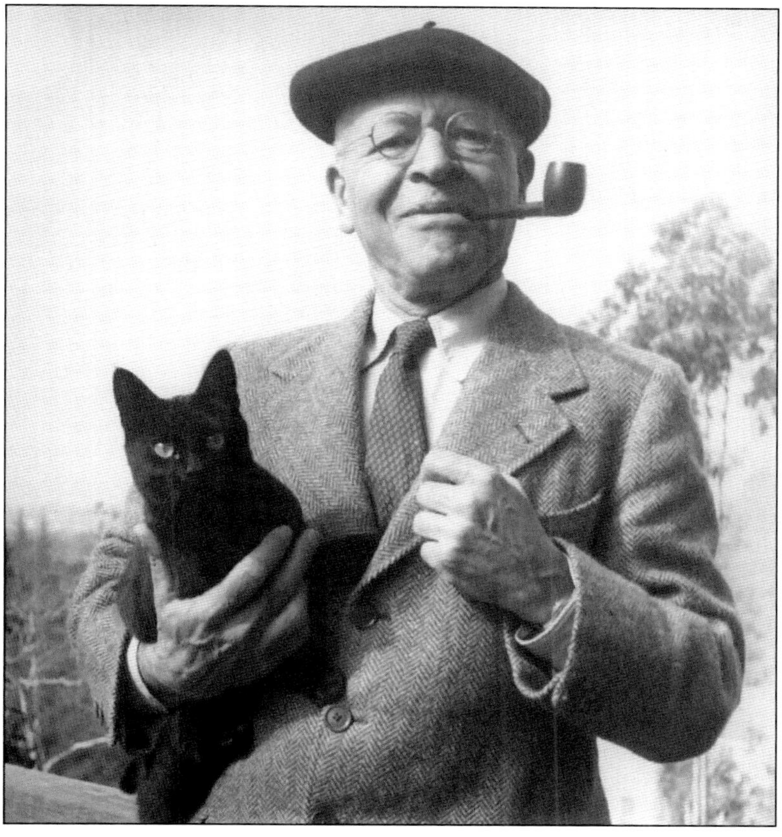

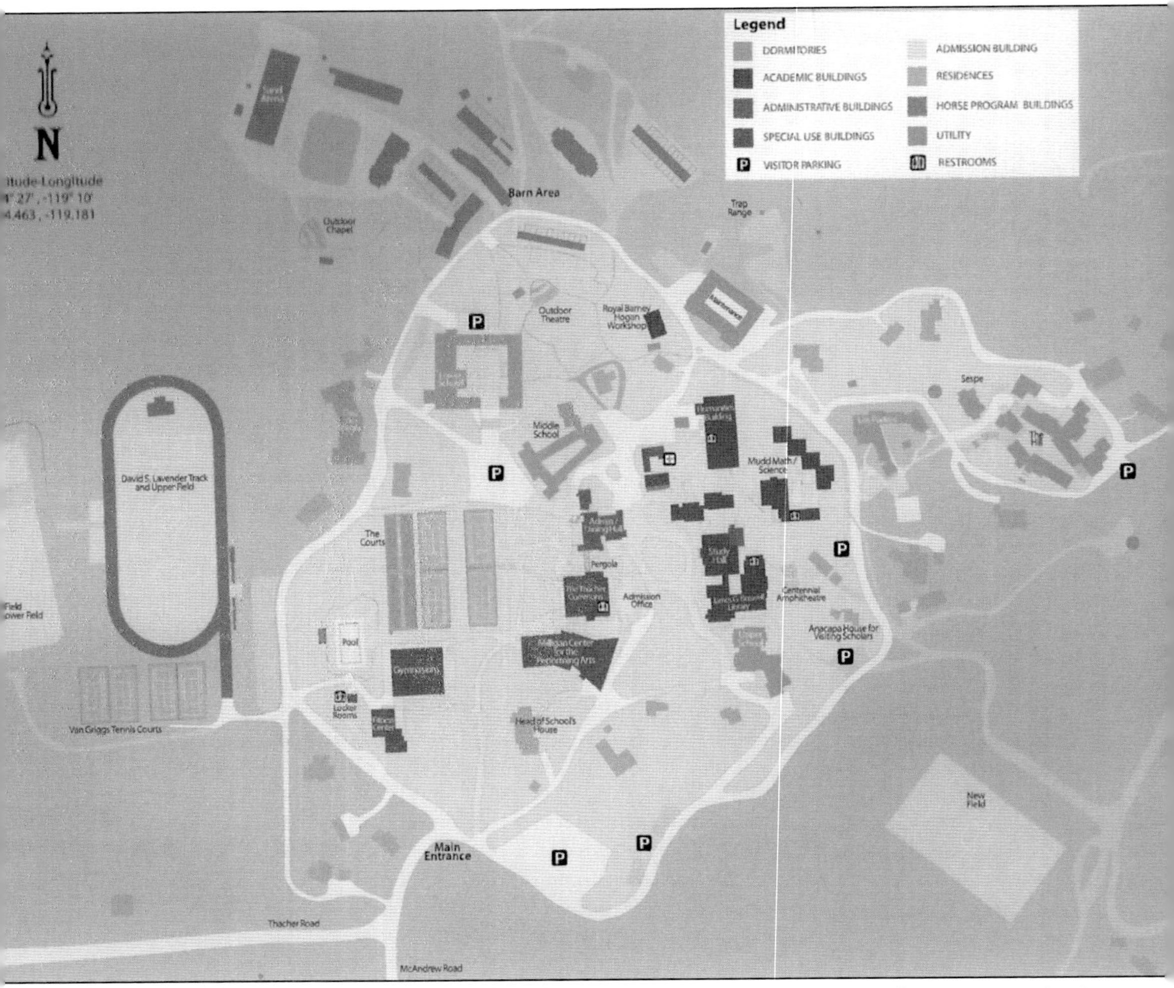

This is a layout of The Thacher School from 2012. Thacher has certainly grown in the last 70-plus years (compare with the diagram on page 23) to a size of over 400 acres. Buildings like the Mudd Science Building and the new humanities center have come, and structures like the Rough-House, the Lamb Auditorium, and the shacks on Beadleville Hill have gone. Thacher is no longer a male bastion. However, it retains its iconic characteristics. It is still the school on the hill. It is still nestled between the Los Padres National Forest and a sea of orange and avocado trees. It still has horses and athletes and artists and scholars. And most significantly, it still fosters the central importance of character as the defining part of a person's life.

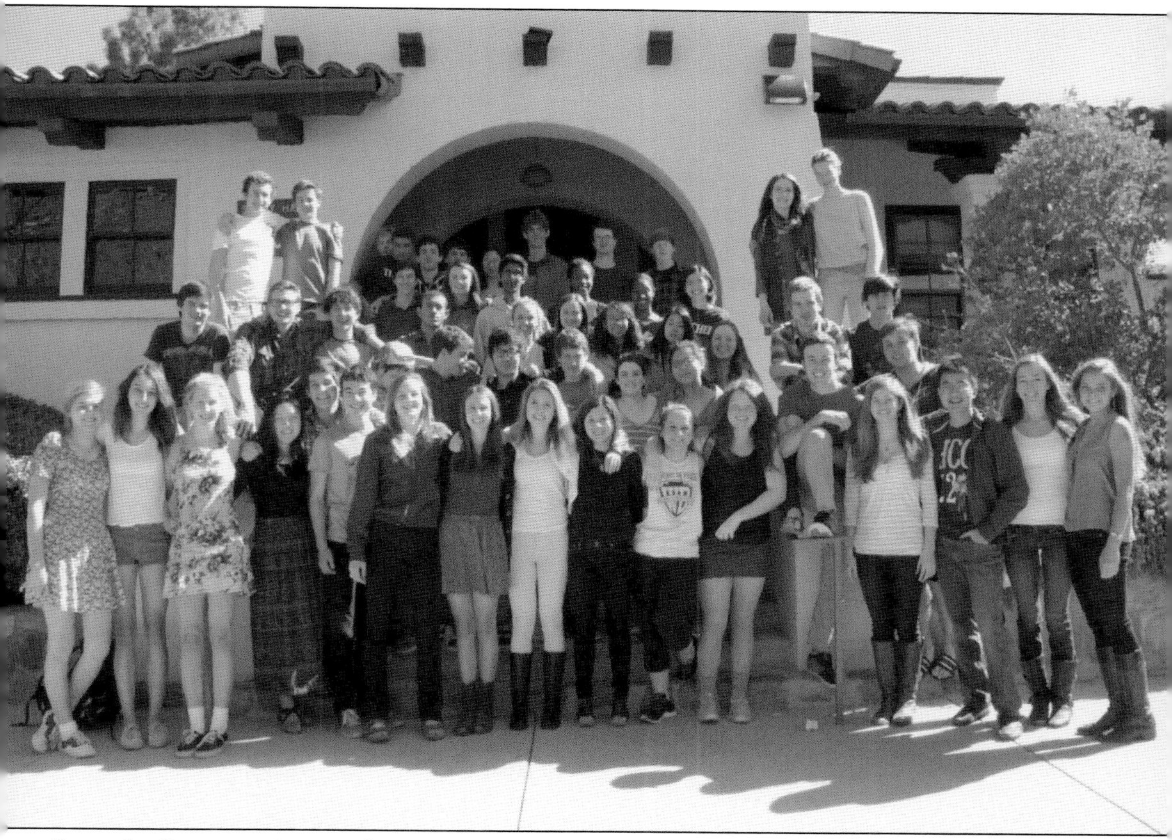

From the first experiences of Henry Farnam as a boarding student being tutored at Sherman Thacher's Casa de Piedra orange ranch to The Thacher School's graduating class of 2014 (shown above in their junior year), there have been 125 years of excellence in education, spurred on by notions of "honor and fairness and kindness and truth." Sherman Thacher started out as an orange rancher and ended up founding an educational institution that, by virtue of the graduates it has produced, has made its mark not only on the Ojai Valley, but also on the nation. This is truly an amazing story and an enduring legacy.

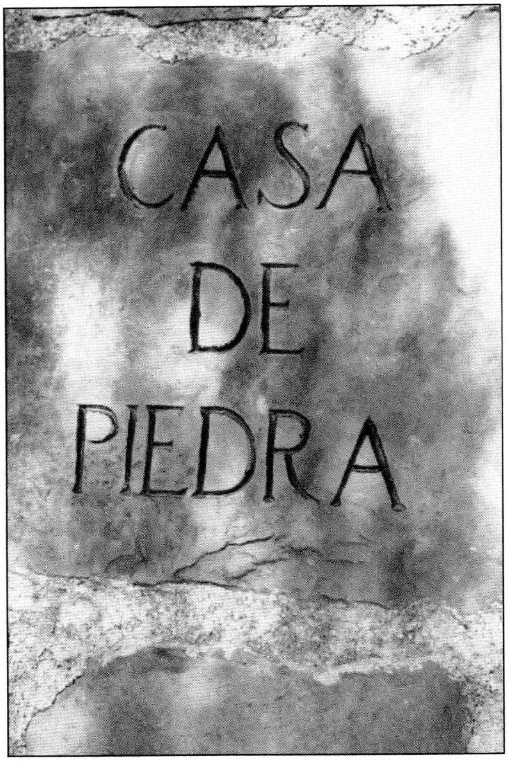

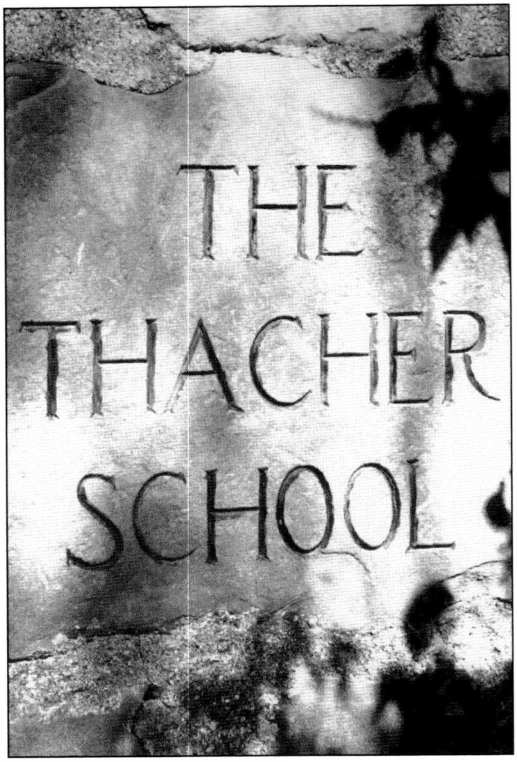

May old Casa Piedra not fade from our hearts,
'Til our hearts cease their restless tattoo!
May honor, and fairness, and kindness, and truth
Be ours 'til life's struggle is through.

May the stamp of the School be stamp of our lives,
Whose honesty carries us on,
To do the best work in the world that we can,
'Til the best we can do is all done.

BIBLIOGRAPHY

El Archivero, 1893–2012.
Fry, Patricia L. *The Ojai Valley—An Illustrated History*. Ojai, CA: Matilija Press, 1983.
Hoye, Richard, Jane McClenahan, Tom Moore, and the Ojai Valley Museum. Images of America: *Ojai*. Charleston, SC: Arcadia Publishing, 2007.
Hoye, Richard, Tom Moore, Craig Walker, and the Ojai Valley Museum. Postcard History Series: *Ojai*. Charleston, SC: Arcadia Publishing, 2010.
Huyler, John S. *The Stamp of the School*. Seattle, WA: Special Child Publications, 1994.
Makepeace, LeRoy McKim. *Sherman Thacher and His School*. New Haven, CT: Yale University Press, 1941.
Nicholson, W.G., ed. *The Taft-Thacher Letters*. Madison, CT: Summer Hill Books, 1985.
Sherman, F. Barreda. *Memoirs of an Old Boy*. Ojai, CA, The Thacher School.